3D Studio MAX 2

Effects Magic

3D Studio MAX 2

Effects Magic

BY
GREG CARBONARO

JEFFREY ABOUAF
STEVEN ALEXANDER
JAYESH KAPADIA
KIM LEE

iv

3D Studio MAX 2 Effects Magic

Copyright © 1998 by New Riders

International Standard Book Number: 1-56205-883-5

Library of Congress Catalog Card Number: 98-84784

Printed in the United States of America

First Printing: August 1998

00   99   98   4   3   2   1

Trademarks

Warning and Disclaimer

Executive Editor
Alicia Buckley

Acquisitions Editor
Laura Frey

Development Editor
Juliet MacLean

Software Development Specialist
Adam Swetnam

Project Editor
Kevin Laseau

Copy Editor
San Dee Phillips

Technical Editor
Michael Todd Anderson
Larry Minton

Cover Designer
Aren Howell

Book Designer
Gary Adair

Production
Michael Henry
Linda Knose
Tim Osborn
Staci Somers
Mark Walchle

Contents at a Glance

Part III: Atmospheric and Terrestrial Realism

Weather Conditions

Natural Disasters

Part IV: Explosions and Pyrotechnics

Mass Destruction

Weapons Firepower

Fires, Glows, and Sparks

Smoke and Steam

Contents

Part III: Atmospheric and Terrestrial Realism

Weather Conditions

Part IV: Explosions and Pyrotechnics

Mass Destruction

Warhead Explosion 279

Atomic Bomb Mushroom Cloud 289

Shattering Geometry 299

Weapons Firepower

About the Authors

Greg Carbonaro's design and product development career spans over fifteen years. Designer of more than twenty video games, he holds numerous software copyrights as well as both design and utility patents. He is a Kinetix certified instructor for 3D Studio MAX and a faculty member at Pratt Institute of New York where he teaches 3D computer graphics and animation. Greg is also co-author of the XtraActive MAX tutorial series. His creative and technical background includes 3D and special effects animation, CD-ROM and video game development, 3D Web site design, and both toy and consumer products development. Currently Greg is a 3D graphics consultant for a Manhattan-based multimedia design company and an independent director of product development for a computer accessory manufacturing company. Greg can be reached by email: imagine@ibm.net or creative@mindless.com.

Jeffrey Abouaf is a fine artist, designer and instructor, whose experience includes television animation and design for print and online. He is a contributing author to *Inside 3D Studio MAX 2*, volumes I and III and follows industry developments in 3D graphics, animation and virtual reality as a conference reporter and product reviewer for several publications, including Computer Graphics & Applications (IEEE), InterActivity, CGI, and CyberEdge Journal. He holds BA, MFA and JD degrees. He teaches 3D Studio MAX at San Francisco State's Multimedia Studies Program and the Academy of Art in San Francisco. He authored online tutorials for Kinetix for 3D Studio MAX R2, and spends substantial time exploring 3DS MAX as a fine art tool. He can be reached at jabouaf@ogle.com; www.ogle.com.

Jeff would like to sincerely thank those individuals and companies who graciously contributed product and support to him on this project, in particular, the staff and developers at Kinetix, the Yost Group, LaVina, Mark and Beau at Digimation, Jim Lammers at Trinity, Dolores at Rem Infographica, Photron, Eyeon, and Adobe. These products keep it fun.

Steven Alexander is a freelance animator and an instructor at several universities in the New York City region. He teaches the advanced undergraduate animation classes at the Pratt Institute in Brooklyn, NY. At The Pratt Manhattan campus, an Autodesk Training Center, he is an Autodesk Certified Instructor. He can also be found teaching at the College of Aeronautics in Queens, NY. Steve is also co-author of the XtraACTIVE Max CD Tutorials, http://www.3dstudiomax.com, and is a contributing author to *Inside 3D Studio Max 2 Volume I*. You can contact Steve at salexand@pratt.edu or 110370.1041@compuserve.com.

Jayesh Kapadia is a graduate of the School of Visual Arts Computer department who has worked on numerous CD titles and infomercials. His love for video games, drafting, and sculpting is what sparked his interest in 3D modeling and animation. Currently, he is the leading artist/designer for ReAllis Inc, which consists of a small group of game developers who will very shortly be releasing their first real-time 3D action game.

Kim Lee has been working with 3D Studio products since its DOS days with release 3. During his early years in the industry he spent time as a demo artist at various trade shows and worked in the New York area for clients like Met Life and Hasbro. He is currently a senior animator at Curious Pictures in New York where he has been involved on projects for clients such as Nick at Nite, Captain Crunch and IBM. He is on the Kinetix Training Specialist team, which is a group of top level instructors recruited by Kinetix to train other instructors and large entertainment accounts around the world. He teaches computer animation at Pratt Institute and is one of the co-founders of the Metro New York 3D Studio MAX users group. He is a beta tester for Kinetix as well as many third-party plug-in developers such as Digimation, REM Infografica, and Lambsoft.

Acknowledgments

New Riders offers a special thanks to the following teachers and students at ITT Tech of Indianapolis:

Lynn Lowder
Dianna Kitzinger
Juan Francisco Castro
Chris Crawford
Mike Fearrin
Anthony W. Kendall
Gus Powell III
Jim Reynolds
Kevin Seewer
Jeff Solenberg

Dedications

Dedicated to the one who makes my happiness possible, the incredible love of my life—Patty

—Greg Carbonaro

To Annette and any virtual humans I sacrificed in these experiments.

—Jeffrey Abouaf

I would like to dedicate my efforts for this book to my Wife Terry Ann and my two daughters, Brandice and Katrina. They have put up with a missing dad for the duration of this project and the work I did for the Inside 3d Studio Max 2 *book. Thanks girls! I would also like to acknowledge the support and friendship of Greg Carbonaro. Greg has been a great influence to me as well as a trusted friend. Thanks Smithers!*

—Steven Alexander

I thank my parents for their eternal support and understanding; Kai and Lori for their unbiased critiques; Frank Delise for the brainstorming; Dena thanks for the encouragement; Patti for your support and patience; Brendan, Max, Joe, Rochelle, Damon, Eric and Lewis for their creative criticism; Steve Katz for the infinite inspiration and advice.

—Kim Lee

Tell Us What You Think!

As the reader of this book, *you* are our most important critic and commentator. We value your opinion and want to know what we're doing right, what we could do better, what areas you'd like to see us publish in, and any other words of wisdom you're willing to pass our way.

As the Executive Editor for the computer animation team at Macmillan Computer Publishing, I welcome your comments. You can fax, email, or write me directly to let me know what you did or didn't like about this book—as well as what we can do to make our books stronger.

Please note that I cannot help you with technical problems related to the topic of this book, and that due to the high volume of mail I receive, I might not be able to reply to every message.

When you write, please be sure to include this book's title and author as well as your name and phone or fax number. I will carefully review your comments and share them with the author and editors who worked on the book.

Fax: 317-817-7070

E-mail: graphics@mcp.com

Mail: Executive Editor
            Computer Animation
            Macmillan Computer Publishing
            201 West 103rd Street
            Indianapolis, IN 46290 USA

Introduction

How did they do that? This question served as the basis for the planning of the content in this book. My goal was to inspire both the beginner as well as the seasoned MAX animator with stunning special effects that would make this book a necessary reference in any serious animator's personal library. I consulted with some of the industries top 3D talent to develop the effects that would be part of an animator's Wish Book. Some of the world's best 3D minds with well over 100 years of combined computer graphics experience collaborated to develop the treasure trove of technical knowledge contained within these pages. Together we created a masterpiece brimming with real-world examples of stunning computer graphics.

The content in this book is concise and to the point—we do not waste words on unimportant information or fluff. Every effect has been refined to contain only powerfully distilled content. The result is an animator's recipe book of truly fine special effects. This is not a tutorial, although it is my opinion that the information presented in this book provides the best possible learning experience. You will be working first-hand with the same techniques employed by experts, nothing has been held back, you will learn the top special effects tricks as revealed by master animators. Whether you're a novice or an expert, this book has more to offer you than anything you have ever experienced before—hundreds of real world solutions to animations toughest challenges. This is not theoretical information; this is the real thing, real results, real animations from the world's best animators.

Just follow the steps as they are laid out for you in logical order, entering all the values exactly as indicated, and you will easily reproduce every stunning animation. All of the effects include numerous screenshots, giving you a complete visual road map through the effect, showing where you should be at any given point in time. On the companion CD-ROM, we also include all the necessary pre-load files, models and maps as well as the actual completed MAX file as constructed by the author. The final piece of this powerful reference library includes fully rendered high-resolution images as well as full-length AVI's of each effect. With all of these powerful learning aids at your side, you will effortlessly assimilate this knowledge and be able to easily re-combine these techniques for use in your own animations.

All of the animators that contributed effects to this book were asked to design effects that would raise a question in the minds of the people who view them: How did he do that? To that end, we have achieved our goal. Each of the contributors was presented with a copy of the other's completed animations and without fail the same question came up time and again. How did he do that? Here's a sidenote to that question that I found very interesting: There is a general consensus among each of the effect's contributors that this very book will be part of his own reference library.

Organization of the Book

This book is probably unlike most other books you have encountered on MAX. It is a Recipe Book, and as such it is not a serial read. It's truly random access. Each effect is a self-contained entity, complete unto itself. Feel free to bounce around the book, pick and choose what you like. A wealth of powerfully distilled knowledge awaits you in each section. Keep it near your computer as a quick problem-solving reference for new animation challenges. Each effect contains complete directions, including what maps and files to copy and pre-load. You'll also find some author insights and ideas along with actual screenshots illustrating the effect creation process. Its almost as if you were sitting there along side the author while the effect was created.

Re-Creating the Effects

MAX is a complex canvas. The infinite combination and variation of settings can be finely tuned to multiple decimal place precision. This is one reason MAX is such a powerful tool for the creation of subtle artistic nuances. The effect's designers went to great lengths to tweak all the settings to create optimal animations. It is absolutely essential that you follow the effect recipe exactly or your results might not look like the original. We suggest that you start your effect design process by using the values in the book, and then once you have gotten it to work, jump in and fine tune it to your liking.

These effects are not meant to be the final word on a given topic but rather they are meant to be the beginning, to serve as a springboard for your imagination. In each step of the effects we give you the exact values as entered by the effect's creator; we do not give you the MAX default value setting however. This was done so that the book would not be full of a lot of redundant superfluous information. The downside to this is that your MAX default values might have been set to something other than default by you during some previous work; these non-default values will often create an animation output that doesn't look like the intended result. Fortunately there is an easy remedy for this, before starting any new effect from this book, simply shut MAX down and then re-start it. This will return all settings to their default values.

During the re-creation of each effect, it will be necessary to precisely place, rotate, or otherwise transform objects. It will be much easier to do this if you use the Transform Type-In dialog box (see Figure 1).

To use the Transform Type-In dialog box:

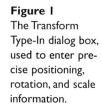

1. Select the object you wish to effect.

2. Decide what type of transformation you will be performing, moving/positioning, rotating or scaling.

3. Select the appropriate transform button in the tool bar (see Figure 2).

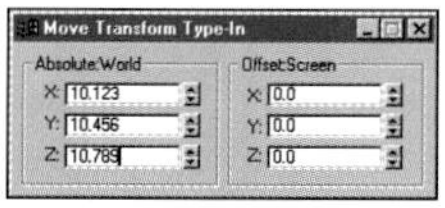

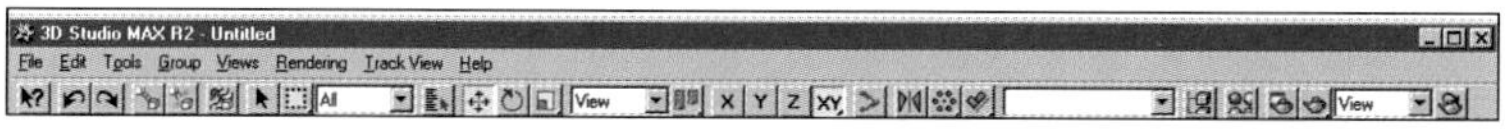

Figure 1
The Transform Type-In dialog box, used to enter precise positioning, rotation, and scale information.

Figure 2
Activating the "select and move" button in the toolbar.

4. Go to the "Tools" drop-down menu at the top of the screen.

5. Click "Tools" to have the menu drop down and select the first menu choice, Transform Type-In.

Once selected, a small dialog box will appear in the center of the screen. This small input box is the Transform Type-In dialog and will allow you to enter exact positioning information for X, Y and Z coordinated positions based on world coordinates. The same technique and type of dialog box can be used to input rotation and scaling information as well. To do this, click either the "Select and Rotate" or "Select and Scale" buttons in the toolbar at the start of the process.

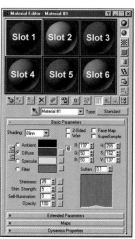

When entering the values for the X, Y, and Z coordinates, use the tab to move to the next field. An important note needs to be highlighted here: When you enter the value for the last field, usually the Z value, its is essential that you hit enter before closing the dialog. If you do not, your last value will not be entered. This could have a very negative effect on your animation and could be a difficult error to find.

Throughout the book you will be using the Material Editor (see Figure 3). Various steps will call out the usage of specific slots within the materials editor. Most effects utilize the standard materials editor layout which is represented by the 1 through 6 slot configuration which is known as the 3×2 Sample Window layout.

Figure 3
Material Editor standard 3×2 Sample Window layout.

Other effects require the use of more slots and so call for the 5×3 Sample Window layout. The logical numbering of the slots in this slot configuration are indicated in Figure 4.

At the beginning of each effect in the pre-configuration area you will be asked to set the materials editor Sample Windows setting to either 3×5 or 5×3. This will ensure that when the effect calls for you to use slot 10 you will know which slot that is. To set the Sample Windows simply open the Material Editor and right-click on any slot; this will bring up a selector dialog that will allow you to select either the 3×5 or 5×3 Sample Window settings (see Figure 5).

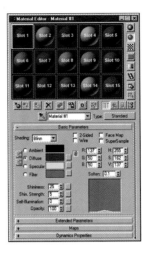

Figure 4
Material Editor standard 5×3 Sample Window layout.

Essentials and Usage of the CD-ROM

Because this book is unlike other books you have used for MAX, it actually mandates the use of the accompanying CD-ROM. That is, if you intend to duplicate the effects as presented. Most effects presented in this book have an accompanying MAX pre-load set up file as well as essential map files. Without these files it would be difficult if not impossible for you to duplicate these effects. At the start of each effect you will be instructed to copy all associated effects' map files to your MAX maps sub-directory. It is essential that you perform this step otherwise MAX will not find the textures it needs at render time. After you have completed this it will also be necessary for you to load the effect's associated MAX pre-load files which contains any necessary models, backgrounds and or animation information needed for you to complete the effect.

Figure 5
Sample Window layout selector dialog.

The CD-ROM contains the fully completed MAX files as originally constructed by the effect's authors. If you find that your effect is not coming out as you expected, we recommend you consult the author's original file for some insight. The CD-ROM also contains high resolution images of all the effects as well as a full length animation of each. For optimal viewing of the animations it is recommended that you copy them to a temp folder on your hard drive before playing them.

PART I

Water Effects

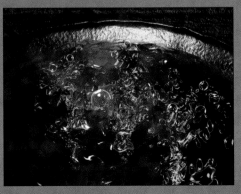

Calm Ocean Surface

by Greg Carbonaro

A good material is the foundation of many great effects. This scene is a perfect example of that. The water material used here is exceedingly simple yet dramatically effective. The proper placement of sunlight reflections and the feel of a gently rolling ocean create a very nice, calm, and realistic illusion.

Note

All position and rotational information is based on absolute world coordinates. When creating objects, use keyboard entry when possible. When positioning objects, use the Transform Type-In dialog box located in the Tools menu. These techniques ensure proper object placement and orientation.

Leave any settings that are not listed in the example at the MAX default values. Create objects in the Top viewport, unless otherwise indicated.

Preconfiguration

1. Before beginning this effect, please reset *or* restart MAX.

2. Copy the Calm Ocean project map files from the accompanying CD-ROM to the MAX maps subdirectory.

3. Load the Clouds.max file from this project's pre-load subdirectory on the CD-ROM. The animation length has been preset to 300 frames.

4. Open the Materials Editor: right-click in any material slot and make sure Sample Windows are set to 5×3.

You should now see a cloud backdrop in your perspective viewport.

Environment Setup

Now you're going to add a fog atmosphere, which will make objects fade at the horizon in the distance.

1. Add the fog atmosphere effect:
   Color = (R = 105, G = 138, B = 239)
   Fog Background = off

Modeling and Materials

Create a cylinder object that will serve as the ocean surface. The cylindrical shape provides unique geometry that compliments the water surface movement generated by the Noise material animation that you will add later.

Ocean Object Creation

1. Activate the Top viewport.

2. Create a standard primitive cylinder in the Top viewport roughly centered in the viewport. Then use the Transform Type-In dialog box to position it at x = 6, y = 191, z = 0. Set the following:
   Radius = 1500
   Height = 4
   Cap Segments = 30
   Sides = 40

3. Name the object **Ocean**.

Ocean Material

1. In the Material Editor, make material slot 1 active and set the Material Type to Standard.

2. Set the Basic parameters as follows:
   Ambient = (R = 0, G = 0, B = 0)
   Diffuse = (R = 0, G = 0, B = 15)
   Shininess = 40
   Shin. Strength = 30

3. Set the Amount for the Bump slot to 20. Click the Bump map slot and set the Map Type to Noise. Set the Noise Parameters:
   Noise Type = turbulence
   Size = 45

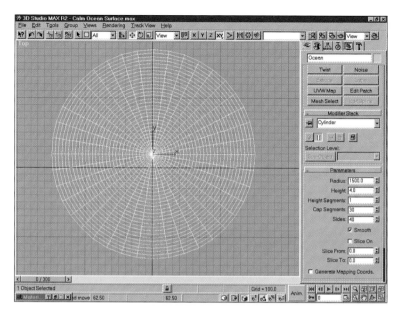

Figure I
A flattened cylinder with tons of cap segments is created to enable smooth wave deformation and a slightly curved horizon line.

4. Set the Noise Coordinate Offset Animation. Animate the x and y coordinates:
   Frame 0 (Keyframe 1) x and y = 0
   Frame 300 (Keyframe 2) x and y = 50

5. Animate the z coordinate:
   Frame 0 (Keyframe 1) z = 0
   Frame 300 (Keyframe 2) z = 150

6. Set the Amount for the Reflection slot to 55. Click the Reflection map slot and set the Map Type to Bitmap. Click Bitmap and assign the Sky.jpg file. Set the following:
   Coordinates Mapping = Shrink-wrap Environment

7. Name the material **Ocean Surface**.

8. Apply the Ocean Surface material to the Ocean object.

Note

To animate the x, y and z coordinates, turn Animate on. At frame 0, set x, y, and z to 0. Move the Time Slider to Frame 300 and set x to 50, y to 50 and z to 150. Turn Animate off.

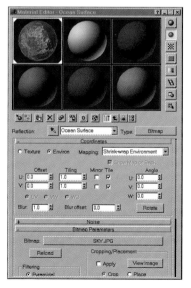

Figure 2
Creating the Ocean Surface material.

Water Surfaces

Ship Object

1. Merge the TunaclVL.max file into the scene by using the Merge command located in the File drop-down menu. The file can be found in the project's Pre-load directory on the CD-ROM.

After the file is loaded, you will see a ship on the water. If you move the Time Slider, you will note that it already has its animation assigned.

Animation Technique

Now add the space warp that will generate the rolling ocean waves.

1. Create a Geometric/Deformable space warp ripple in the Top viewport just outside the ocean surface object roughly at the 5 o'clock position. Use the Transform Type-In to position it at x = 953, y = -1189, z = 0. Set the following:
    Amplitude1 = 15
    Amplitude2 = 15
    Wave length = 125
    Decay = 0.001
    Circles = 20
    Segments = 20
    Divisions = 15

2. Animate the Phase as follows:
    Frame 0 (Keyframe 1) Phase = 0
    Frame 300 (Keyframe 2) Phase = 5

3. Bind the space warp to the cylinder named Ocean.

Lighting Setup

Next, create the lighting effects for the scene.

1. Create an omni light in the Top viewport just outside the ocean surface object roughly at the 1 o'clock position. Then use the Transform Type-In to position it at x = 336, y = 1596, z = 169. Set the following:
    Color = (R = 180, G = 180, B = 180)
    Multiplier = 5.5

2. Name the omni light **Sun Light**.

3. Create an omni light in the Top viewport just outside the ocean surface object roughly at the 5 o'clock position. Then use the Transform Type-In to position it at x = 423, y = -1074, z = 163. Set the following:
    Color = (R = 180, G = 180, B = 180)
    Multiplier = 1.3
    Cast Shadows = on

Note

To animate Phase, turn Animate on. At Frame 0, set Phase to 0. Move the Time Slider to Frame 300 and set the Phase to 5. Turn Animate off.

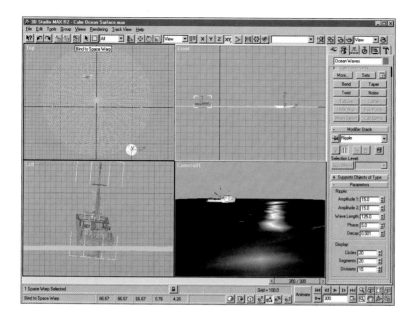

Figure 3
Creating the ripple space warp that produces the waves and binding it to the ocean surface.

4. Name the omni light **Front Light**.

5. Create a target spot light in the Top viewport just outside the ocean surface object roughly at the 1 o'clock position. Then use the Transform Type-In to position it at x = 386, y = 1695, z =174. Position the target at x = -113, y = 846, z = 29. Set the following:
   Color = (R = 180, G = 180, B = 180)
   Multiplier = 5.5
   Cast Shadows = on
   Use Raytraced Shadows = on

6. Name the object **Shadow Spot**.

Camera Setup

The final step is to set up the camera through which you will view the finished effect.

1. Create a target camera at x = -14, y = -800, z =120. Position the target at x = -10, y = -259, z = 33. Set the following Environmental Ranges:
   Near Range = 700
   Far Range = 2388

Water Surfaces

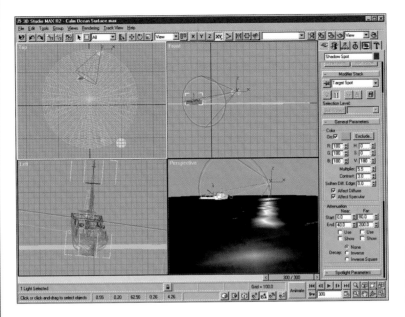

Figure 4
Creating the various lights to illuminate the scene.

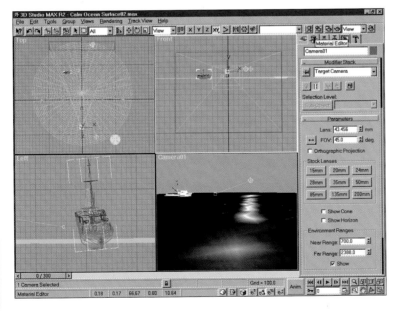

Figure 5
Completed Calm Ocean Surface effect. The camera environmental range works in conjunction with the environmental fog to create a misty horizon line.

You can find the final MAX file, CalmOceanSurface.max, in this project's Scene folder and the final AVI file in the Images folder.

Choppy Ocean Surface

by Greg Carbonaro

F or a truly raging ocean scene, good material will do most of the work for you. The water material used for this effect requires a high degree of surface turbulence on both the macro and micro scales. You can accomplish this by using several ripples and multilevel Noise in the Bump map channel. The proper placement of sunlight reflections and the feel of the rolling ocean create a very realistic illusion.

Note

All position and rotational information is based on absolute world coordinates. When creating objects, use keyboard entry when possible. When positioning objects, use the Transform Type-In dialog box located in the Tools menu. These techniques ensure proper object placement and orientation.

Leave any settings that are not listed in the example at the MAX default values. Create objects in the Top viewport, unless otherwise indicated.

Preconfiguration

1. Before beginning this effect, please either reset *or* restart MAX.

2. Copy the Choppy Ocean project map files from the accompanying CD-ROM to the MAX maps subdirectory.

3. Set the animation length to 300 frames.

4. Open the Material Editor. Right-click in any material slot and make sure Sample Windows are set to 3×2.

Environment Setup

In this section you are going to set the background color and add a fog atmosphere, which will add a slightly misty ambience to the scene.

1. In the Rendering drop-down menu under Environment set the Background Color (R = 230, G = 242, B = 247).

2. Add a fog atmosphere effect:
   Color = (R = 230, G = 242, B = 247)
   Fog Background = Off
   Standard Far% = 75

Modeling and Materials

You will now create a cylinder object that will serve as the ocean surface. The cylinder geometry provides unique geometry that compliments the water surface movement generated by the noise material animation that you will add later.

Ocean Object Creation

1. Activate the Top viewport.

2. Create a standard primitive cylinder roughly centered in the Top viewport and then use the Transform Type-In dialog box to position it at x = 6, y = 191, z =0. Set the following:
   Radius = 1500
   Height = 4
   Cap Segments = 30
   Sides = 40

3. Name the object **Choppy Ocean** (see Figure 1).

Ocean Material

1. In the Material Editor, make material slot 1 active and set the Material Type to Standard.

2. Set the Basic Parameters as follows:
   Ambient = (R = 100, G = 141, B = 147)
   Diffuse = (R = 0, G = 0, B = 0)
   Specular = (R = 229, G = 229, B = 229)
   Shininess = 40
   Shin. Strength = 30
   Soften = 0.25

3. Set the Amount for the Bump slot to 30. Click the Bump map slot and set the Map Type to Mix.

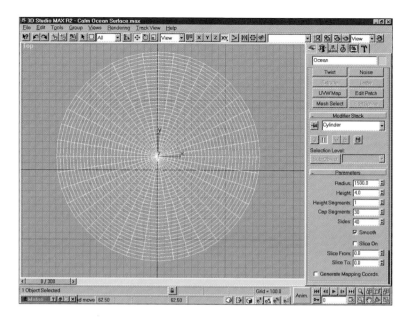

Figure 1
A flattened cylinder with a lot of cap segments is created to enable dramatic wave deformation.

4. Set the Noise parameters for Map1:
   Noise Type = turbulence
   Size = 90

5. Animate the Noise coordinates. Animate the X and Y coordinates as follows:
   Frame 0 (Keyframe 1) X and Y = 0
   Frame 300 (Keyframe 2) X and Y = 50

6. Animate the Z coordinate as follows:
   Frame 0 (Keyframe 1) Z = 0
   Frame 300 (Keyframe 2) Z = 150

7. Set the Noise parameters for Map2:
   Noise Type = turbulence
   Size = 25

8. Animate the Noise coordinates. Animate the X and Y coordinates as follows:
   Frame 0 (Keyframe 1) X and Y = 0
   Frame 300 (Keyframe 2) X and Y = 150

9. Animate the Z coordinate as follows:
   Frame 0 (Keyframe 1) Z = 0
   Frame 300 (Keyframe 2) Z = 450

10. Set the Amount for the Reflection slot to 65. Click the Reflection map slot and set the Map Type to Bitmap. Click

Note

To animate the x, y, and z coordinates, turn Animate on. At Frame 0, set X, Y and Z to 0. Move the Time Slider to Frame 300 and set x to 50, y to 50 and z to 150. Turn Animate off.

Water Surfaces

Bitmap and assign the Sky.jpg file. Set the following:
Coordinates Mapping = Shrink-wrap Environment

11. Name the material **Choppy Surface**.

12. Apply the Choppy Surface material to the Choppy Ocean object (see Figure 2).

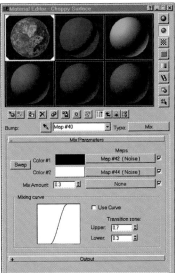

The extra turbulence is added by using a Mix map on the Bump level and adding another layer of Noise on a smaller, more turbulent scale.

Animation Technique

Now you are going to add the space warps that will generate the choppy ocean waves.

1. Create a Geometric/Deformable space warp ripple at x = 1276, y = −492, z = 0. Set the following:
Amplitude1 = 10
Amplitude2 = 10
Wave Length = 259
Circles = 20
Segments = 20
Divisions = 15

2. Animate the Phase as follows:
Frame 0 (Keyframe 1) Phase = 0
Frame 300 (Keyframe 2) Phase = 5

3. Bind the space warp to the cylinder named Choppy Ocean.

4. Create a Geometric/Deformable space warp ripple in the Top viewport on the edge of the ocean surface object roughly at the 12 o'clock position. Then use the Transform Type-In to position it at x = 24, y = 1646, z = 0. Set the following:
Amplitude1 = 8
Amplitude2 = 8
Wave Length = 303
Circles = 20
Segments = 20
Divisions = 15

Note

To animate the X,Y and Z coordinates, turn Animate on. At frame 0, set X,Y and Z to 0. Move the Time Slider to frame 300 and set X to 150,Y to 150 and Z to 450. Turn Animate off.

Figure 2
This material differs from a calm ocean surface in that it is much more turbulent at the mirco level.

5. Animate the Phase as follows:
   Frame 0 (Keyframe 1) Phase = 0
   Frame 300 (Keyframe 2) Phase = 5

6. Bind the space warp to the cylinder named Choppy Ocean.

7. Create a Geometric/Deformable space warp ripple in the Top viewport on the edge of the ocean surface object roughly at the 8 o'clock position. Then use the Transform Type-In to position it at x = –1326, y = –495, z = 0. Set the following:
   Amplitude1 = 11
   Amplitude2 = 11
   Wave Length = 150
   Circles = 20
   Segments = 20
   Divisions = 15

8. Animate the Phase as follows:
   Frame 0 (Keyframe 1) Phase = 0
   Frame 300 (Keyframe 2) Phase = 5

9. Bind the space warp to the cylinder named Choppy Ocean.

10. Create a Geometric/Deformable space warp ripple in the Top viewport on the edge of the ocean surface object roughly at the 4 o'clock position. Then use the Transform Type-In to position it at x = 1276, y = –493, z = 0. Set the following:
    Amplitude1 = 10
    Amplitude2 = 10
    Wave Length = 259
    Circles = 20
    Segments = 20
    Divisions = 15

11. Animate the Phase as follows:
    Frame 0 (Keyframe 1) Phase = 0
    Frame 300 (Keyframe 2) Phase = 5

12. Bind the space warp to the cylinder named Choppy Ocean.

13. In the Choppy Ocean modifier stack, set the flexibility of each of the 3 ripple bindings to 1.5.

Lighting Setup

Next, you will create the lighting for the scene.

1. Create an omni light in the top viewport just outside the ocean surface object roughly at the 1 o'clock position. Then use the

Note

To animate Phase, turn Animate on. At Frame 0, set Phase to 0. Move the Time Slider to Frame 300 and set the Phase to 5. Turn Animate off.

Transform Type-In to position it at x = 336, y = 1596, z = 169.
Set the following:
Color = (R = 180, G = 180, B = 180)
Multiplier = 5.5

2. Name the omni **Sun Light** (see Figure 3).

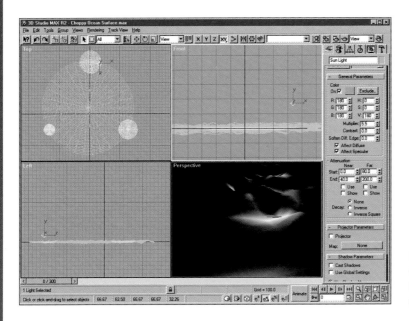

Figure 3
Creating the sun-
light that will illu-
minate the scene.

Camera Setup

The final step is to set up the camera through which you will view the
finished effect.

Create a target camera at x = −14, y = −771, z = 282. Position
the target at x = −10, y = −259, z = 33 (see Figure 4). Set the
Environmental Ranges:
Near Range = 700
Far Range = 2388

The combination of three ripple modifiers used in this effect produces a
nice pattern of wave interference and a very tumultuous surface. The
water material used in this effect was almost identical to the one used in
the calm ocean surface effect except for one key difference: the choppy
material required an additional layer of Noise to produce a higher degree
of micro level water turbulence. You can find the final MAX file,
ChoppyOceanSurface.max, in this project's Scene folder and the final
AVI in the Images folder.

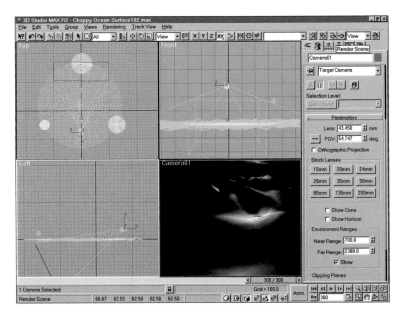

Figure 4
Completed
Choppy Ocean
Surface effect. A
slight hazy effect is
created by the
camera's environ-
mental range.

Swift Moving River

by Kim Lee

O ne of the hardest effects for any 3D artist to achieve is moving water. Because nearly everyone knows what flowing water looks like, you need to pay special attention to the subtle nuances of both the animation and material elements of this effect. In this chapter, you harness the procedural noise functions of the Material Editor to simulate the chaotic beauty found in a swiftly flowing river. Also, you see how to use the second UVW channel to create whitecaps on the tip of waves. You will utilize the built-in ray-tracing capabilities of MAX R2 to re-create realistic reflection and refraction on the surface of the water. Using the following techniques, you will be able to create river effects of various intensities for various project requirements.

Note

All position and rotational information is based on absolute world coordinates. When creating objects, use keyboard entry when possible. When positioning objects, use the Transform Type-In dialog box located in the Tools menu. These techniques ensure proper object placement and orientation.

Leave any settings that are not listed in the example at the MAX default values. Create objects in the Top viewport, unless otherwise indicated.

Preconfiguration

1. Before beginning this effect, please reset *or* restart MAX.

2. Copy the project map files from the accompanying CD-ROM to the MAX maps subdirectory.

Create the River Object

First you will need to create the geometry for the surface of the river.

1. Create a QuadPatch at x = 0, y = 0, z = 0. Set the following parameters:
Length = 250
Width = 35
Length Segments = 6

2. Rename the QuadPatch **River**.

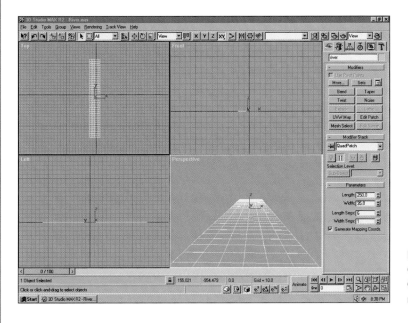

Figure 1
Creating a QuadPatch for the river geometry.

3. Add an Edit Patch modifier to the Modifier Stack and deselect the Sub-Object button. Set Topology Steps to 45. This increases the complexity of the object for future deformations.

4. Place an Edit Mesh modifier to the Modifier Stack and deselect the Sub-Object button to transform the Patch object to a polygonal mesh object.

5. Add a Displace modifier to the Modifier Stack and set the following:
Strength = 2

6. In the Image section of the Displace Parameters, click None under the label MAP and choose a Noise map.

7. In the Material Editor, click-and-drag the button now labeled Map #1 (noise) from the command column to the first material sample slot. Select Instance in the Instance (Copy) Map dialog box.

8. Rename the Material in slot 1 **Displacement**.

9. Set the Noise parameters:
   Noise Type = Fractal
   Size = 2

   The surface of our river object will now have a wave-like distortion.

10. Turn Animate on and go to Frame 100. Set the following:
    Y Offset = –50
    Phase = 10

11. Close the Material Editor and turn Animate off.

12. Add a UVW Map modifier to the Modifier Stack. Set the following parameters:
    Mapping = Planar
    Channel = 2
    Alignment = Y

13. Click Fit in the Alignment section of the UVW modifier.

14. In the Front viewport, zoom on the mapping gizmo. Adjust Length in the Alignment section of the UVW modifier to around 1.3 with the intent of fitting the mapping gizmo to encompass the highest wave.

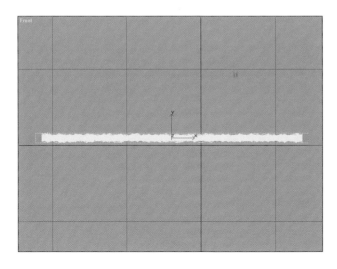

Figure 2
Proper alignment of the UVW mapping gizmo to create whitecaps.

15. In the Top viewport, create a Spline line in the shape of a shallow letter S. Merge the Line01 shape from the preconfiguration file.

16. Select the River object and add a Path Deform World Space modifier to its stack.

17. Click Pick Path and select the line shape.

18. Click Move to Path and select a Path Deform Axis of Y. Set the following:
Percent = 50
Rotation = 90

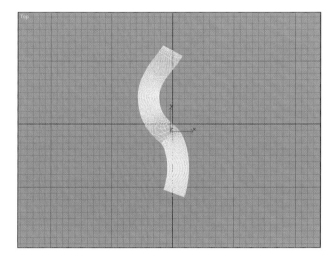

Figure 3
River geometry after applying Path Deform.

The River object is now deformed into the shape of a generic river and has an animated surface displacement resembling a flowing current. Render a preview to see the results thus far.

Create a Generic Landscape

1. Create a QuadPatch in the Top viewport at −6.497, 4.648, −5.141 so that it is centered on the river object. Set the following:
Length = 240
Width = 240
Length Segments = 1
Width Segments = 1

2. Rename the object **Land**.

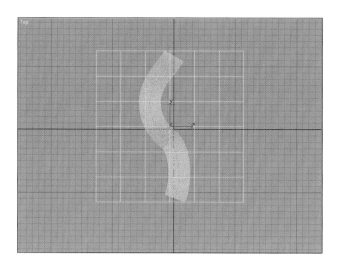

Figure 4
Correct positioning
of Land geometry.

3. Add an Edit Patch modifier to the Modifier Stack and deselect
the Sub-Object button. Set the following:
Steps = 80

4. Add an Edit Mesh modifier to the Modifier Stack and deselect
the Sub-Object button. This converts the patch object to polygonal geometry.

5. Create a displacement bitmap for the land object that matches
the contours of the river object. Click Render Scene and set the
Output Size to 500×500. Click Close.

6. Activate the Top viewport. Right-click the viewport label and
select Show Safe Frame. Zoom and pan the Top view so that the
objects fall squarely within the outer yellow safe frame box. (See
Figure 6.)

7. Render the Top view and save the image. Return to the Render
dialog box and set Output Size to 320×240.

8. In the Top viewport turn off Show Safe Frame and click Zoom
Extents.

9. Select the Land object and in the Modifiers tab add a Displace
modifier to the stack.

10. In the Image section of the Displace Parameters, click None
under Bitmap and select Land_Disp.tga from the file selection
box. Set the following:
Strength = 20

Note

*You would now nor-
mally save your MAX
R2 scene file and
open a bitmap-based
editing program, such
as Photoshop or
Painter. This is where
you will use the saved
bitmap as a guide to
paint a Displacement
map. File
Land_Disp.tga provid-
ed in this project's
Maps folder was cre-
ated in this manner.*

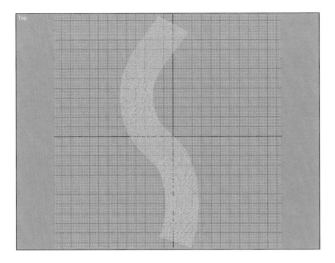

Figure 5
Proper view align-
ment with safe
frame.

11. Switch to a Perspective view in Smooth+Highlights mode.
Make sure the reference coordinate system is set on View.

12. Move the land object up and down, constraining to the Z axis,
until it looks similar to the following image.

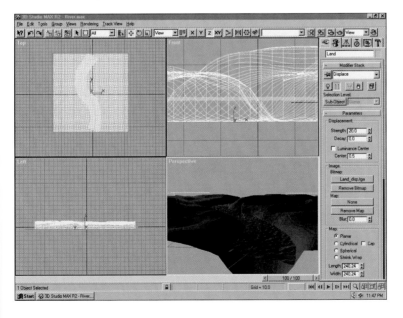

Figure 6
Correct alignment
of Land and River
objects.

Create the Environment

In this section you will create the environment for the scene.

Lights and Camera

1. Create an omni light in the Top viewport near the upper-left corner of the Land object at x = –92, y = 130, z = 41. Set the following:
   Color = (H = 0, S = 0, V = 255)
   Multiplier = 2
   Cast Shadows = On

2. Name this light **Sun**.

3. Create an omni light in the Top viewport and place it near the lower-right corner of the Land object at x = 102, y = –115, z = 54. Set the following:
   Color = (H = 0, S = 0, V = 50)
   Multiplier = 1.0

4. In the Top viewport, create a target camera over the lower-right portion of the landscape aimed toward the upper-left to frame the scene looking across the length of the river. Position the camera at x = 35, y = –94, z = 13. Position the target at x = –63, y = 67, z = –4.

5. Change the Perspective view to a Camera view.

Create Background

1. Select Environment from the Rendering drop-down menu.

2. Click None under Environment Map and select Bitmap from the list.

3. In the Material Editor, drag and drop the Map#2(Bitmap) button from the Environment dialog box to the second Material sample slot. Choose Instance as your copy method.

4. In the Material Editor, change the name of slot 2's material to Backdrop and set the following:
   Environ Mapping: = Screen

5. Go down to Bitmap Parameters and click the blank button next to Bitmap. Select sunset90.jpg and click OK.

6. Select the Camera viewport and select Background Image from the Views drop-down menu. Set the following options:
   Use Environment Background = Checked
   Display Background = Checked

You should now have all of the geometry and surrounding environment built.

Creating Materials

Now all you need to do is create and assign materials.

Create the Ground Material

1. In the Material Editor, activate material slot 3. Set the following parameters:
   Shininess = 10
   Shin. Strength = 5

2. Click the Diffuse map slot and set the Map Type to Bitmap. Click Bitmap and assign the file dirtgray.jpg. Set the following parameters:
   U Tiling = 8
   V Tiling = 8

3. Toggle on the Show Map in Viewport button and return to the material level. Drag the Diffuse map slot to the Bump Slot. Specify to copy as an Instance.

4. Name this material **Ground** and apply it to the Land object.

Create the Water Material

1. In the Material Editor, select a free sample slot and name it **Water**.

2. Set the Basic Parameters as follows:
   Ambient = (R = 9, G = 44, B = 77)
   Specular = (R = 255, G = 255, B = 255)
   Shininess = 60
   Shin. Strength = 100
   Opacity = 80

3. Click the Diffuse map slot and set the Map Type to Gradient. Name the map **Gradient 1**. You will be nesting multiple identical gradients to create a sharper border between blue (the main diffuse color of our water) and white (the whitecaps of our waves).

4. Set the following for Gradient 1:
Color #2 = (R = 88, G = 114, B = 144)
Color #3 = (R = 88, G = 114, B = 144)
Texture Mapping: = Explicit UVW 2
Color 2 Position = 0.4

5. Click the Color #1 map slot of Gradient 1 and set the Map Type to Gradient.

6. Repeat steps 4 and 5 twice, naming each new gradient— Gradient 2 and Gradient 3 respectively. On Gradient 3, do not place another gradient into Color #1.

7. Set the Amount for the Bump slot to 30 (see Figure 7). Click the Bump map slot and set the Map Type to Noise. Set the Noise parameters:
Noise Coordinates = UVW1
V Tiling = 2
Noise Type = Fractal
Size = 0.01

8. Turn Animate on and go to frame 100. Set the following:
V Offset = –1
Phase = 10

9. Turn Animate off.

10. Set the Amount for the Reflection slot to 30. Click the Reflection map slot and set the Map Type to Raytrace.

11. Click on Options and turn off Global Antialiasing. Click Close. (See Figure 8.)

12. Apply the material to the River object.

13. Render the effect. It should look something like the file river.avi.

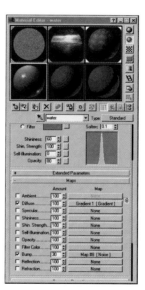

Note

You used UVW1 mapping this time instead of XYZ because you want the Noise Bump map to flow down along the path of the river like the Displacement map. However, if you use XYZ coordinates here, you would see the Bump texture move in a straight line from the origin of the river to its end without following any of the river's bends.

Figure 7
Creating the water material.

Figure 8
Using Raytrace for reflections.

With a little experimentation, you should find it quite easy to drastically alter the intensity of the river flow. Note that by continuing to nest gradients, you can make the border of the whitecaps more abrupt. By merely adjusting the Offset, Phase, and Strength/Amount parameters of the Noise maps used for both Displacement and Bump, you can animate the river as a placid flow to an angry torrent.

You can find the final MAX file, River.max, in this project's Scene folder and the final AVI in the Images folder.

Note

Because the water in this river is relatively deep and flowing quickly we would probably not be able to see far into its depths from our current vantage point. Therefore it is not absolutely necessary to apply a refraction map. However, feel free to place a ray-trace material type into this channel.

Raindrop Ripples

by Steve Alexander

In this effect, you will create a moody, drizzly scene with a shallow pool of water, rippled with rain drops. The rain drops are created with a particle system with the right amount of transparency set to the material so that the rain is subtle. You will create the ripples with a modifier, based on a flat object with many length and width segments. We'll use a background picture to help with the setup.

Note

All position and rotational information is based on absolute world coordinates. When positioning objects in your scene, always use the Transform Type-In dialog box located in the Tools menu. This ensures proper object orientation.

Leave any settings that are not listed in the example at the MAX default values. Create objects in the Top viewport, unless otherwise noted.

Preconfiguration

Load the RainStart.max scene from this project's Pre-load folder on the accompanying CD-ROM.

This file has a background image into which you'll blend the effect.

Objects and Materials
Puddle Creation

1. Create a standard primitive box anywhere in the Top viewport and place it at x = 0, y = −48, z = −9. Set the following:
   Length = 125
   Width = 125
   Height = 0
   Length Segments = 16
   Width Segments = 16

2. Name the box **Puddle**.

3. Select the Puddle and add a Ripple modifier:
   Wave Length = 4.5
   Decay = 0.35

Note

At this point, you should set the length and width segments to a lower number to help keep modeling and setup at a better speed. The final number for this object will be 96 segments. Another method of keeping the modeling environment at a manageable level is to set the segments to their final number, and setting the object's properties to be as visible as a bounding box.

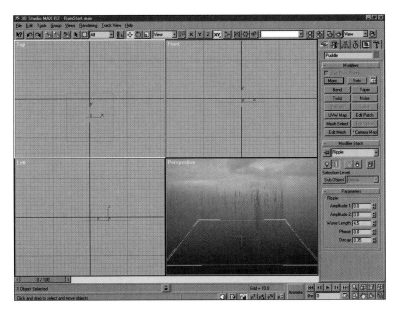

Figure 1
The ripple on the surface object.

Blizzard Particle System Creation

1. Create a particle system Blizzard anywhere in the Top viewport and place it at x = 0, y = 30, z = 65. Set the following:
   Length = 100
   Width = 100
   Rotation: y = 11.5

2. In the Particle Generation rollout, set the following:
   Use Total = 150
   Emitter Stop = 150
   Display Until = 150
   Life = 13
   Size = 2

The scene now contains the surface and a particle system, which will act as the rain for the scene.

Animation

In this section you will animate the ripple so that it looks like the rain-drops are hitting the surface.

1. Turn on Animate. At Frame 22, set the following:
   Amplitude 1 = 0.75
   Amplitude 2 = 0.75
   Phase = −1.0

2. With Animate still on, go to Frame 45, and set the following:
   Amplitude 1 = 0
   Amplitude 2 = 0
   Phase = −2.0

3. Turn off Animate. Press the Edit Stack button on the Modify panel, and select the ripple from the list. Make 10 copies of the ripple.

4. In the Modify panel, select the first rip-ple in the stack and change it to the Sub-Object Center level. Move the cen-ter of the ripple. Repeat this for all the ripple centers in order to create the 'drops' falling at different places.

Figure 2
The Edit Modifier Stack dialog box with the ripple copies.

5. In the Track View, select the keys for the first ripple and copy them so that the last keys are at the end of the animation.

6. Select all the keys for the second ripple. Copy the keys and move them so that key #1 starts at a frame other than Frame 1. Do this for all the ripples so that there will be a staggered effect for the start and end of each ripple. See Figure 3.

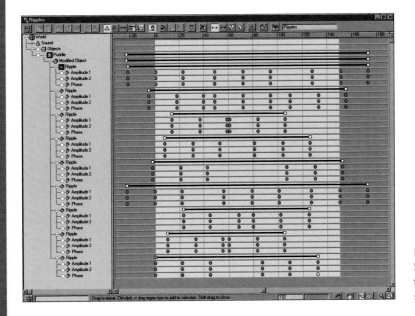

Figure 3
Staggered ripples for a random splash effect.

At this point the ripple centers should be at different places on the surface object and the animations for each should be staggered so that the ripples do not appear to happen simultaneously.

Camera Setup

Next, set up the camera through which you will view the finished effect.

1. Create a target camera anywhere in the Top viewport and place it at x = 0, y = –100.0, z = 3.25. Position the target at: x = 0, y = 0, z = –4.

2. Make a viewport a Camera view.

Creating the Rain Drops Material

1. In the Material Editor, make Slot 1 active and set the Material Type to standard material.

2. Set the Basic Parameters as follows:
   Ambient = (R = 230, G = 230, B = 230)
   Diffuse = (R = 230, G = 230, B = 230)
   Specular = (R = 230, G = 230, B = 230)
   Self Illumination = 50
   Opacity = 70

3. Name the material **Rain Drops**. Assign it to the particle system.

Creating the Water Material

1. In the Material Editor, make slot 2 active and set the Material Type to Standard.

2. Set the Basic Parameters:
Ambient = (R = 125, G = 130, B = 145)
Diffuse = (R = 125, G = 130, B = 145)
Opacity = 15

3. Name the material **Water**. Assign it to the surface object.

You can find the final MAX file, RainFinal.max, in this project's Scene folder and the final AVI in the Images folder.

Splash Impact

by Greg Carbonaro

U pon first examination, a Splash Impact appears as a complex jumble of activity. In reality, you can break the effect down into a linear sequence of distinct events. Of course, there is some overlap as the events occur, but it is a linear sequence nonetheless. In this effect, you will re-create a splash sequence by combining and animating the parameters of several overlapping space warps and modifiers simultaneously.

Leave any settings that are not listed in the example at the MAX default values. Create objects in the Top viewport, unless otherwise indicated.

Preconfiguration

1. Before beginning this effect, please reset *or* restart MAX.

2. Copy the Splash Impact project map files from the accompanying CD-ROM to the MAX maps subdirectory.

3. Load the Meteorite.max file from the projects pre-load subdirectory on the CD-ROM. The Animation length is pre-set to 300 frames.

4. Open the Materials Editor. Right-click in any material slot and make sure Sample Windows are set to 3×2.

You will now see a background sky map in your perspective viewport. This Environmental map (ArubaOcean.tif) will require some fine-tuning in the Material Editor, which you will do in the next section. The scene also contains an animation of a large meteorite falling from the sky.

Environment Setup

Now you are going to set up the scene's atmosphere and fine-tune the Environmental background settings.

1. Open the Environment dialog (Rendering/Environment) and add a Fog atmospheric effect. Set the following Fog parameter:
Color = (R = 120, G = 154, B = 228)

2. Copy (drag and drop an instance) of the Background Environment map ArubaOcean.tif to the Fog Environment Opacity Map slot (see Figure 1).

3. Open the Material Editor and copy (drag and drop an instance) of the Background Environment map ArubaOcean.tif to slot 2 of the Material Editor.

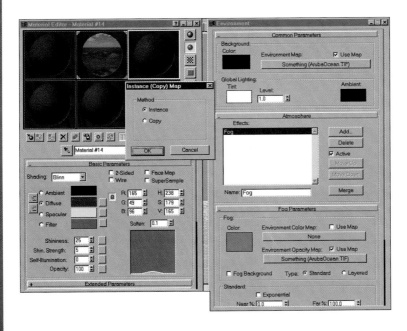

Figure 1
Copy instances of the ArubaOcean.tif map to both the Fog Environment Opacity map as well as Slot 2 of the Material Editor.

4. In the Material Editor, set the following for this map:
Coordinates: Environmental = On
Mapping = Screen

5. In the Output rollout, set the following parameter:
Output Amount = 1.39

If you look at your viewport, the most apparent change is that you have lightened up the background slightly. What is not so obvious is that you have also added a slightly hazy fog. This fog will only become apparent when you add the water to the scene and render the image later.

Modeling and Materials

Next you will be creating a flattened cylinder object. This cylinder will become your ocean after you apply a special water material that you'll be creating in a subsequent section.

Creating the Ocean Surface

1. Activate the Top viewport.

2. Create a standard primitive cylinder approximately in the center of the viewport, then use the Transform Type-In to position it precisely at x = 6, y = 191, z = 0. Set the parameters as follows:
   Radius = 1500
   Height = 4
   Height Segments = 1
   Cap Segments = 100
   Sides = 100
   Smooth = On
   Generate Mapping Coordinates = On

3. Name the object **Ocean**.

Creating the Ocean Surface Water Material

1. In the Material Editor, make material slot 1 active and set the Material Type to Standard.

2. Set the Basic Parameters as follows:
   Ambient = (R = 45, G = 55, B = 65)
   Diffuse = (R = 122, G = 112, B = 92)
   Specular = (R = 255, G = 255, B = 255)
   Filter = (R = 41, G = 24, B = 14)
   Shininess = 62
   Shin. Strength = 100
   Opacity = 30

3. In the Extended Parameters rollout, set the following:
   Refract Map/RayTrace IOR = 1.3

4. Set the Amount of the Bump slot to 20. Click the Bump map slot and set the Map Type to Noise. Set the Noise parameters as follows:
   Coordinates = XYZ
   Y Tiling = 4

Noise Type = Turbulence
Size = 45

5. Animate the Noise X,Y,Z Coordinates Offsets:
Frame 0 (Keyframe 1) = (x = 0, y = 0, z = 0)
Frame 300 (Keyframe 2) = (x = 50, y = 50, z = 150)

6. Set the Amount for the Refraction slot to 40. Click the Refraction slot and set the Map Type to Thin Wall Refraction. Set the following parameter:
Bump Map Effect = 2

7. Name the material **WaterSurface**.

8. Apply the WaterSurface material to the Ocean object.

Note

To animate the Noise, turn Animate on. At Frame 0, set X Offset to 0, Y Offset to 0, and Z Offset to 0. Move the Time Slider to Frame 300. Set X Offset to 50, Y Offset to 50, and Z Offset to 150. Turn Animate off.

You should now see the Ocean object in your viewport with the WaterSurface material applied.

Ocean Surface Animation

Now you are going to animate the ocean by adding a modifier and some space warps. First add a Noise modifier, which will create some chaotic surface movement. Then add a Ripple space warp to produce gentle rolling waves.

Normal Ocean Surface

1. Apply a Noise modifier to the Ocean object. Set the following parameters:
Seed = 45643
Scale = 10
Fractal = On
Roughness = 0.25
Strength = (z = 10)
Animate Noise = On

2. Open Track View and expand the hierarchy tree to display the Strength track for the Noise modifier. Create the following animation keys:
Frame 0 (Keyframe 1) Strength = (x = 0, y = 0, z = 0)
Frame 90 (Keyframe 2) Strength = (x = 0, y = 0, z = 0)
Frame 91 (Keyframe 3) Strength = (x = 0, y = 0, z = 40)
Frame 180 (Keyframe 4) Strength = (x = 0, y = 0, z = 0)

3. Select all the Strength keys and set their In and Out tangents to Linear.

4. Activate the Top viewport.

5. Create a Geometric/Deformable Ripple space warp on the edge of the Ocean object roughly at the 5 o'clock position, then use the Transform Type-In to position it precisely at x = 983, y = −1159, z = 0. Set the following parameters:
   Amplitude 1 = 15
   Amplitude 2 = 15
   Wavelength = 125
   Decay = 0.001

6. Animate the Ripple's Phase:
   Frame 0 (Keyframe 1) Phase = 0
   Frame 300 (Keyframe 2) Phase = 5

7. Set the Display parameters:
   Circles = 20
   Segments = 20
   Divisions = 15

8. Name the ripple **Ocean Waves**.

9. Bind the Ocean Waves ripple to the Ocean object.

Note

To animate the Phase, turn Animate on. At Frame 0, set Phase to 0. Move the Time Slider to Frame 300. Set Phase to 5. Turn Animate off.

Impact Wave

Now you are going to add another Ripple space warp. This is the Ripple that will dramatically deform the Ocean surface to simulate the splash impact.

1. Activate the Top Viewport.

2. Create a Geometric/Deformable Ripple space warp in the center of the Ocean object, then use the Transform Type-In to position it precisely at x = 44.872, y = 217.707, z = 0. Accept the default MAX name Ripple01. Set the following parameters:
   Amplitude 1 = 54
   Amplitude 2 = 54
   Wave Length = 375
   Phase = 0
   Decay = 1

3. Turn Animate on. Advance to Frame 90 and shift-right click the Decay spinner to create a key.

4. Advance to Frame 91 and set the following parameter:
   Decay = 0

5. Advance to Frame 115 and shift-right click the Wave Length spinner to create a key.

6. Advance to Frame 190 and shift-right click the Amplitude 1 and Amplitude 2 spinners to create keys.

7. Advance to Frame 225 and set the following parameters:
Amplitude 1 = 0
Amplitude 2 = 0
Decay = 0.01

8. Advance to Frame 300 and set the following parameters:
Wave Length = 750
Phase = −10
Decay = 1

9. Open Track View and expand the hierarchy tree to display the tracks for the Ripple01 object. For each track, select all the animation keys and set their In and Out tangents to Linear. Each track must be done separately to properly set the tangent types.

10. Turn Animation off.

11. Set the Ripple Display Parameters (see Figure 2):
Circles = 17
Segments = 47
Divisions = 4

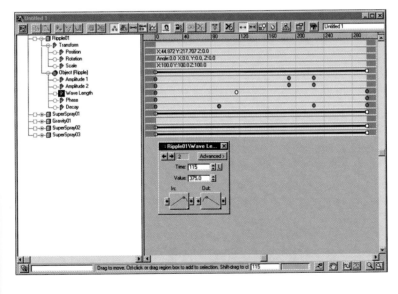

Figure 2
When setting up the ripple animation keyframes, be sure to set the In and Out tangent curves as indicated in the text.

12. Bind the Ripple01 ripple to the Ocean object.

13. Create a Geometric/Deformable Displace space warp at x = 42.471, y = 213.54, z = 95.893. Accept the default name Displace01. Set the following parameters:
Decay = 1.75
Map = Spherical

> **Length** = 125
> **Width** = 125
> **Height** = 125

14. Open Track View and expand the hierarchy tree to display the Strength track for the Displace01 object. Create the following animation keys:
Frame 0 (Keyframe 1) Strength = 0
Frame 90 (Keyframe 2) Strength = 0
Frame 93 (Keyframe 3) Strength = 200
Frame 98 (Keyframe 4) Strength = 0

15. Select all the Strength keys and set their In and Out tangents to Linear.

16. Bind the Displace01 space warp to the Ocean object.

17. Create a Geometric/Deformable Displace space warp in the Top viewport roughly centered on the Ocean object. Then, use the Transform Type-In to position precisely at x = 46.848, y = 213.54, z = −112.376 and the Transform Type-In to rotate the Displace space warp to x = 90, y = 0, z = 0. Set the following:
Decay = 1.5
Map = Spherical
Length = 125
Width = 300
Height = 300

18. Accept the default name Displace02.

19. Open Track View and expand the hierarchy tree to display the Strength track for the Displace02 object. Create the following animation keys:
Frame 0   (Keyframe 1) Strength = 0
Frame 96   (Keyframe 2) Strength = 0
Frame 101 (Keyframe 3) Strength = 250
Frame 132 (Keyframe 4) Strength = 0

20. Select all the Strength keys and set their In and Out tangents to Linear.

21. Bind the Displace02 space warp to the Ocean object.

If you were to render the scene at this point you would find that most of the water's animation has been completed. As the meteorite impacts the water, a violent ripple/noise wave upheaval dramatically deforms the ocean surface, then slowly and rhythmically the impact subsides into calm rolling waves.

Splashing Water Creation

Now you're going to add the finishing touch. You'll use a few particle systems to create sprays of gushing and splashing water.

1. Create a Super Spray particle system in the Top viewport roughly at the center of the Ocean, then use the Transform Type-In to position it precisely at x = 14.847, y = 26.361, z = −168.699. Accept the MAX-assigned default name Super Spray01.

2. Set the Basic Parameters:
   Off Axis = 45
   Off Axis Spread = 3
   Off Plane Spread = 180
   Icon Size = 124

3. Set the Particle Generation parameters:
   Use Rate = 300
   Speed = 40
   Speed Variation = 50
   Emit Start = 89
   Emit Stop = 94
   Display Until = 120
   Life = 15
   Life Variation = 4
   Size = 15
   Size Variation = 25
   Grow For = 0
   Fade For = 0

4. Set the Particle Type parameters:
   Standard Particles = Tetra

5. Set the Particle Rotation parameters:
   Spin Time = 45
   Direction of Travel/MBlur = On
   Stretch = 4

6. In the Top viewport, create a Gravity space warp at x = −1600, y = 1350, z = 0. Set the following:
   Icon Size = 275

7. Bind the Gravity space warp to Super Spray01.

8. Create a Super Spray particle system in the Top viewport roughly at the center of the Ocean, and then use the Transform Type-In to position it precisely at x = 14.847, y = 26.361, z = −168.699 and accept the MAX-assigned default name Super Spray02.

9. Set the Basic Parameters:
Off Axis = 25
Off Axis Spread = 3
Off Plane Spread = 180
Size = 124

10. Set the Particle Generation parameters:
Use Rate = 150
Speed = 30
Speed Variation = 50
Emit Start = 106
Emit Stop = 112
Display Until = 160
Life = 30
Life Variation = 4
Size = 15
Size Variation = 25
Grow For = 0
Fade For = 0

11. Set the Particle Type parameters:
Standard Particles = Tetra

12. Set the Particle Rotation parameters:
Spin Time = 45
Direction of **Travel/MBlur** = On
Stretch = 4

13. Bind the Gravity space warp to Super Spray02.

14. Create a Super Spray particle system in the Top viewport roughly at the center of the Ocean, then use the Transform Type-In to position it precisely at x = 14.847, y = 26.361, z = −168.699 and accept the MAX–assigned default name Super Spray03.

15. Set the Basic Parameters:
Off Axis = 20
Off Axis Spread = 3
Off Plane Spread = 180
Size = 124

16. Set the Particle Generation parameters:
Use Rate = 75
Speed = 23
Speed Variation = 50
Emit Start = 139
Emit Stop = 143
Display Until = 180

Life = 30
Life Variation = 4
Size = 15
Size Variation = 25
Grow For = 0
Fade For = 0

17. Set the Particle Type parameters:
Standard Particles = Tetra

18. Set the Particle Rotation parameters:
Spin Time = 45
Direction of Travel/MBlur = On
Stretch = 4

19. Bind the Gravity space warp to Super Spray03.

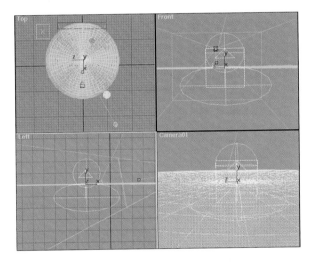

Figure 3
Creation of the splash Super Sprays.

The three particle systems you created should be located in the center of the Ocean surface object and visible in your viewport.

Creating the Splash Material

Next you will create the material that will be applied to these particles.

1. In the Material Editor, make material slot 3 active and set the Material Type to Standard.

2. Set the Basic Parameters as follows:
Ambient = (R = 45, G = 55, B = 65)
Diffuse = (R = 122, G = 112, B = 92)
Specular = (R = 255, G = 255, B =255)
Filter = (R = 41, G = 24, B = 14)

Shininess = 62
Shin. Strength = 100
Opacity = 30

3. In the Extended Parameters rollout, set the following:
Refract Map/RayTrace IOR = 1.3

4. Set the Amount for the Bump slot to 75. Click the Bump map slot and set the Map Type to Noise. Set the Noise parameters as follows:
Coordinates = UVW1
V Tiling = 4
V Offset = 0
Noise Type = Regular
Size = 0.05

5. Animate the V Coordinate Offset:
Frame 0 (Keyframe 1) V Offset = 0
Frame 300 (Keyframe 2) V Offset = −13

6. Animate the Noise Phase:
Frame 0 (Keyframe 1) Phase = 0
Frame 300 (Keyframe 2) Phase = 20

7. Set the Amount for the Reflection slot to 75. Click the Reflection map slot and set the Map Type to Reflect/Refract.

8. Set the Amount for the Refraction slot to 40. Click the Refraction map slot and set the Map Type to Thin Wall Refraction. Set the following parameter:
Bump Map Effect = 2

9. Name the material **WaterSplash**.

10. Apply the WaterSplash material to the Super Spray01, Super Spray02, and Super Spray03 particle systems.

Note

To animate both the V Offset and the Phase, turn Animate on and advance to Frame 300. Set V Offset to −13 and Phase = 20. Turn Animate off.

Once the material is applied and the animation is complete, all you need to do is add the lights and camera.

Lighting Setup

Next, you will create the lighting for this scene.

1. In the Top viewport Create an omni light roughly at the 12 o'clock position relative to the Ocean object, then use the Transform Type-In to position it precisely at x = 212, y = 8828, z = 5553. Set the following parameters:
Multiplier = 2.75
Cast Shadows = On

2. Name the omni light **Sun Light**.

3. In the Top viewport create a target spotlight in front of and pointing at the Ocean object, then use the Transform Type-In to position the body precisely at x = 1381, y = − 2420, z = 5116. Next use the Transform Type-in to Position the target at x = − 29, y = 84, z = 19. Set the following:

Multiplier = 2
Hotspot = 40
Falloff = 42
Cast Shadows = On
Shadow Map Size = 2048

4. Name the target spot **Shadow Spot01**.

Camera Setup

The final step is to set up the camera through which you will view the finished effect.

In the Top viewport create a target camera in front of and pointing at the Ocean object, then use the Transform Type-In to position the body precisely at x = −13.6, y = − 801, z = 120. Next use the Transform Type-In to Position the target at x = − 10, y = − 259, z = 33.5.

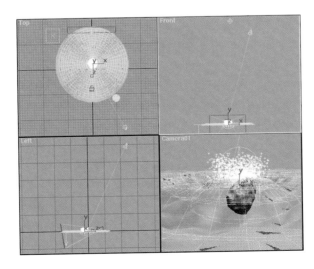

Figure 4
Completed Splash
Impact effect.

After completing this effect go back and study the sequence of events. As you can see, a splash animation has a precise well defined and definitive linear sequence.

You can find the final MAX file, SplashImpact.max, in this project's Pre-load folder and the final AVI file in the Images folder.

Violent Boiling

by Greg Carbonaro

Something as seemingly simple and everyday as boiling water is among the most difficult things to capture in an animation. The physical nature of boiling is extremely complex and chaotic, and yet it has unique visual characteristics that are both recognizably common and yet absolutely unique in all of nature. It is a true tribute to the power of an animation program that enables an animator the creative flexibility to reproduce such difficult imagery. In this effect, you create boiling water using a combination of refraction mapping, particle systems, and Displacement space warps.

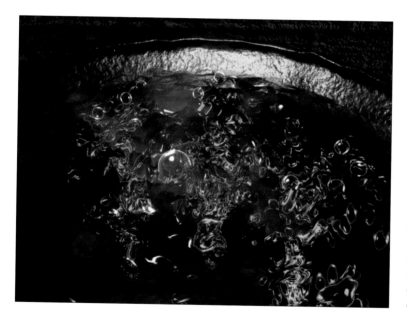

Note

All position and rotational information is based on absolute world coordinates. When positioning objects in your scene, always use the Transform Type-In dialog box located in the Tools menu. This ensures proper object orientation.

Leave any settings that are not listed in the example at the MAX default values. Create objects in the Top viewport, unless otherwise indicated.

Preconfiguration

1. Before beginning this effect, either reset *or* restart MAX.

2. Copy the Violent Boiling project map files from the accompanying CD-ROM to the MAX maps subdirectory.

3. Load the file Kettle.max from this project's Preload subdirectory on the CD-ROM. This file consists of a kettle located within a fireplace. The animation length is already set to 300.

4. Open the Materials Editor, right-click in any material slot and make sure Sample Windows are set to 3×2.

Modeling and Materials

In this section, you create a boiling water surface by using a cylinder, Noise modifier, and spherical Displacement space warps. You create the bubbles in the water by using particle systems and steam vapors by using particle systems. Finally, you create materials for the water surface, bubbles, and steam.

Creating the Water Surface

1. Create a standard primitive cylinder located at the center of the neck of the kettle. Use the Transform Type-In dialog box to position the cylinder at x = 0.547, y = −42.573, z = −0.286. Set the following parameters:
   Radius = 92.5
   Height = 2.2
   Height Segments = 2
   Cap Segments = 64
   Sides = 64
   Smooth = On
   Generate Mapping Coords. = on

2. Name the object **WaterSurface**.

3. Add a Noise modifier to WaterSurface (see Figure 1). Set the following Noise Parameters:
   Seed = 3453
   Scale = 6.5
   Fractal = Checked
   Roughness = 0.5
   Strength: z = 6.5
   Animate Noise = Checked

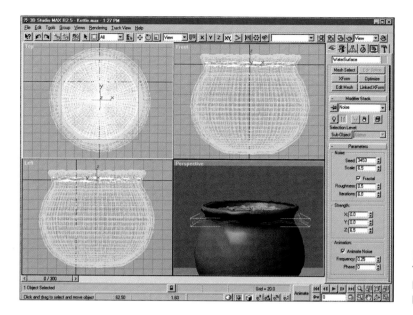

Figure 1
The water surface located within the kettle.

At this point, the scene consists of a rough water surface located within the kettle.

Creating the Water Surface Material

1. In the Material Editor, activate material slot 1 and set the Material Type to Standard. Click Background to turn on background display in the material slot.

2. Set the Basic Parameters as follows:
   Ambient = (R = 45, G = 55, B = 65)
   Diffuse = (R = 122, G = 112, B = 92)
   Specular = (R = 255, G = 255, B = 255)
   Filter = (R = 41, G = 24, B = 14)
   Shininess = 62
   Shin. Strength = 100
   Opacity = 30

3. Set the Amount for the Bump slot to 30. Click the Bump slot and set the Map Type to Noise. Set the Noise Parameters as follows:
   Coordinates = UVW1
   V Tiling = 4
   Noise Type = Turbulence
   Size = 0.2

4. Turn Animate on and at Frame 0 set W Offset to 0. Move the Time Slider to Frame 300 and set W Offset to −7.5. Turn Animate off.

5. Set the Amount for the Refraction slot to 40. Click the Refraction slot and set the Map Type to Thin Wall Refraction. Set the following parameters:
Refraction: **Bump Map Effect** = 2

6. Name the material **WaterSurface**.

7. Apply the WaterSurface material to the WaterSurface object (see Figure 2).

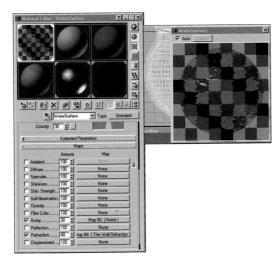

Figure 2
Creating a refraction water surface.

At this point, the water surface has now been assigned its material.

Bubble Creation

1. Create a Super Spray particle system located in the upper portion of the kettle. Use the Transform Type-In dialog box to position the particle system at x = 14.847, y = 26.361, z = −168.699.

2. Set the Basic Parameters as follows:
Off Axis = 4
Off Axis Spread = 12
Off Plane Spread = 180
Icon Size = 20
Percentage of Particles = 50

3. In the Particle Generation rollout, set the following:
Use Rate = 3
Speed = 3
Emit Start = –50
Emit Stop = 300
Display Until = 300
Life = 58
Size = 3
Grow For = 30
Fade For = 0

4. Set the Particle Type parameters as follows:
Standard Particles = Facing

5. Set the Particle Rotation parameters as follows:
Spin Time = 60
Spin Variation = 33
Phase = 180
Phase Variation = 100

6. Set the Bubble Motion parameters as follows:
Amplitude = 1.6
Amplitude Variation = 20
Period = 8
Period Variation = 40
Phase = 180
Phase Variation = 100

7. Accept the MAX–assigned default name SuperSpray01.

At this point, the scene now contains the water surface and one of the particle systems that you use to generate the bubbles.

Bubble Material

1. In the Material Editor, activate material slot 2 and set the Material Type to Standard. Set the Sample Type to the cube.

2. Set the Basic Parameters as follows:
Shading = Phong
Face Map = On
Ambient = (R = 97, G = 46, B = 26)
Diffuse = (R = 227, G = 218, B = 215)
Specular = (R = 252, G = 253, B = 254)
Filter = (R = 255, G = 255, B = 255)
Shininess = 0
Shin. Strength = 0
Soften = 0

3. Set the Amount for the Opacity slot to 100. Click the Opacity slot and set the Map Type to Bitmap. Set the following Bitmap Parameters:
   Bitmap = bubbles.tif

4. Name the material **Bubbles**.

5. Apply the Bubbles material to the SuperSpray01 particle system (see Figure 3).

At this point, the particle system that will be used to generate the bubbles has been assigned a material.

Creating More Bubbles

1. Copy the SuperSpray01 particle system to the right of the center of the kettle. Use the Transform Type-In dialog box to position the particle system at x = 51.819, y = –38.697, z = –168.699, and accept the default name SuperSpray02.

2. Edit the SuperSpray02 particle system. In the Particle Generation rollout, set the following parameters:
   Seed = 3323

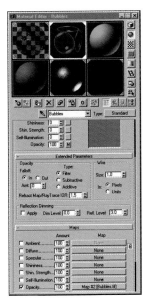

Figure 3
Creating a bubble surface material.

3. Copy the SuperSpray01 particle system slightly to the left and down. Use the Transform Type-In dialog box to position the particle system at x = –44.644, y = 11.424, z = –168.699, and accept the default name SuperSpray03.

4. Edit the SuperSpray03 particle system, and in the Particle Generation rollout, set the following parameters (see Figure 4):
   Seed = 25000

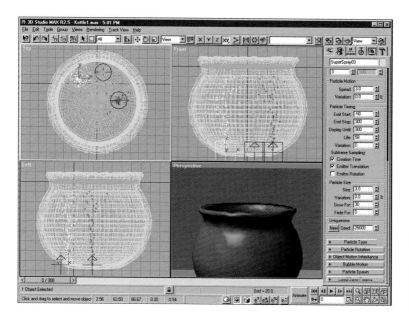

Figure 4
The location of the three particle systems, creating the small bubbles.

At this point, the scene contains the water surface and particle systems used to create the small bubbles.

Creating Bigger Bubbles

1. Copy the SuperSpray01 particle system to the center of the kettle. Name the SuperSpray **SuperSprayBigBubbles**. Set the position at x = −6.054, y = −34.188, z = −168.699.

2. Edit the **SuperSprayBigBubbles** particle system. In the Particle Formation section of the Basic Parameters rollout, set the following parameters:
   Off Axis Spread = 36

3. In the Particle Generation rollout, set the following parameters (see Figure 5):
   Use Total = 75
   Emit Start = 30
   Size = 5
   Size Variation = 100
   Seed = 3323

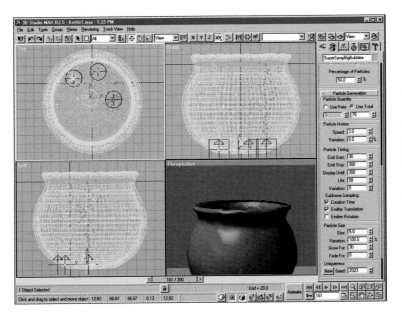

Figure 5
By setting the life of the bubbles appropriately, they appear to pop as they breach the surface. Combined with the varying size and inter-twined chaotic movement, these face mapped bubbles create a convincing boiling mixture.

At this point, the scene contains the water surface and the particle systems used to create the bubbles.

Creating the Hot Steam Vapor

1. Create a standard primitive cylinder located at the center of the neck of the kettle. Use the Transform Type-In dialog box to position the cylinder at x = 0.547, y = –42.573, z = –13.37. Set the following parameters:
   Radius = 92.5
   Height = 10
   Height Segments = 1
   Cap Segments = 1
   Sides = 16

2. In the Modify panel, click Edit Stack and select to convert to an Editable Mesh. Turn on Sub-Object Vertex, select the bottom vertices in the Front viewport, and click Delete in the Miscellaneous section of the rollout to delete the vertices. Turn off Sub-Object mode.

3. Right-click the object, select Properties, and turn off Renderable.

4. Name the object **Steam Emitter**.

5. Create a PArray to the side of the kettle. The position of the PArray icon and its size do not matter. Set the following parameters:
   Pick Object = Steam Emitter
   Particle Formation = Over Entire Surface

6. In the Particle Generation rollout, set the following parameters:
   Use Rate = 2
   Speed = 3
   Divergence = 10
   Emit Stop = 300
   Display Until = 300
   Life = 50
   Size = 18
   Grow For = 0
   Fade For = 40

7. Set the Particle Type parameters as follows:
   Standard Particles = Facing

8. Set the Bubble Motion as follows:
   Amplitude = 1.6
   Amplitude Variation = 20
   Period = 8
   Period Variation = 40
   Phase = 180
   Phase Variation = 100

9. Name the PArray **Steam**.

At this point, the scene contains the water surface and the particle systems used to create the bubbles and the steam.

Creating the Steam Material

1. In the Material Editor, make material slot 3 active and set the Material Type to Standard. Set the Sample Type to the cube.

2. Set the Basic Parameters as follows:
   Face Map = On
   Ambient = (R = 0, G = 0, B = 0)
   Diffuse = (R = 255, G = 255, B = 255)
   Shininess = 0
   Shin. Strength = 0
   Self-Illumination = 100

3. Set the Extended Parameters as follows:
   Falloff: Amt = 85

4. Set the amount for the Diffuse slot to 100. Click the Diffuse slot and set the Map Type to Noise. Set the Noise Parameters as follows:
Noise Type = Turbulence
Size = 20

5. Swap Color #1 with Color #2.

6. Set the amount for the Opacity slot to 100. Click the Opacity slot and set the Map Type to Mask.

7. In the Mask map, click the Map slot and set the Map Type to Noise.

8. Set the following Noise Parameters:
Noise Type = Turbulence
Size = 20

9. Swap Color #1 with Color #2.

10. Return to the Mask map, click on the Mask slot, and set the Map Type to Gradient.

11. Set the following Gradient parameters:
Gradient Type = Radial

12. Swap Color #1 with Color #3.

13. Name the material **Steam**.

14. Apply the Steam material to the Steam PArray (see Figure 6).

At this point, the scene contains the water surface and the particle systems used to create the bubbles and the steam. You have defined materials and applied them to the water surface and the particle systems.

Water Surface Displacement

In this section, you merge a set of Displacement space warps into the scene. When bound to the water surface, they deform it like bubbles seething through the water surface.

1. Merge the Displacements.max file from this project Preload directory on the CD-ROM. Select all objects to merge.

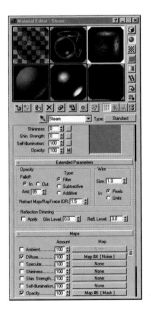

Note

These 22 Displacement space warps load with a simple linear animation. They are all linked together and move in a linear fashion through the surface of the water over the 300-frame animation.

Figure 6
Creating the Steam material.

2. Bind all 22 Displacement space warps to the WaterSurface object (see Figure 7).

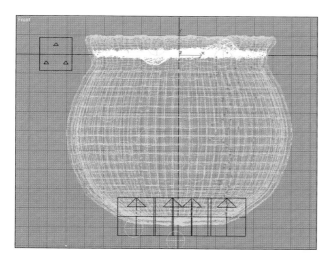

Figure 7
Spherical
Displacement space
warps animated
through the water
surface simulate
the effect of large
air bubbles during
boiling.

At this point, the scene is completed except for the addition of a camera and some lights.

Lighting Setup

In this section, you add the lighting to the scene.

1. Create an omni light at the center of the kettle. Use the Transform Type-In dialog box to position the light at x = 0.547, y = −42.573, z = −79.967. Set the omni light parameters as follows:
    Color = (R = 205, G = 217, B = 220)
    Multiplier = 0.5
    Projector = On

2. Click the Projector Map slot and set the Map Type to Bitmap. Drag the Project Map slot to slot 4 in Material Editor. Choose method Instance. Set the following Bitmap parameters:
    Coordinates = Texture
    Blur = 2
    Bitmap = DUSKCLD5.tga

3. Click the Exclude button and select Both (Illumination and Shadow Casting). Select the following objects for exclusion: Kettle, Steam, SuperSpray01, SuperSpray02, SuperSpray03, SuperSprayBigBubbles, and WaterSurface.

4. Create an omni light behind the kettle by Wall01. Us the Transform Type-In dialog box to position the light at x = −4.98, y = 113.43, z = −155.91. Set the omni light parameters as follows:
    Color = (R = 237, G = 101, B = 54)
    Multiplier = 7
    Attenuation: Far Use = On
    Far Start = 185
    Far End = 266
    Cast Shadows = on
    Use Shadow Maps = on

5. Click the Exclude button and select Both (Illumination and Shadow Casting). Select the following objects for exclusion: Kettle, Kettle01, Steam, SuperSpray01, SuperSpray02, SuperSpray03, SuperSprayBigBubbles, and WaterSurface.

6. Accept the default name Omni02.

7. Create a target spot light with the body located in front of the fireplace and the target located near the center of the kettle. Position the light at x = −192, y = −413, z = 422 and position the target at x = 20, y = −24, z = 0. Set the following spot light parameters:
    Multiplier = 2
    Hot Spot = 29
    Falloff = 60

8. Click the Exclude button and select Both (Illumination and Shadow Casting). Select the following object for exclusion: Kettle01.

At this point, the scene is completed except for the addition of a camera (see Figure 8).

Camera Setup

In this section, you add the camera to the scene.

1. Create a target camera with the body immediately in front of the fireplace and the target near the center of the kettle. Position the camera at x = 4, y = −370, z = 56. Position the target at x = 4, y = −12, z = −17. Set the following camera property:
    Lens = 35

2. Turn Animate on and move the Time Slider to Frame 150. Position the camera body at x = 4, y = −152, z = 89. Turn Animate off (see Figure 9).

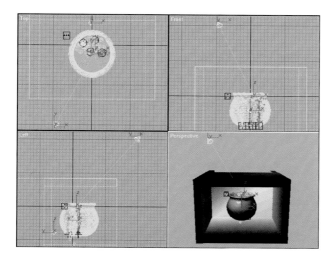

Figure 8
The placement of
the lights.

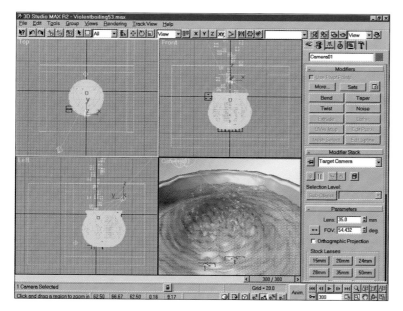

Figure 9
Completed Violent
Boiling animation.

You can find the final MAX file, ViolentBoiling.max, in this project's
Preload folder and the final AVI file in the Images folder.

Water Surfaces

Sunlit Underwater Surface

by Greg Carbonaro

If you were a scuba diver looking up toward the surface of the water, a sunlit underwater surface is essentially what you would see. It's a very distinctive effect that requires fine-tuned settings to produce a realistic, natural look. This is the beginning of a five-step effects series geared toward creating a visually dynamic underwater setting. In the steps outlined in this effect, you reproduce one of the four Underwater Ambiance effects in the series: "Sunlit Underwater Surface." In successive effects examples, you explore "Caustic Light Projections on Underwater Objects," "Murky Sea Floor Ambiance," "Dancing Volumetric Light Rays," and "Volumetric Spot and Flood Lights." When combined together, these four effects create a highly realistic underwater environment.

Note

All position and rotational information is based on absolute world coordinates. When creating objects, use keyboard entry where possible. When positioning objects, use the Transform Type-In dialog box located in the Tools menu. These techniques ensure proper object placement and orientation.

Leave any settings that are not listed in the example at the MAX default values. Create objects in the Top viewport, unless otherwise indicated.

Preconfiguration

1. Before beginning this effect, either reset *or* restart MAX.

2. Copy the project map files from the accompanying CD-ROM to the MAX maps subdirectory.

3. Load the file floor.max from the project preload directory on the CD-ROM. The animation length has been preset to 200 frames.

4. In the Material Editor, right-click in any material slot and make sure Sample Windows is set to 3×2.

At this point, you should see a simple sea floor on your screen.

Environment Setup

In this section, you create the underwater depth and distance cue.

1. Add an atmospheric fog effect.
   Fog: **Environmental Color Map**: Map #1 (Gradient)
   Use Map = on

2. In the Material Editor, make material slot 1 active.

3. Use Get Material to set the Material Type to Gradient. Set the Gradient Parameters as follows:
   Coordinates: Environ = on, Mapping = screen
   Color #1 = (R = 65, G = 115, B = 150)
   Color #2 = (R = 40, G = 95, B = 130)
   Color #3 = (R = 20, G = 70, B = 100)

4. Name the material **Depth Gradient**.

5. Copy the Depth Gradient material as Instance to the Fog Parameters – Environment Color Map slot in the Environment dialog box.

Note

Step 5 can be accomplished by having the Material Editor and the Rendering Environment dialog box open at the same time. You must drag and drop the gradient from slot 1 to the color map selector. This is the same color map selection bar that you assigned a gradient to in Step 1.

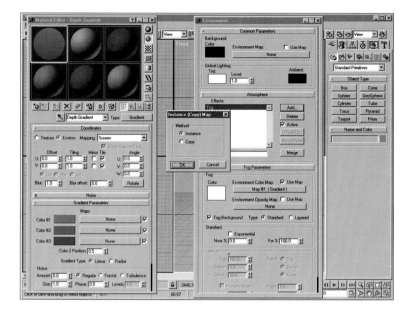

Figure 1
Copy the Depth
Gradient material
as Instance.

Modeling and Materials

Now create the ocean surface object and materials.

Ocean Surface Object Creation

1. Activate the Top viewport.

2. Create a standard primitive box in the Top viewport roughly
   centered over the ocean floor object, and then use the Transform
   Type-In dialog box to position the primative box at x = 0, y = 0,
   z = 50. Set the following:
   Length = 7000
   Width = 15000
   Height = 5
   Generate Mapping = on

3. Name the box **Ocean Surface**.

At this point, you should see an extremely large box many times the size
of the ocean floor object in the viewport.

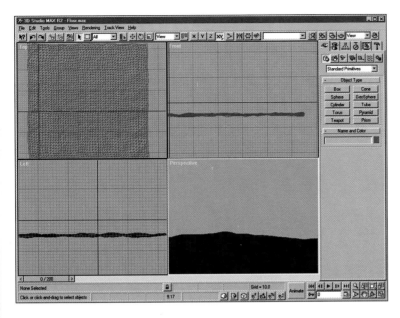

Figure 2
The Ocean Surface object.

Ocean Surface Material

1. In the Material Editor, make material slot 2 active.

2. Set the Basic Parameters as follows:
   Shading = Phong
   Ambient = (R = 65, G = 115, B = 145)
   Diffuse = (R = 65, G = 115, B = 145)
   Shininess = 20
   Shin. Strength = 95
   Soften = 0

3. Set the Amount for the Bump map channel to 30. Click the Bump map channel and set the map Type to Noise. Set the Noise Parameters as follows:
   Noise Type = Turbulence
   Size = 10

4. Animate the coordinates' Z Offset:
   Frame 0 (Keyframe 1) Z Offset = 0
   Frame 300 (Keyframe 2) Z Offset = 60

   Return to the parent level of the material.

5. Set the amount for the Reflection map channel to 100. Click the Reflection map channel and set the type to Bitmap. Select Sky.jpg as the bitmap. Set the coordinates:
   Environ = on
   Mapping = Spherical

6. Name the material **Under Surface**.

7. Apply the Under Surface material to the Ocean Surface object.

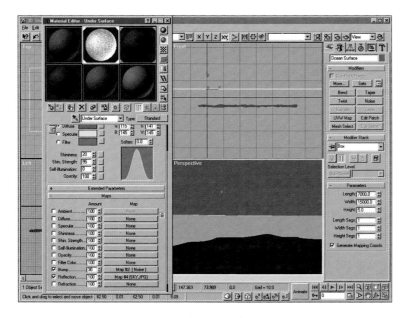

Figure 3
This material and its z-axis coordinate noise animation are the keys to this effect.

You have just created the sparkly underwater surface, and if you were to render it right now, you would see that the effect is starting to come together. You need to do a few more things, however, to fine-tune and complete the image.

Lighting Setup

In this section, you create the bright, glowing sunlight that glistens on the water surface.

1. Create an omni light in approximately the center of the Top viewport and then use the Transform Type-In dialog box to position the light at x = 300, y = 0, z = 30:
Color = (R = 250, G = 250, B = 250)
Multiplier = 2

2. Exclude the Ocean Floor from Shadow Casting and Illumination.

3. Name the omni light **Sun Light**.

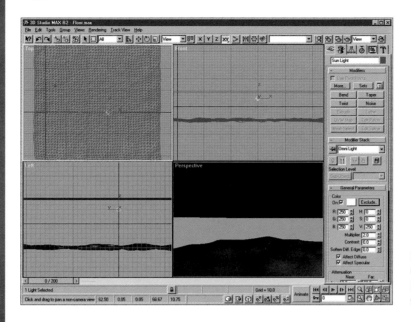

Figure 4
Create an omni
light in the Top
viewport.

Camera Setup

The final step is to set up the camera through which you will view the
finished effect.

> Create a target camera in the Top viewport, pointing toward the
> center of the ocean floor object and then use the Transform
> Type-In dialog box to position the body at x = 120, y = –50,
> z = 0. Position the target at x = 220, y = 0, z = 0. Set the
> Environmental Ranges:
> **Near Range** = 75
> **Far Range** = 345
> **Show** = checked

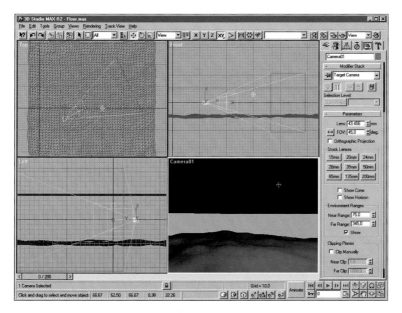

Figure 5
Create a target
camera in the Top
viewport.

The camera environmental ranges used here work in conjunction with
the Rendering Fog Environment to create underwater depth and distance fade.

Caustic Light Projections on Underwater Objects

by Greg Carbonaro

This is part two of a four-step effects series geared toward creating visually dynamic underwater settings. Part one of the Underwater Ambiance effects series was explored in a previous section "Sunlit Underwater Surface." In the steps outlined here, you reproduce the necessary setup and settings to create caustic light highlights and shadows under water, a vital visual element in any underwater scene. In successive effects examples, you explore "Murky Sea Floor Ambiance," and "Dancing Volumetric Light Rays." When combined together, these four effects create a highly realistic underwater environment.

Note

All position and rotational information is based on absolute world coordinates. When creating objects, use keyboard entry where possible. When positioning objects, use the Transform Type-In dialog box located in the Tools menu. These techniques ensure proper object placement and orientation.

Leave any settings that are not listed in the example at the MAX default values. Create objects in the Top viewport, unless otherwise indicated.

Preconfiguration

1. Before beginning this effect, either reset or restart MAX.

2. Copy the Caustic Light project map files from the accompanying CD-ROM to the MAX maps subdirectory.

3. Load the SunLit.max scene from the project's preload directory on the CD-ROM. (This effect was created in the previous effects example "Sunlit Underwater Surface.") The animation length has been preset to 200 frames.

4. Merge the Ship object into the scene from the project's preload directory.

5. In the Material Editor, right-click in any material slot and make sure Sample Windows is set to 3×2.

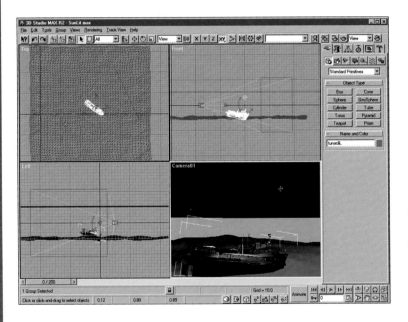

Figure 1
This preloaded scene was created in the previous effects section "Sunlit Underwater Surface."

At this point, you should see a scene containing the sea floor and a ship.

Materials

You now need to create an interesting, natural-looking sea floor.

Sea Floor Material

1. In the Material Editor, make material slot 3 active.

2. Set the Material Type to Standard.

3. Set the Basic Parameters:
   Shading = Phong
   Shininess = 0
   Shin. Strength = 0
   Soften = 0

4. In the Maps area, set the Diffuse map to an RGB tint type and in the Tint Parameters, use sandwave.jpg as the map.

5. Go back up to the RGB tint level of the material and set the Tint Parameters:
   Red = (200, 100, 100)
   Green = (100, 200, 100)
   Blue = (100, 100, 200)

6. Go up to the parent level of the material and copy the Diffuse map channel to the Bump map channel: Set the Bump map amount to 185.

7. Name the material **Sea Floor Sand**.

8. Apply the Sea Floor Sand material to the Ocean Floor object.

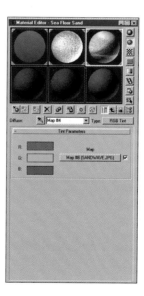

Figure 2
Set the Tint Parameters in the Material Editor.

9. Set the Object properties:
Ocean Surface Object Cast Shadow = off

Caustic Light Projectors

The spotlights you are about to create serve as projectors that cast the sea water caustic lighting effects.

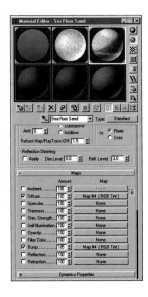

1. Create a target spotlight in the Front viewport pointing down toward the sea floor. Use the transform Type-In dialog box to position the light at x = 180, y = –95, z = 128. Position the target at x = 220, y = 0, z = 0. Set the following:
Color = (R = 145, G = 195, B = 230)
Multiplier = 2

Figure 3
Copy the Diffuse map channel to the Bump map channel.

2. Click the Exclude button and select Both (Illumination and Shadow Casting). Select the Ocean Floor and Ocean Surface objects for exclusion.

3. Set the Spotlight Parameters:
Hotspot = 90
Falloff = 92
Projector = on
Map = Noise
Cast Shadows = on

4. Copy the spotlights projector map Noise as an Instance to slot 4 of the Material Editor.

5. Name the target spot **Caustic Ship Light**.

6. Create a target spotlight in the Front viewport pointing down toward the sea floor. Use the Transform Type-In dialog box to position the light at x = 265, y = −28, z = 350. Position the target at x = 265, y = −28, z = −77. Set the following:
   Color = (R = 180, G = 180, B = 180)
   Multiplier = 2

7. Click the Exclude button and select Illumination. Select the Ship and Ocean Surface objects for exclusion.

8. Set the Spotlight Parameters:
   Hotspot = 100
   Falloff = 102
   Projector = on
   Map = Noise
   Cast Shadows = on

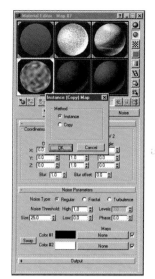

Figure 4
Drag and drop an Instance of the lights projector Noise map to slot 4 of the Material Editor.

9. Copy the spotlights projector map Noise as an Instance to slot 5 of the Material Editor.

10. Name the target spotlight **Light Floor**.

Caustic Light Projector Materials

1. In the Material Editor, make material slot 4 active.

2. Set the Noise coordinates:
   UVW1 = on

3. Animate the coordinates:
   Frame 0 (Keyframe 1) W Offset = 0
   Frame 200 (Keyframe 2) W Offset = 0.1

4. Set the Noise Parameters:
   Noise Type = Turbulence

5. Set the Noise Threshold parameters:
   High = 0.835
   Size = 0.02

6. Swap color #1 with color #2.

7. Name the material **Ship Caustic**.

8. In the Material Editor, make material slot 5 active.

9. Animate the coordinates:
Frame 0 (Keyframe 1) W Offset = 0
Frame 200 (Keyframe 2) W Offset = 70

10. Set the Noise Parameters:
Noise Type = Turbulence

11. Set the Noise Threshold parameters:
High = 0.75
Size = 10

12. Swap color #1 with color #2.

13. Name the material **SeaFloor Caustic**.

When you render the animation, you will see a very convincing under-water caustic light effect dramatically illuminating the ocean floor and ship with its noisy turbulent characteristics.

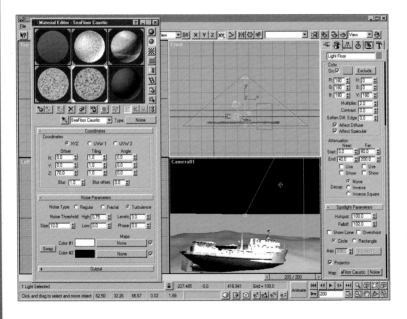

Figure 5
The completed caustic light projections on Underwater Objects effect.

Murky Sea Floor Ambiance

by Greg Carbonaro

This is part three of a four-step effects series geared toward creating visually dynamic underwater settings. Parts one and two of the Underwater Ambiance Effects series were explored in the previous sections "Sunlit Underwater Surface" and "Caustic Light Projections on Underwater Objects." In the steps outlined here, you reproduce the necessary setup and settings to create a murky underwater sea floor, another vital visual element in any underwater scene. In the successive effects example, you explore "Dancing Volumetric Light Rays." When combined together, these four effects create a highly realistic underwater environment.

Note

All position and rotational information is based on absolute world coordinates. When creating objects, use keyboard entry where possible. When positioning objects, use the Transform Type-In dialog box located in the Tools menu. These techniques ensure proper object placement and orientation.

Leave any settings that are not listed in the example at the MAX default values. Create objects in the Top viewport, unless otherwise indicated.

Preconfiguration

1. Before beginning this effect, either reset *or* restart MAX.

2. Copy the murky sea floor project map files from the accompanying CD-ROM to the MAX maps subdirectory.

3. Load the CausticLight.max file from the project's preload directory on the CD-ROM. (This effect was created in the previous effects example "Caustic Light Projections on Underwater Objects.") The animation length has been preset to 200 frames.

4. In the Material Editor, right-click any material slot and make sure Sample Windows are set to 3×2.

At this point, your scene should contain a sea floor, sea surface, ship, and various lights and cameras.

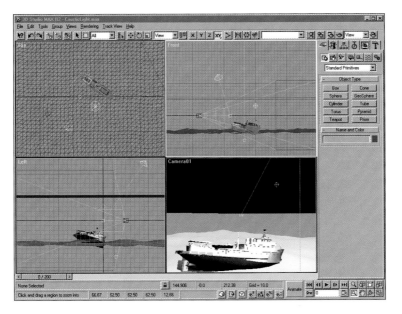

Figure 1
This preloaded scene was created in a previous effects section, "Caustic Light Projections on Underwater Objects."

Creating the Murky Sea Floor

Now create the gizmo that contains the murky sea floor ambiance.

1. Create an Atmospheric apparatus Helper cylgizmo in the Top viewport in approximately the center of the ocean floor object; use the Transform Type-In dialog box to position it at x = 271, y = 26, z = −48. Set the following:
Radius = 165.5
Height = 8.2

2. Name the cylgizmo **Murky Floor**.

3. In the Rendering Environment, add an Atmospheric effect
Volume fog to the scene:
Pick Gizmo = Murky Floor
Soften Gizmo Edges = 1

4. Set the Volume parameters:
Color = (R = 155, G = 150,
B = 140)
Density = 50
Fog Background = Off

5. Set the Noise Parameters:
Type = Fractal
Uniformity = 0.6
Levels = 6
Size = 15
Wind Strength = 0.2
Wind From The = Left

6. Animate the Noise Phase:
Frame 0 (Keyframe 1) phase = 0
Frame 200 (Keyframe 2) phase = 2

Figure 2
The Environment
dialog box in which
you add an
Atmospheric effect.

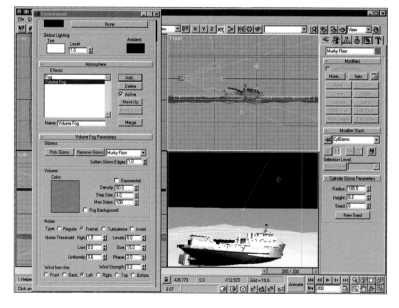

Figure 3
The Noise Phase
animation causes
the volume fog
contained within
the cylgizmo to
move in a slow, bil-
lowing fashion.

Underwater Ambiance

Dancing Volumetric Light Rays

by Greg Carbonaro

This is the final part of a four-step effects series geared toward creating visually dynamic underwater settings. Parts one, two, and three of the Underwater Ambiance Effects series were explored in the preceding sections, "Sunlit Underwater Surface," "Caustic Light Projections on Underwater Objects," and "Murky Sea Floor Ambiance." In the steps outlined here, you reproduce the necessary setup and settings to create dancing rays of sunlight, another vital visual element in any underwater scene. When you combine this final effect with the previous four, you can create a highly realistic underwater environment.

Note

All position and rotational information is based on absolute world coordinates. When creating objects, use keyboard entry where possible. When positioning objects, use the Transform Type-In dialog box located in the Tools menu. These techniques ensure proper object placement and orientation.

Leave settings that are not listed in the example at the MAX default values. Create objects in the Top viewport, unless otherwise indicated.

Preconfiguration

1. Before beginning the effect, either reset or restart MAX.

2. Copy the Dancing Volumetric Sunlight Rays project map files from the accompanying CD-ROM to the MAX maps subdirectory.

3. Load the MurkySea.max file from the project preload directory on the CD-ROM. (This effect was created in the previous effects example "Murky Sea Floor Ambiance.") The animation length has been preset to 200 frames.

4. In the Material Editor, right-click in any material slot and make sure Sample Windows are set to 3×2.

At this point, you should see the ocean floor, ship, associated lights, and a camera.

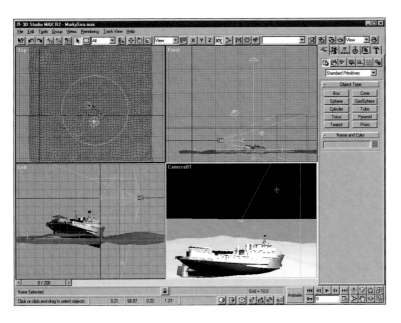

Figure 1
This preloaded scene was created in a previous effect, "Murky Sea Floor Ambiance."

Volume Light Projector

In this section, you create multiple shafts of moving volumetric light with a single spotlight and a projector bitmap.

1. Create a target spotlight in the Front viewport pointing down. Use the Transform Type-In dialog box to position the body at x = 130, y = –74, z = 126. Position the target at x = 215, y = –11, z = –28. Set the following:
   Color = (R = 255, G = 255, B = 255)
   Multiplier = 4

2. Set the Attenuation parameters:
   Far Start = 0
   Far End = 305
   Use = on

3. Click the Exclude button and select Both (Illumination and Shadow Casting). Select the Ocean Surface object for exclusion.

4. Set the Spotlight Parameters:
   Hotspot = 73
   Falloff = 92
   Projector = on
   Map = Bitmap
   Cast Shadows = on

5. Copy the spotlight's projector map bitmap as an Instance to slot 6 in the Material Editor.

6. Name the target spot **Light Rays**.

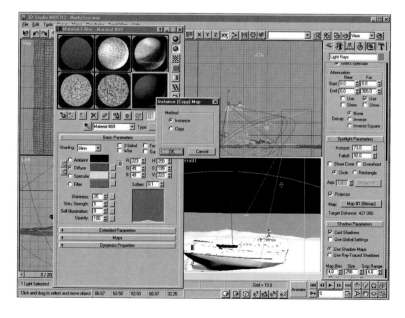

Figure 2
Drag and drop an Instance of the lights projector bitmap map to slot 6 of the Material Editor.

Volume Light Material

Now you can set up the projector bitmap to produce the multiple light rays.

1. In the Material Editor, make material slot 6 active.

2. Set the Bitmap coordinates:
   Blur = 2

3. Animate the coordinates W angle:
   Frame 0 (Keyframe 1) W angle = 0
   Frame 300 (Keyframe 2) W angle = 60

4. Set the Bitmap Parameters:
   Bitmap = "volumask.gif"

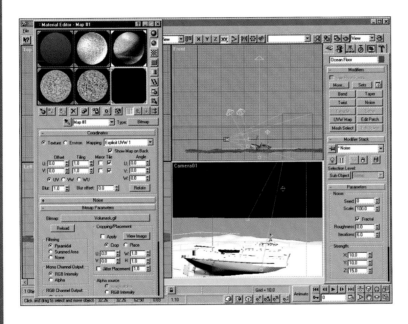

Figure 3
Set the Bitmap Parameters.

5. Set the Output:
   Output Amount = 2
   Bump Amount = 2

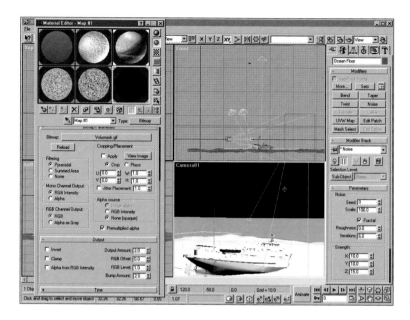

Figure 4
Set the Output in
the Material Editor.

Volumetric Light Rays

You are now going to create the actual dancing light rays by making the
projector spotlight you created volumetric.

1. Select the Rendering drop-down menu and open the
   Environment dialog box.

2. Under Atmosphere, add a volume light.

3. Under Volume Light Parameters, select the Light Rays spotlight.
   Set the following:
   Filter Shadows = High
   Noise Threshold: High = 0

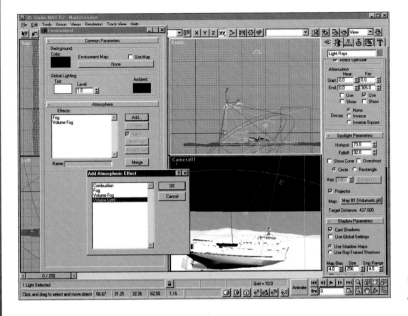

Figure 5
Add a volume light.

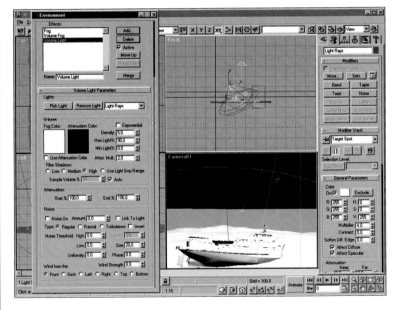

Figure 6
Set the Volume
Light Parameters.

When you render the animation, be prepared for moderately long render
times. Volumetric lights are notorious for bogging down even the fastest
machines. The final imagery and the sense of realism it can introduce
into your animations, however, is well worth the wait.

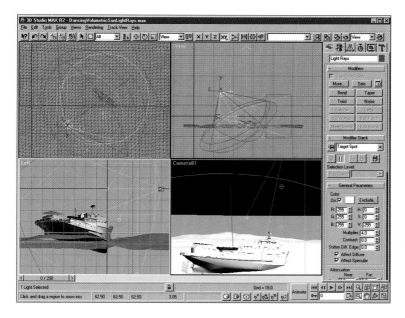

Figure 7
The completed
Dancing Volumetric
Light Rays effect.

Underwater Bubbles Effect

by Jay Kapadia

The effect of bubbles rising from the ocean floor has two qualities to note: The bubbles vary and animate in size and shape, and their overall movement is effected by underwater currents. The following effect provides an underwater scene and illustrates how to build and animate the rising bubbles. This scene makes extensive use of noise in building scene geometry, the environment, lighting, materials, and bubble motions. The bubbles emit as MetaParticles from a Blizzard particle system and as Standard sphere particles from a PArray particle system (to add bubble motion).

You build the underwater environment by using a QuadPatch with a Noise modifier for the ocean floor, and as background, an environmental map (spherical mapping) made from a gradient with Noise. Standard fog is applied, using the same gradient as an Environmental Color Map. Although the scene includes a volumetric light, it is turned off for this exercise because of the effect it has on the standard fog bubble particles. Deconstructing the MAX file for this exercise can be helpful if you are unfamiliar with techniques common to underwater scenes.

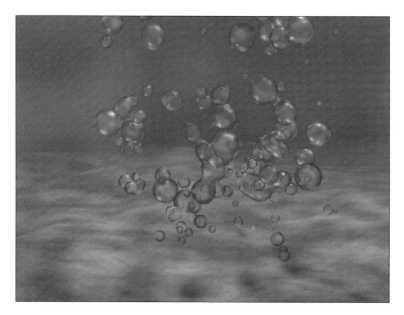

Note

All position and rotational information is based on absolute world coordinates. When positioning objects in your scene, always use the Transform Type-In dialog box located in the Tools menu. These techniques ensure proper object orientation.

Leave any settings that are not listed in the example at the MAX default values. Create objects in the Top viewport, unless otherwise noted.

1. Load bubble.max from this project's Preload folder on the accompanying CD-ROM. This is an underwater scene containing general lighting and an animated camera (see Figure 1).

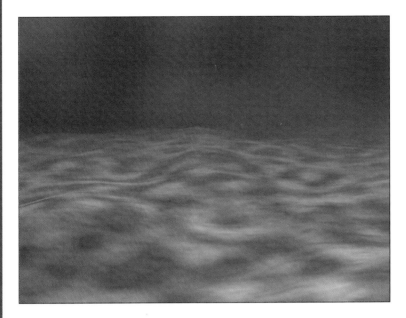

Figure 1
The beginning underwater scene.

Add Bubbles to the Scene

MetaParticles in the Blizzard particle system work well to create the deforming bubbles rising from the ocean floor.

1. Create a Blizzard particle system so that it appears in the fore-ground in the camera viewport, at or just below the QuadPatch. Use the Transform Type-In dialog box to position the QuadPatch at x = 12, y = –65, z = 0. Set the following:
Width = 120
Length = 60
Viewport Display: Percentage of Particles = 100

2. Rotate the emitter 180 degrees along the y-axis so particles emit upward.

3. Under Particle Generation, set the following:
Use Rate = checked, 3

4. Turn Animate on, advance to Frame 10, and set Use Rate to 0. Advance to Frame 20 and set Use Rate to 3. Advance to Frame 40 and set Use Rate to 0.

5. Open Track View and expand the hierarchy tree to show the tracks for Blizzard01. The Use Rate values set in Step 4 are stored in the track labeled Birth Rate. Highlight the Birth Rate track, click the Out-of-Range icon, and select Cycle (in and out). Select the Birth Rate keys, right-click on a key, and adjust the In and Out settings each to the Step (square) setting. This results in particles emitted in bursts (see Figure 2).

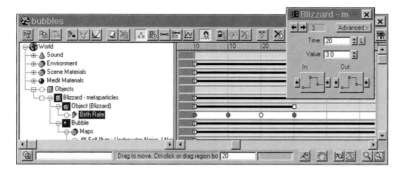

Figure 2
Animating the Birth Rate settings in Track View creates burst particle emissions.

6. Under Particle Generation, set the following:
Speed = 3.0
Variation = 10.0
Tumble = 1.0
Emit Stop = 100
Life = 50
Variation =10
Particle Size = 15.0
Variation = 75
Grow For = 10
Fade For = 0

7. Under Particle Type, select MetaParticles and set the following:
Tension = 0.5
Automatic Coarseness = checked

For the second particle system, you need Bubble Motion capability and particles emitting from a surface. This feature is not present in Blizzard, but is with the PArray particle system. PArray requires a geometric object for the emitter.

8. In the Top viewport and concentric with the Blizzard emitter, draw a rectangle at x = 12, y = –65, z = 0. Set the following:
Length = 100
Width = 150

9. Add an Edit Mesh Modifier and position it below the sea floor.

10. Create a PArray particle system and select the rectangle from Step 7 as the Object-Based Emitter. Set the following:
   Particle Formation = At Distinct Points
   Total = 20
   Viewport Display: Percentage of Particle = 100%

11. In Track View, copy the Birth Rate track from the Blizzard particle system to the Birth Rate track for PArray.

12. In the Modify panel of the Particle Generation rollout, set the following:
   Speed = 3.0
   Variation = 50
   Divergence = 10.0
   Emit Stop = 100
   Life = 50
   Variation = 10
   Particle Size = 5.0
   Variation = 75
   Grow For = 10
   Fade For = 0

13. Under Particle Type, choose Standard Particles, Sphere.

14. Under Bubble Motion, set the following:
   Amplitude = 10.0
   Amplitude Variation = 25.0
   Period = 30
   Period Variation = 10
   Phase = 55
   Phase Variation = 10

At this point, you should see two particles streams mixing, a larger set made up of MetaParticles and a smaller one of standard spheres (see Figure 3).

Bubble Material

The next step is to create the material for the bubbles.

1. In the Material Editor, select an empty slot and set the Material Type to Standard.

2. Set the Basic Parameters as follows:
   2-Sided = checked
   Diffuse = (H = 151, S = 164, V = 156)
   Filter = (H = 151, S = 164, V = 156)
   Shininess = 40
   Shin. Strength = 100
   Self-Illumination = 80
   Opacity = 70

Figure 3
Frame 50 of the animation, showing the two particle systems before applying materials.

3. Under Extended Parameters, set the following:
   Falloff = In
   Amt. = 100

4. Copy as an instance the Water Noise map used for the target spotlight projector map to the Bubble Self-Illumination, Shininess, and Opacity map channels. Set the Amount in each channel to 50. Name the material **Bubble** (see Figure 4).

Figure 4
Copy the Water Noise map from the Material/Map Browser to the Self-Illumination, Shininess, and Opacity map slots for the Bubble material in the Material Editor. Note this is the same map used as a Projector spot on Spot - water pattern in the scene.

5. In the Material Editor, select an empty slot and create another Noise map material. Set the following:
   X, **Y**, and **Z Tiling** = 4.0
   Blur = 2.0
   Noise Type = Regular
   Size = 20.0
   Noise Threshold: High = 0.49, Low = 0.35

6. Turn Animate on. At Frame 0, set Phase to −1.0. Advance to Frame 100 and set Phase to 2.0. Turn Animate off.

7. Set the Noise colors as follows:
   Color #1 = (H = 43, S = 8, V = 218)
   Color #2 = (H = 151, S = 164, V = 56)

8. Copy this map as an Instance to the Bubble Reflection map channel. Set the Amount to 20.

9. Copy this map again to the Filter Color map. Set the Amount to 100.

10. Label the material **water reflection map**.

11. Assign the Bubble material to the Blizzard and PArray particle systems (see Figure 5).

12. In the Front viewport, create another target spot above the scene and at an angle, illuminating the bubbles as they rise. Use the Transform Type-In dialog box to position the light at x = 119, y = −39, z = 363. Label it **Spot-bubbles** and set the following:
   Color = (H = 101, S = 10, V = 204) (see Figure 6)

Figure 5
The final materials used for the bubbles and the bubble environment.

13. Click the Exclude/Include button. Set to Include, Both, and select only the PArray and Blizzard particle systems.

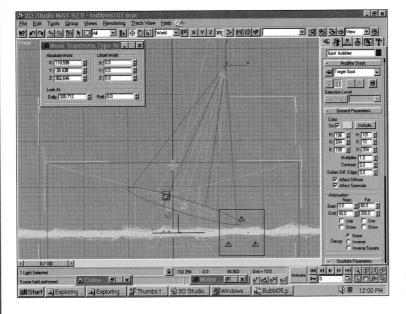

Figure 6
Create a target spot to illuminate the bubbles from above.

14. Set the following Spotlight parameters:
Falloff = 45

15. Set the following Shadow parameters:
Cast Shadows = checked
Use Global Settings = checked

16. Clone this target spot and place it below the sea floor and at an angle so that it illuminates the particles from underneath. Use the Transform Type-In dialog box to position it at x = –203, y = –39, z = –228. Label it **Spot – bubbles low**. Deselect Cast Shadows (see Figure 7).

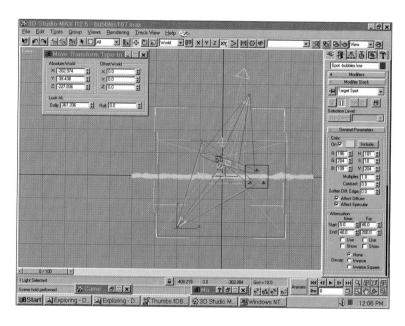

Figure 7
Clone the bubble illuminating spot and place it below the ocean floor for additional illumination.

Render the sequence. The final max file is included on the accompanying CD-ROM in this project's Scene folder as bubbles_final.max, and the final animation (Bubbles6.avi) is in the Images folder.

The shininess and brilliance of reflections off the bubbles is strongly affected by the fog density and camera environment settings. Also, if you want to add volume lights to the scene, you need to add an Environment Opacity map to the Standard Fog or use another fog solution.

Air Bubbles, Small and Large

by Jeff Abouaf

Both small and large air bubbles are key effects for making any underwater scene believable. Your vision is limited when you are underwater, therefore, having bubbles at different distances from the camera and some fading in the background produces a realistic effect of depth. The motion of the bubbles also helps break up the dark, dull background. Bubbles in general are good for movement. They can show currents, for instance. You also can use this effect to make smoke come out of the back of an engine or even a cigarette.

Preconfiguration

1. Copy the Air project map files from the accompanying CD-ROM to the MAX maps subdirectory.

2. Load the air.max file from this project's Pre-load folder on the accompanying CD-ROM.

At this point you should see a scene containing an underwater vehicle and a free spot. The animation is preset to 200 frames.

Creating a Bubble Particle System

In this section you are going to create the bubbles coming out of the engines.

1. Press K to switch the viewport to back. Create a Super Spray with an icon size of 30. Now position Super Spray01 behind the motor01 at x = −108.01, y = 1445.95, z = 50.11.

2. In the Particle Formation box of the Basic Parameters rollout, set the following:
    Off Axis Spread = 15
    Off Plane = 90
    Off Plane Spread = 30

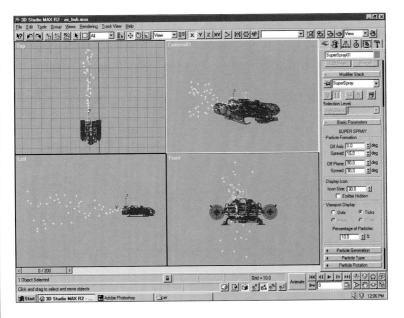

Figure 1
The position of Super Spray01 and the values changed in the Basic Parameters rollout.

3. In the Particle Motion box of the Particle Generation rollout, set the following:
    Speed = 15
    Variation = 5

4. In the Particle Timing box set the following:
Emit Start = −50
Emit Stop = 500
Display Until = 500
Life = 300
Variation = 20

5. In the Particle Size box, set the following:
Size = 3
Variation = 60

Note

Three is the basic size of the bubble. The higher the variation, the more varied the size of the bubbles.

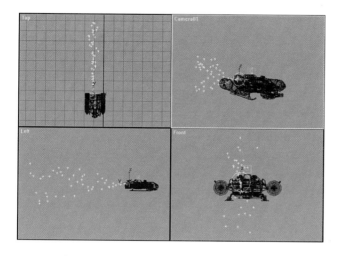

Figure 2
The parameters under the Particle Generation rollout.

6. In the Particle Type rollout, click Facing.

7. Link Super Spray01 to the Dummy01.

At this point you have created a particle system that will spray out bubbles randomly.

Creating Rising Bubbles

As everyone knows bubbles in water rise to the surface, so you will be using a Gravity space warp to create this effect.

1. Create a Gravity space warp at x = −88.8, y = 1388. 2, z = 103.0. Bind it to Super Spray01, and make it point up (see Figure 3):
Strength = 0.05

Note

I like to keep space warps close to the particle systems they are affecting. It makes it easier when you have multiple space warps affecting multiple particle systems.

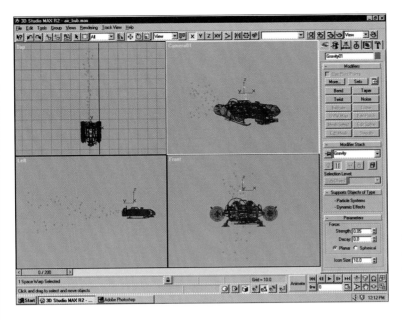

Figure 3
The placement of the Gravity space warp and the changed parameters.

2. Link the Gravity Space Warp to Dummy01.

At this point, as the ship moves along blowing out bubbles, the bubbles should rise out of the camera viewport.

Creating the Bubble Material

In this section, you are going to create the material for the bubbles.

1. In the Materials Editor, activate slot 3 and create a material called bubbles.

2. In the Basic Parameters rollout, turn on face map.

3. Set the Basic Parameters as follows:
   Ambient = (R = 0, G = 0, B = 0)
   Diffuse = (R = 0, G = 0, B = 0)
   Specular = (R = 0, G = 0, B = 0)
   Filter = (R = 0, G = 0, B = 0)
   Shininess = 0
   Shin. Strength = 0
   Soften = 0

4. Click the opacity slot and choose bitmap.

5. Load a file called bubbles.tif.

Note

If your machine begins to slow down, change the Percentage of Particles to display set at 2 percent. This enables you to work faster because your CPU won't have to update as many particles in the viewport.

6. Apply the bubbles material to the Super Spray01 (see Figure 4).

7. Clone Super Spray01 and place it behind motor02 at x = −65.47, y = 1445.95, z = 50.11. Click the New Seed button in the Particle Generation rollout.

The speed at which the bubbles are generated makes the vehicle look like it's moving fast. The slower the bubbles come out, the slower the apparent speed of the vehicle.

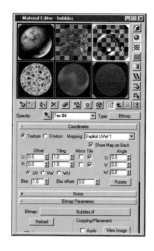

Figure 4
Loading the bubbles.tif image.

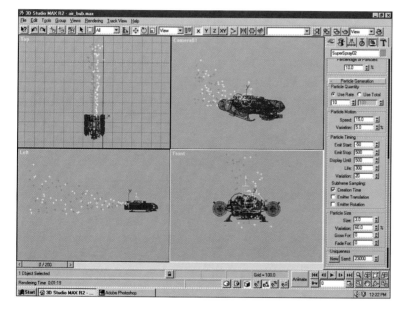

Figure 5
The position of the second Super Spray.

Water Fountain

by Greg Carbonaro

There are several challenges that you need to address when creating the Water Fountain effect. First, you must create a convincing water surface by utilizing a refraction mapped material, an underwater reflector, and a sky projector spotlight. For the actual fountain water you must utilize refraction mapping, as well as reflection mapping to create sparkly translucent water. To achieve this lively effect, you will use tetra particles with no motion blur; although the animation is beautiful, there is a minor tradeoff—the still images suffer because the tetra particles are easy to pick out. That said, this effect is about animation not stills. Beautiful imagery can be accomplished with instanced geometry instead of tetra particles, but that would require a tremendous amount of render time.

Note

All position and rotational information is based on absolute world coordinates. When creating objects use keyboard entry when possible. When positioning objects use the Transform Type-In dialog box located in the Tools menu. These techniques ensure proper object placement and orientation.

Leave any settings that are not listed in the example at the MAX default values. Create objects in the Top viewport, unless otherwise indicated.

Preconfiguration

1. Before beginning this effect, please reset *or* restart MAX.

2. Copy the Water Fountain project map files from the accompanying CD-ROM to the MAX maps subdirectory.

3. Load the Fountain.max file from this project's Pre-load folder on the CD-ROM. The animation length has been pre-set to 300 frames.

4. Open the Material Editor and right-click in any material slot to make sure Sample Windows are set to 3×2.

At this point, you should see a scene containing a fountain, a wall, and the ground.

Modeling and Materials

The first part of the effect is created with some basic modeling techniques and the application of specially designed materials.

Creating the Water Surface

1. Right-click in the Top viewport to activate it.

2. Create a standard primitive cylinder in the center of the fountain at x = 0.547, y = −42.573, z = −0.286. Set the parameters as follows:
   Radius = 100
   Height = 3.5
   Height Segments = 2
   Cap Segments = 32
   Sides = 50
   Smooth = on
   Generate Mapping Coordinates = on

3. Name the object **FountainWater** (see Figure 1).

Water Surface Material

1. In the Material Editor, make material slot 1 active and set the Material Type to Standard

2. Set the Basic parameters as follows:
   Shading = Blinn
   Ambient = (R = 45, G = 55, B = 65)
   Diffuse = (R = 122, G = 112, B = 92)
   Specular = (R = 255, G = 255, B = 255)

Filter = (R = 41, G = 24, B = 14)
Shininess = 62
Shin. Strength = 100
Opacity = 30

3. Set the amount for the Bump slot to 50. Click the Bump map slot and set the map Type to Noise. Set the Noise parameters as follows:
Coordinates = UVW1
V Tiling = 4
Noise type = turbulence
Size = 0.02

4. Animate the coordinates:
Frame 0 (Keyframe 1) W offset = 0
Frame 300 (Keyframe 2) W offset = −0.75

5. Return to the Parent level of the material. Set the Amount for the Refraction slot to 40. Click the Refraction slot and set the map type to Thin Wall Refraction. Set the following:
Refraction: Bump Map Effect = 2.0

6. Name the material **WaterSurface**.

7. Apply the WaterSurface material to the FountainWater object.

The FountainWater object now has a realistic, bumpy, refractive surface.

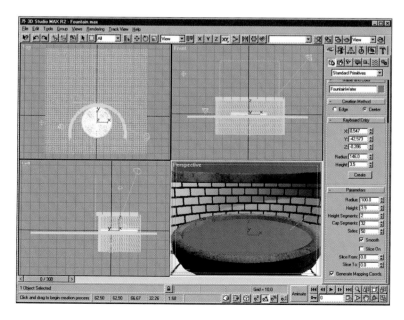

Figure 1
Creating the water surface.

Sky Reflector Creation

1. Right-click the Top viewport to activate it.

2. Create a standard primitive cylinder at the center of the fountain slightly below the water object at x = 0.14, y = −42.573, z = −6.808. Set the parameters as follows:
   Radius = 100
   Height = 2
   Height Segments = 2
   Cap Segments = 6
   Sides = 25
   Smooth = on

3. Add a UVW Map modifier to the cylinder object. Set mapping to Box.

4. Name the object **SkyReflector** (see Figure 2).

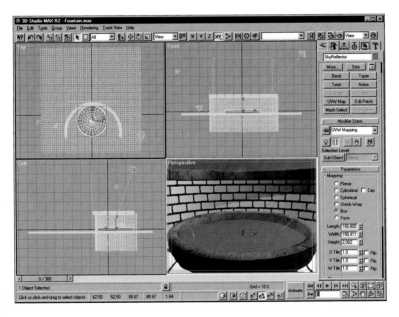

Figure 2
The SkyReflector object.

This Sky Reflector object will serve as a projection screen for a sky map that will illuminate the water surface creating a nice water reflect/refract effect.

Sky Reflection Projector Light

In this section, you will create the lighting effects for the scene.

1. Create a target spot light use the Transform Type-In to position the body at x = 0.5, y = −42.6, z = 164.3. Position the target at x = 0.5, y = −42.6, z = 5.0. Set the spotlight parameters as follows:
   Hotspot = 75.4
   Falloff = 82.3
   Projector = on
   Map = bitmap
   Cast Shadows = on

2. Click the Exclude button and select Both (illumination and shadow casting). Select the following objects for exclusion: BackdropScreen, Fountain, FountainWater, Ground, Nozzle01, TopRail, and Wall.

3. Open the Material Editor then drag and drop an Instance of the projector Bitmap to slot 5.

4. In the Material Editor slot 5, click the Bitmap button and choose the file Sky.jpg. Set the Coordinate parameters as follows:
   U Tiling = 0.5
   V Tiling = 0.5

5. Set the Output parameters as follows:
   Output Amount = 2.0
   RGB Level = 1.25

6. Name the map **SkyReflection**.

You now have a spotlight that projects a sky image onto only the SkyReflector (see Figure 3).

Creating the Water Fountain

You will now create the particle system that simulates the spraying water.

1. Create a super spray particle system at the center of the water at x = −0.19, y = −40.053, z = 2.548. Use the Transform Type-In for positioning.

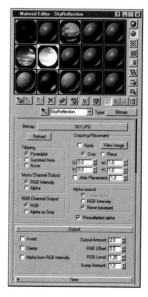

Figure 3
The SkyReflection map.

2. Set the Basic Parameters as follows:
   Off Axis = 6
   Off Axis Spread = 6
   Off Plane = 0
   Off Plane Spread = 180
   Icon Size = 20

3. Set the Particle Generation parameters as follows:
   Use Rate = 6
   Particle Motion: Speed = 5

4. Set the Particle Timing parameters as follows:
   Emit Start = –75
   Emit Stop = 300
   Display Until = 300
   Life = 75
   Variation = 10

5. Set the Particle Size parameters as follows:
   Size = 6
   Variation = 20
   Grow For = 0
   Fade For = 75

6. Set the Particle Type parameters as follows:
   Standard Particles = tetra

7. Set the Particle Rotation spin speed control:
   Spin Time = 45
   Direction of Travel/mblur = on

8. Set the Particle Spawn parameters as follows:
   Spawn Trails = selected
   Multiplier = 5
   Variation = 40
   Direction Chaos = 5
   Speed Chaos Factor = 85
   Fast = selected
   Scale Chaos Factor = 175
   Up = selected
   Lifespan Value Queue = 5, 4, 4, 8, 6, 8, 12, 10

9. Name the Super Spray **Spurt01** (see Figure 4).

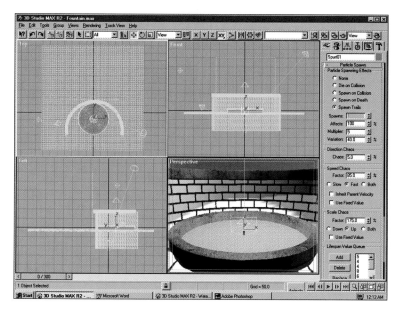

Figure 4
The Spurt01 Super
Spray.

10. Set the Cast Shadow property of the Super Spray to off.

11. In the Top viewport, create a Gravity space warp at any convenient location; you can use x = 145, y = 125, z = 0. Set the following parameters:
    icon size = 65 (optional information)
    strength = 0.09

12. Bind the Gravity space warp to Spurt01.

13. In the Top viewport, create a Deflector space warp centered on the water object at x = 0.547, y = –42.573, z = 1.953. Set the parameters as follows (see Figure 5):
    Bounce = 0.15
    Width = 200
    Length = 200

14. Bind the Deflector space warp to the Spurt01 Super Spray.

The effect now includes "water" particles that spurt and bounce like a fountain.

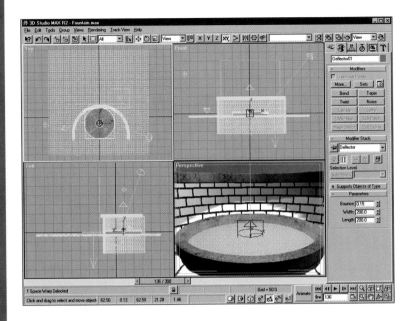

Figure 5
Creating a
Deflector space
warp.

Creating the Water Fountain Material

Use a custom material to change the particles from simple particles to "water."

1. In the Material Editor, make material slot 2 active and set the Material Type to Standard.

2. Set the Basic parameters as follows:
   Shading = Blinn
   Ambient = (R = 45, G = 55, B = 68)
   Diffuse = (R =123, G = 113, B = 94)
   Specular = (R = 255, G = 255, B = 255)
   Filter = (R = 41, G = 25, B = 12)
   Shininess = 62
   Shin. Strength = 100
   Opacity = 30

3. Set the Amount for the Bump slot to 75. Click the Bump map slot and set the map Type to Noise. Set the Noise parameters as follows:
   Coordinates = UVW1
   V Tiling = 4
   Noise Type = regular
   Size = 0.05

4. Animate the Phase:
   Frame 0 (Keyframe 1) Phase = 0
   Frame 300 (Keyframe 2) Phase = 20

5. Animate the coordinates:
   Frame 0 (Keyframe 1) W Offset = 0
   Frame 300 (Keyframe 2) W Offset = −13

6. Set the Amount for the Reflection map slot to 75. Click the empty slot and choose the Reflect/Refract type.

7. Set the Amount for the Refraction map slot to 40. Click the empty slot and choose the Thin Wall Refraction type. Set the parameters:
   refraction: bump map effect = 2.0

8. Name the material **WaterFountain**.

9. Apply the WaterFountain material to the Spurt01 object.

At this point, the basic particles take on more realistic properties—reflection and refraction, like real water.

Camera Setup

The final step is to set up the camera through which you will view the finished effect.

1. Create a target camera using the Transform Type-In position the camera in front of the fountain looking at Spurt01 at x = −2, y = −259, z = 75. Position the target at x = −1, y = −1, z = 16. Set the following:
   Lens = 35mm

2. Change the Perspective viewport to Camera01 (see Figure 6).

After you render this effect, you will be surprised by the realism. The greatest challenge to an animator is to mimic reality.

You can find the final MAX file, WaterFountains.max, in this project's Pre-load folder and the final AVI file is in the Images folder.

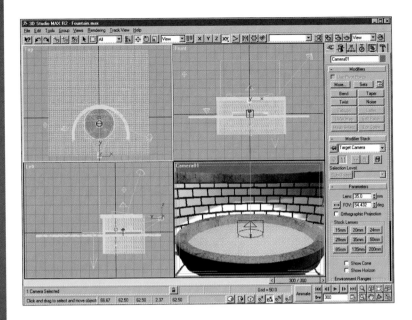

Figure 6
Completed Water
Fountain effect.

Fire Hose Spray and Impact

by Kim Lee

To create this effect you will utilize the Super Spray particle system and its spawning capabilities to create water bursting out of a fire hose. Making the water gush from the hose, crash against the wall, and splash onto the floor will be fairly straightforward with the proper use of motion blur. However, the little details are what make an effect really look convincing. For example, you must make the wall and floor look progressively wetter as the water spray passes over and across different areas of their surfaces. To do this requires the creation of some reasonably complex materials and several custom animated masks.

Note

All position and rotational information is based on absolute world coordinates. When creating objects, use keyboard entry when possible. When positioning objects, use the Transform Type-In dialog box located in the Tools menu. These techniques ensure proper object placement and orientation.

Leave any settings that are not listed in the example at the MAX default values. Create objects in the Top viewport, unless otherwise indicated.

Preconfiguration

1. Before beginning this effect, please reset *or* restart MAX.

2. Copy the Hose project map files from the accompanying CD to the MAX maps subdirectory.

Create the Hose and Environment Objects

You will be creating a hose by lofting a circle shape over a NURBS point curve path.

Creating the Hose

1. In the Front viewport, create a NURBS point curve roughly in the shape of the letter S.

2. Create a spline circle shape:
   Radius = 4

3. Create 3 dummy objects and position them along the curve where the NURBS points lie. Place them near the end of the hose where you will place the nozzle, with Dummy01 at the far right end and Dummy03 closer to the middle of the curve. Rotate the dummy at the end of the NURBS curve so that it is parallel to the end of the curve.

Note

Using this type of curve for the path rather than a spline eliminates the problems of bézier handle orientation at animation time. Instead of simply toggling the NURBS curve as renderable, using a loft provides the option of animating the hose to appear as if water were rushing into it and filling it out. I have chosen not to use this, but if you choose to do so, simply animate the scale deformation of the loft.

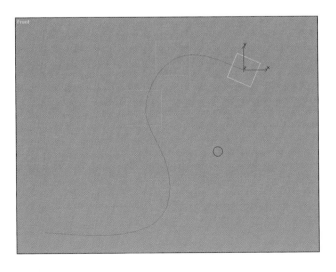

Figure I
Creating the hose shape.

4. Select the NURBS curve and toggle on Sub-Object\Point mode. Select the right-most point.

5. With the Sub-Object still selected, add a Linked XForm modifier to the stack. Click Pick Control Object and select the Dummy01 object.

6. Add an NCurve Sel modifier to the stack and toggle on the Sub-Object button. Select the point to the left of the previous one.

7. With Sub-Object still selected, add a Linked XForm modifier to the stack. Click Pick Control Object and select the Dummy02 object.

8. Repeat steps 6 and 7 for the next point to the left and use Dummy03 as the control object.

9. With the NURBS curve selected, choose the Create tab of the command column and click Geometry. Select Loft Object from the drop-down list and click Loft.

10. Click Get Shape in the Creation Method rollout and select the circle shape.

11. Name the object **Hose**.

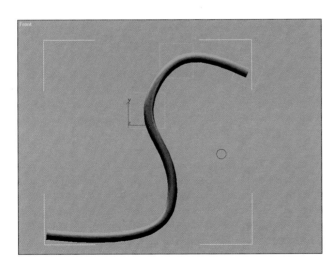

Figure 2
The Hose object.

Create the Nozzle

1. In the Front viewport, create a spline line shape like the one in the following figure. This will be the profile of our nozzle object (see Figure 3).

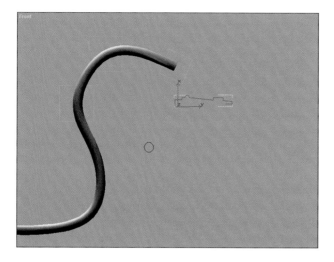

Figure 3
Creating the profile
of the nozzle.

2. Apply a Lathe modifier to the stack. Set the following:
   Segments = 36
   Direction = Y
   Min button = selected

3. Rename the object **Nozzle**.

4. Using the Move and Rotate tools, orient the Nozzle object at the end of the Hose object.

5. With the nozzle selected, click the Link tool and link the Nozzle object to Dummy01.

You should now have a completed hose object that can be animated by manipulating the dummy objects.

Create the Environment

Now create the floor and wall objects for the water to splash onto.

1. In the Top viewport, create a QuadPatch object with the following parameters:
   Length = 2000
   Width = 1000

> **Length Segments** = 1
> **Width Segments** = 1

2. Rename the object **Floor** (see Figure 4) and orient it at
   x = –20.734, y = 91.79, z = –152.266.

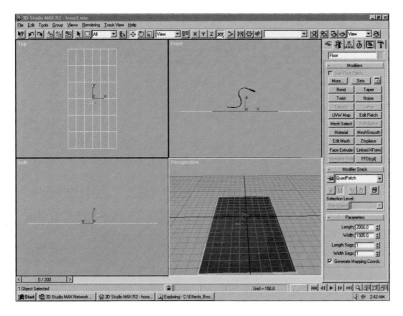

Figure 4
Positioning the floor.

3. In the Front viewport, turn on Angle snap and while holding
   down the shift key, rotate the floor object 90 degrees counter
   clockwise around the z axis. Name the cloned object **Wall**.

4. Change the wall object's width to approximately 500 and move it
   so that it is oriented at x = 449.034, y = 91.79, z = 85.998.

Create the Particle System

1. Set the animation length to 200. From the Create panel, select
   Particle Systems and click Super Spray. In the Left viewport, click
   to create the particle system emitter.

2. Orient the Super Spray object (see Figure 5).

3. Link the SuperSpray01 object to Dummy01.

4. With SuperSpray01 selected, select the Modify tab in the com-
   mand column. Set the Basic Parameters:
   Off Axis Spread = 8.0
   Off Plane Spread = 180
   Percentage of Particles = 5.0

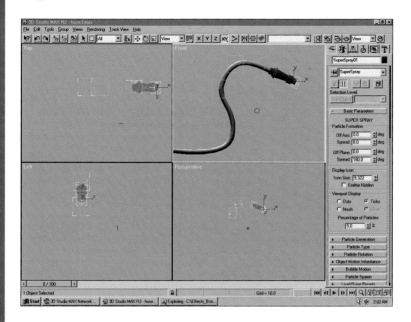

Figure 5
Positioning the
Super Spray.

5. Set the Particle Generation parameters:
   Use Rate = 20
   Speed = 30
   Speed Variation = 0
   Emit Start = 24
   Emit Stop = 200
   Display Until = 200
   Life = 100
   Life Variation = 0
   Size = 8
   Size Variation = 10
   Grow For = 0

   Make Sure all of the Subframe Sampling boxes are checked.

6. Set the Particle Type parameters:
   Particle Type = Standard Particles
   Standard Particles = Tetra

7. Set the Particle Rotation parameters:
   Spin Axis Controls = Direction Of Travel/Mblur
   Stretch = 2

8. Set the Particle Spawn parameters:
   Spawn on Collision = selected
   Spawns = 2 (one for the Wall and then one for the Floor)
   Affects = 100

Multiplier = 3
Direction Chaos = 50
Scale Chaos: Factor = 50
Scale Chaos: Down = selected
Lifespan Value Queue = 20 and 10

Create Space Warps

1. In the Create panel, select the Space Warps button and choose Particles and Dynamics from the drop-down menu. Select Gravity and click anywhere in the Top viewport to create a Gravity space warp. Set the following:
   Strength = 0.6

2. Select the Bind to Space Warp tool. Select the SuperSpray01 object and click and drag to the Gravity01 object.

3. Create a Deflector space warp in the Left viewport that overlaps the wall object.

4. Use the Align tool to align the Deflector exactly over the wall object in all three axis. In the Modify panel, set the following:
   Bounce = 0.2

5. Bind the SuperSpray01 object to the Deflector01 object.

6. Create a Deflector space warp in the Top viewport that overlaps the Floor object.

7. Align the Deflector over the floor object in all three axis. In the Modify panel, set the following:
   Bounce = 0.4

8. Bind the SuperSpray01 object to the Deflector02 object.

You should now have a particle created that will react to any animation applied to the hose while colliding realistically with the surrounding wall and floor objects.

Animate the Hose

I have chosen to animate the hose dipping down toward the floor before rising up and then swaying back and forth from left to right. As the exact animation of the hose will be different depending on the animator, I will not go into great detail as to the steps taken. The only instruction here is: animate the dummy objects to animate the hose. Realize that Dummy01, when rotated, will control the rotation of both the nozzle and the Super Spray objects. You might find that hiding the particle systems while animating the hose will increase interactivity speed. However, remember to preview the motion with the particles visible to ensure that their reaction with the space warps is satisfactory.

Create Materials

Water Material

With this material you will need to create the look of fast moving white, frothy water. This look is more dependent on the motion blur than any tricks with materials.

1. In the Material Editor, select an empty material slot. Name the slot **Water Particles**.

2. Set the Basic parameters:
   Ambient = (R = 255, G = 255, B = 255)
   Diffuse = (R = 255, G = 255, B = 255)
   Specular = (R = 255, G = 255, B = 255)

3. Apply the material to the Super Spray particle system.

4. Right-click the particle system, select Properties from the pop-up menu, and in the Motion Blur area select Image and set the Multiplier to 3.0.

5. Save the scene as **FireHose.Max**.

Create the Floor Material

Next you need to create a material for the floor.

1. In the Material Editor, select an empty slot, set the Material Type to Blend and click OK.

2. Name this material **Floor**.

3. Click the Material 1 slot of Floor. Rename this component **Floor Dry**. Click the button next to Diffuse and set the Map Type to Bitmap.

4. Under Bitmap Parameters, select Cement.gif. Set the following:
   U Tiling = 4
   V tiling = 10

5. Navigate to the parent level of the Floor material. Drag and copy the Floor Dry component to the Material 2 slot. Do not choose Instance as Method.

6. Click the Material 2 slot of Floor. Rename this component **Floor Wet**.

7. Set the Basic parameters as follows:
Shininess = 51
Shin. Strength = 100
Opacity = 60

8. In the Maps rollout, click the slot next to Bump. Set the Map Type to Noise. Set the following:
Size = 10

9. Turn Animate on and go to frame 200. Set X Offset to 1000 and Phase to 10. Turn Animate off.

10. Return to the parent level of Floor Wet and click the slot next to Reflection. Set the Map Type to Flat Mirror and in the Flat Mirror parameters under Distortion click Use Bump Map.

Create the Animated Wet/Dry Mask

Now that you have both a dry and wet material for the floor, create the animated wet/dry mask. You will be using our existing particle system to render spheres that will represent globs of water hitting the wall and floor. Please note that this phase can be extremely time consuming when rendering. To help improve performance in the interface you may want to set your Percentage of Particles to a low percentage when we start adjusting the Super Spray parameters.

1. In the Material Editor, drag and copy the Water Particles material into an unused slot. Name the new material **Mask Particle**.

2. Set the Basic parameters:
Self–Illumination = 100

3. Apply the material to the particle system.

4. Select the particle system and go to the Modify panel. Select Super Spray from the Modifier Stack.

5. In the Particle Generation rollout, change the following:
Life = 200
Size = 40

6. In the Particle Type rollout, set the following:
Standard Particle = Sphere

7. In the Particle Rotation rollout, change the following:
Spin Axis Controls = Random

Note

Creating the floor presents a problem. The floor must look progressively wetter wherever the water particles strike it. Setting up a material for the dry floor and making the same floor look wet is easy, but you need to use an animated mask to define where and when the dry floor becomes wet. It is overwhelming to paint by hand a mask based on the positions of each particle that strikes the floor. Instead, let MAX do the work. However, you must temporarily modify the current scene to create these animated masks (one for the wall and one for the floor).

Figure 6
Select Super Spray from the Modifier Stack.

8. In the Particle Spawn rollout, change the second value in the Lifespan Value Queue from 10 to 150.

   To create the animated mask, make the particles stick to the floor once they strike it. To do this, temporarily change the settings for the Floor deflector.

9. Select the Deflector02 space warp and change the following: **Bounce** = 0

   Now you must render only the particles that come in contact with the floor. To do this, harness the clipping plane controls of the cameras in MAX.

10. Create a Free Camera in the Top viewport between the hose nozzle and the wall at x = 216.951, y = −14.277, z = 589.419. Rotate the camera 90 degrees in the Z axis.

11. Rename this **Floor Cam**.

12. In the Modify panel check the Clip Manually checkbox in the Clipping Planes area of the free camera. Use the Front viewport as a guide and increase the Near clip value so that the red line is just above the particles on the floor. Do the same for the Far clip valuebut and make sure that its red line falls just below the floor object. Note: You may need to change the Super Spray's View Display setting to Mesh to actually see the top surface of the sphere particles.

13. Click Select by Name and select the floor, wall, hose and nozzle objects.

14. Click the Display tab and choose Hide Selected.

15. Select the Floor Cam viewport and click Render Scene. Select Active Time Segment and an output size of 320x240. Select your project's maps directory for output. Name the output file **FloorMask.avi** and click Render.

16. When the FloorMask render is done, open the Material Editor and select the Floor material slot. At the Parent level of the material, click the Mask slot.

17. Select Bitmap as the map type and in the Bitmap parameters area select FloorMask.Avi as the bitmap. If you opted to output sequential image files, use an IFL file instead. Turn Show Map In Viewport on and turn off the checkboxes under Tile.

18. Unhide the floor object and apply the new Floor material to it. Close the Material Editor. Change the Floor Cam view to

Note

Depending upon your final output size you might need to render the mask at a higher resolution for a smoother dry/wet edge. To keep things simple, I've rendered as an AVI, but you can also render as sequential image files of the format of your choice.

Perspective and turn on Smooth & Highlights mode in both Top and Perspective views.

19. Apply a UVW Map modifier to the Floor object. Make sure Planar is selected, click Bitmap Fit, and select FloorMask.Avi.

20. Click Sub-Object. Scale, rotate, and move the mapping gizmo so that the map lies directly under the particles that were used to create it. You might need to scrub the timeline back and forth a few times to make sure it looks right.

21. Select Deflector02 and set its Bounce to 0.4.

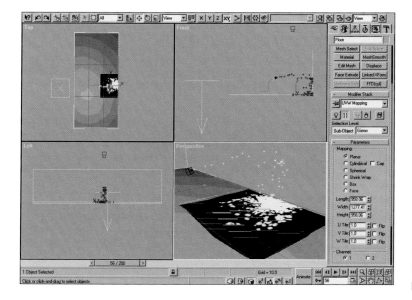

Figure 7
Moving the mapping gizmo.

Create the Wall Material

While we have the settings for our particle system adjusted to create masks, let's create the mask for the wall. The overall technique will be pretty much the same as that for the floor with one addition. Since this will be simulating water on a wall we will need to take into account the fact that water will flow down the wall. Sounds simple enough considering that our particles, bound to a gravity space warp, will move down the wall after their initial collision. However, as the particles flow downward, how can we prevent the part of the wall above them from appearing suddenly dry? This will require rendering at least two passes; one with our particles sticking to the wall upon collision and one with them sliding down after the initial collision. We will need to composite these two passes together in Video Post to create our final wall mask. Depending upon the way you animated the hose, you may find it necessary to render a still image at various points of the animation in order to fill any gaps that appear. These stills will also need to be combined into the final animated mask file.

First we will create a "sticky" water pass.

1. Select the Deflector01 space warp:
   Bounce = 0.0

2. Go to frame 0 and change the Left viewport to a Right view. In the Right viewport, create a Free camera over the top of the SuperSpray icon at absolute world coordinates (1259.239, −83.691, 83.184).

3. Rename this camera **Wall Cam** (see Figure 8).

4. Switch to the Perspective view and press C to change it to the Camera view.

5. Move the time slider to frame 200 and in the Front viewport, move Wall Cam to the right until the particles are in frame and the floor object is aligned with the lower edge of the frame.

6. In the Modify panel, check the Clip Manually checkbox in the Clipping Planes section of the Free camera. Set the Near Clip value to 1. Use the Front viewport as a guide and increase the Far Clip value so that the red line falls just beyond the particles hitting the wall.

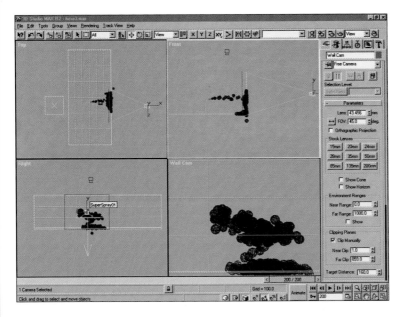

Figure 8
Adjusting the Far Clip value.

7. Select and hide the floor object.

8. Select the Wall Cam viewport and click Render Scene. Use the same settings used for the floor mask. Select your project's maps directory and name the output file **WallMaskA.avi**. Click render.

Next, you will create a "sliding" water pass.

9. Select the Deflector01 space warp and change the following: **Bounce** = 0.2

10. Select the Wall Cam viewport and click Render Scene. Use the same settings used for the floor mask. Select your project's maps directory and name the output file **WallMaskB.avi**. Click render.

Finally, I've created still frames at points in my animation where the WallMaskB.avi leaves gaps behind. I've named these WallMaskC.tga, WallMaskD.tga, and WallMaskE.tga. These frames were rendered from points along the same WallMaskB animation after reviewing the avi and noting frames where the white particles appear to drip down the wall and leave black "holes" behind. If left as is, it would appear that the wall was instantaneously drying up at certain points right after the leading edge of the water flowed by.

Using Video Post to Composite the Masks

Now its time to composite these five elements together in Video Post.

1. Select Video Post from the Rendering drop-down menu.

2. Click Add Image Input Event and then click Files. Choose WallMaskA.avi from the browser window.

3. Repeat Step 2 and choose WallMaskB.avi as the image input event.

4. Select both Image Input Event entries using the shift key.

5. Select the now-enabled Add Image Layer Event button and select Simple Additive Compositor from the drop-down list.

6. Click anywhere in the empty white area in the video post window to deselect all entries. Add another Image input event. This time, select WallMaskC.tga and set the VP start Time to 84 and VP end time to 200. I've chosen frame 84 as a start because that is the frame of the animation where I rendered this particular frame.

7. Repeat step 6 for both WallMaskD.tga and WallMaskE.tga using 100 and 126 respectively for VP start times. Make sure the VP end times for both are 200.

8. Select the Simple Additive Compositor entry. Hold down the Ctrl key and select the WallMaskC.tga entry. Select the Add Image Layer Event button and select Simple Additive Compositor from the drop-down list.

9. Select the upper-most Simple Additive Compositor entry. Hold down the Ctrl key and select the WallMaskD.tga entry. Select the Add Image Layer Event button and select Simple Additive Compositor from the drop-down list.

10. Repeat step 9 for the WallMaskE.tga file.

11. Click anywhere in the empty white area in the Video Post window to deselect all entries and then click Add Image Output Event. Click Files and name the output file WallMask.avi.

12. Click Execute Sequence. Set the range from 0 to 200 and size to 320x240 and click Render.

13. Change the Wall Cam view to Perspective.

Completing the Wall Material

Now that the last animated mask is rendered we need to create a wall material to use it with. We will create the wall material in much the same way we created the floor.

1. In the Material Editor, select an empty slot and set the Material Type to Blend and click OK. Name this material **Wall**.

2. Click the Material 1 slot of Wall. Rename this component **Wall Dry**. Click the button next to Diffuse and select Bitmap.

3. Under Bitmap parameters, select Bricktan.gif as the bitmap. Set the following:
U Tiling = 10
V Tiling = 4

4. Go up to the parent level of Wall Dry and put Brickruf.gif in the Bump slot. Set the following:
U Tiling = 10
V tiling = 4
Bump Amount = 67

5. Navigate up to the parent level of the Wall material. Drag and copy the Wall Dry component to the Material 2 slot. Do not choose Instance as Method.

6. Rename this component **Wall Wet** and set the Basic parameters:
   Shininess = 55
   Shin. Strength = 100
   Opacity = 61

7. Click the slot next to Reflection. Set the Map Type to Flat Mirror. Set Amount to 5.

8. Go to the parent level of the Wall material and select WallMask.avi as the mask. Turn on the Show Map In Viewport button and make turn off the checkboxes under Tile.
   Mapping Coordinate Type: Explicit UVW 2

9. Reveal the Wall object and apply the Wall material to it.

10. Apply a UVW Map modifier to the modifier stack of Wall.
    Planar = selected
    Channel = 1

11. Click Sub-Object and in the Perspective viewport rotate the gizmo 90 clockwise on the X axis. Click the Fit button.

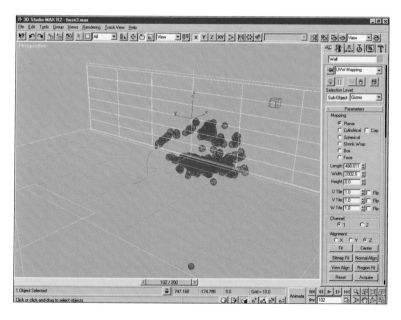

Figure 9
Rotating the gizmo.

12. Apply a second UVW Map modifier to the modifier stack of Wall.
    Planar = selected
    Channel = 2

13. Click Bitmap Fit and select WallMask.Avi.

14. Click Sub-Object and in the Top viewport rotate the gizmo 90 clockwise on the X axis.

15. With the Sub-Object button still selected, move and scale the mapping gizmo so that the map lies directly under the particles that were used to create it. You might need to scrub the timeline back and forth a few times to make sure it looks right.

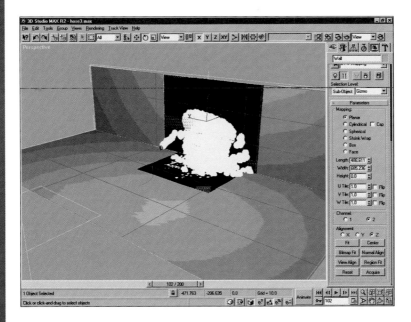

Figure 10
Moving and scaling the mapping gizmo.

16. Set all of the Super Spray parameters back the way they were. Double-check your settings with those in "Create the Particle System," steps 4–8.

Depending on how you implement this effect, certain settings need to change. Like many other effects, the parameters used are highly dependent on the scale at which you build the scene. Also, you can modify many of the techniques here—simulate the look of flowing sheets of water flowing down the side of the wall with a combination of noise maps and gradient masks. This is a rather computationally heavy effect, and it might take quite a while to create with less powerful computers. But as the saying goes, "No Pain No Gain."

Erupting Geyser

by Kim Lee

In this geyser effect, you will re-create the powerful eruption of steam and water associated with geysers such as Old Faithful in Yellowstone. Because not all geysers look the same, you have room for artistic interpretation. Geysers are the result of the super heating of water underground past the point of boiling. To create this, you will add a layer of steam rising from the ground around the actual cone. To create the different types of steam motion, you will employ both a particle approach (for the violent and fast moving steam column) and an environment atmospheric approach.

Create the Environment

1. In the Top viewport, create a QuadPatch at x = 0, y = 0, z = 0). Set the following:
   Length = 200
   Width = 200

2. Rename the QuadPatch **Ground**.

3. Add an Edit Patch modifier to the stack. De-select the Sub-Object button and set the following:
Topology Steps = 50

4. Apply a Mesh Select modifier and again toggle off the Sub-Object button.

5. Add a Displace modifier to the stack (see Figure 1). In the Image section of the Displace parameters, set the following:
Bitmap = Geyser.tga
Strength = 20

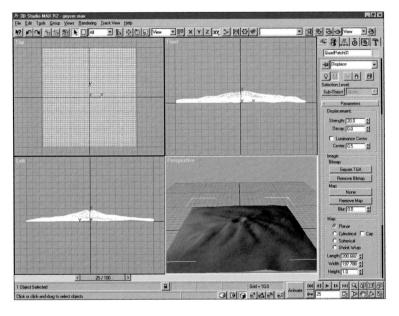

Figure 1
You should now see a shallow crater.

6. Select Environment from the Rendering drop-down menu. Click Environment Map and choose Bitmap.

7. Drag and drop an instance copy of the Environment Map button to an empty slot in the Material Editor.

8. In the Material Editor, rename the material **Background**.

9. Set the Mapping to Screen and select Scene100.tga as the Bitmap.

Camera Setup

1. Create a target camera. Position the camera at x = −128.257, y = −114.934, z = 13.84 and place the target at x = −5.32, y = 14.337, z = 52.098.

2. Change the Perspective view to a Camera view and select Background Image from the View menu.

3. Check the boxes next to Use Environment Background and Display Background.

4. Adjust your camera so that the Camera view is similar to the following figure if it is not already (see Figure 2).

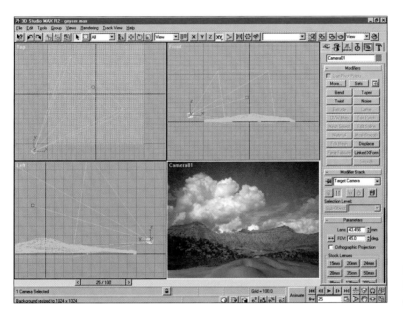

Figure 2
Positioning the camera.

You now have the ground geometry, camera, and background environment set up.

Create the Main Steam/Water Column

Next you will create the main steam/water column.

1. Make the Top viewport a shaded view and create a Super Spray particle emitter at the center of the crater at x = −2.861, y = 3.399, z = 0). Set the Basic Parameters:
   Off Axis Spread = 3.0
   Off Plane Spread = 90

2. In the Particle Generation rollout, set the following:
   Use Rate = 100
   Speed = 5
   Emit Start = 20
   Emit Stop = 100
   Display Until = 100
   Life = 60
   Size = 1.5
   Grow For = 5
   Fade For = 0

3. Set the Particle Type parameters:
   Particle Type = Standard Particles
   Standard Particles = Tetra

4. Set the Particle Rotation:
   Spin Axis Controls = Direction Of Travel/Mblur
   Stretch = 4

5. Rename the Super Spray **Super Spray Geyser**.

6. In the Top viewport, create a Gravity space warp:
   Strength = 0.075

7. Bind the Super Spray Geyser to the Gravity space warp.

8. Create a Wind space warp at x = −130.87, y = −35.663,
   z = 110.96 and orient it so that it blows left to right in the Front
   viewport (see Figure 3). Set the following:
   Strength = 0.025
   Turbulence = 0.5

9. Bind the Super Spray Geyser to the Wind space warp.

10. Right-click the Super Spray particle system and select Properties
    from the drop-down menu. Select Image motion Blur. Set the
    following:
    Multiplier = 2
    Cast Shadows = Off

11. Create a Super Spray particle emitter in the Top viewport at the
    center of the crater just slightly offset from the first emitter. at
    x = 5.384, y = 8.182, z = 11.285. Rename it **Super Spray
    Steam** and set the Basic Parameters:
    Off Axis Spread = 10.0
    Off Plane Spread = 90
    Percentage of Particles = 25.0

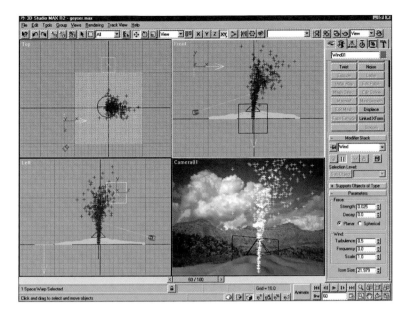

Figure 3
Creating the Wind
space warp.

12. In the Particle Generation rollout, set the following:
Use Rate = 15
Speed = 5
Emit Start = 15
Emit Stop = 100
Display Until = 100
Life = 60
Life Variation = 5
Size = 10
Size Variation = 50
Grow For = 5
Fade For = 0

13. Set the Particle Type parameters:
Particle Type = Standard Particles
Standard Particles = Facing

14. Set the Particle Rotation:
Spin Time = 60
Spin Time Variation = 100
Phase = 25
Phase Variation = 100

15. Open Track View and navigate to the Speed parameter for Super Spray Steam. Set keys at frames 0 and 25 with a value of 5 and another key at frame 35 with a value of 3. Set the in and out tangency types to linear for all keys.

16. Create a second Wind space warp at x = −132.89, y = 8.896, z = 110.96 and orient it so that it blows left to right in the Front viewport. Set the following:
Strength = 4
Decay = 0.034
Turbulence = 0.7

17. Bind the Super Spray Steam to the Wind (see Figure 4).

Note

The Decay value will vary the force of the wind on the particles depending on the relative positions of the Wind space warp and the particles.

Figure 4
Binding Steam to Wind.

18. Right-click the Super Spray Steam particle system and select Properties from the drop-down menu. Turn off Cast Shadows.

You should now see the primary column of steam and water particles erupting into the air.

Create Ground-Level Rising Steam

Now we need to create the steam that rises up slowly from the surface of the ground.

1. Create a SphereGizmo in the Top viewport. Set the following:
   Radius = 50
   Hemisphere = checked

2. Use the non-uniform scale to scale down the helper about 50% on its local Z axis.

3. Using the Shift key and the Move tool, make 3 copies of this object around the base of the crater. Adjust the radius of each SphereGizmo to your liking. (These will be defining the areas of rising steam.)

4. In the Front viewport, raise the helpers so that their bases are just buried in the ground.

5. Select Environment from the Rendering menu. Click the Add button under Atmosphere and choose Combustion.

6. Click the Pick Gizmo button and type **H** to bring up a hotlist. Select all of the SphereGizmo objects and click Pick.

7. Change all three color swatches to white (R = 255, G = 255, B = 255).

8. Use the following settings for the remaining Combustion Parameters (see Figure 5):
   Flame Type = Fireball
   Stretch = 2.0
   Regularity = 0.2
   Flame Size = 10
   Flame Detail = 6.0
   Density = 5.0
   Samples = 15
   Phase = 0
   Drift = 0

9. Turn Animate on and go to Frame 100. Change Phase to 10 and Drift to 50. Turn Animate off.

The steam now has a slow undulating, upward motion.

Create the Materials

Now you need to create some materials for the scene.

Create the Ground Material

1. In the Material Editor, select an empty slot. Rename it **Ground**.

2. Click the Diffuse map slot and set the Map Type to Bitmap. Choose DirtGray.jpg as the map and set the following:
U Tiling = 4
V Tiling = 4

3. Apply the material to the ground object.

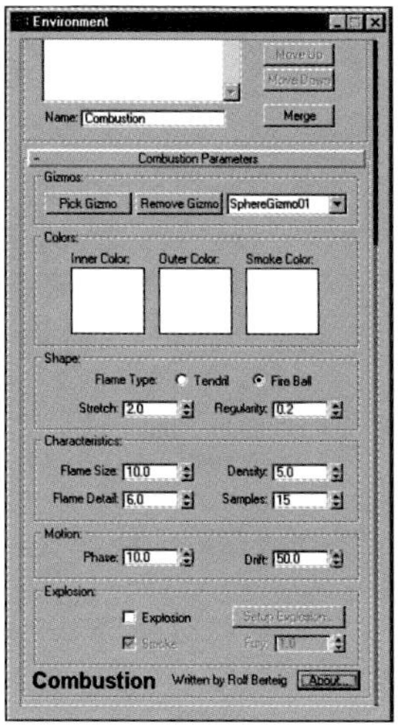

Create the Steam Material

1. Select an unused slot and rename it **Steam**. Set the following:
Ambient = (R = 213, G = 213, B = 213)
Filter = (R = 206, G = 206, B = 206)
Shininess = 0
Shin. Strength = 0
Face Map = checked

2. In the Extended Parameters rollout, set the following:
Falloff: Amt = 50

3. Click the Diffuse map slot and set the Map Type to Gradient. Copy Color #3 to Color #1. Set the following:
Color 2 Position = 0.66
Gradient Type = Radial

4. Set the noise settings:
Type = Fractal
Amount = 0.41
Size = 3.15
Phase = 0.36

Figure 5
Setting the Combustion Parameters.

5. Click the map slot for Color #2 and set the Map Type to Particle Age. Set the Particle Age colors (see Figure 6):
Color #1: Color = (R = 149, G = 149, B = 149), Age = 0
Color #2: Color = (R = 92, G = 92, B = 92), Age = 70
Color #3: Color = (R = 0, G = 0, B = 0), Age = 90

6. Click the Go to Parent button to return to the Gradient parameters. Copy the Particle Age map from the Color#2 slot to the Color #3 slot. Set the Particle age colors:
Color #1: Color = (R = 238, G = 238, B = 238), Age = 0
Color #2: Color = (R = 146, G = 146, B = 146), Age = 70
Color #3: Color = (R = 0, G = 0, B = 0), Age = 90

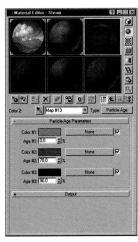

Figure 6
Setting the Particle Age colors.

7. Navigate to the top level of the Steam shader tree.

8. Click the Opacity map slot and set the Map Type to Gradient. Copy Color #3 to Color #1. Set the following:
Color 2 Position = 0.66
Gradient Type = Radial

9. Set the noise settings:
Type = Fractal
Amount = 0.41
Size = 3.15
Phase = 0.36

10. Click the map slot for Color #2 and set the Map Type to Particle Age. Set the Particle age colors:
Color #1: Color = (R = 37, G = 37, B = 37), Age = 0
Color #2: Color = (R = 62, G = 62, B = 62), Age = 70
Color #3: Color = (R = 0, G = 0, B = 0), Age = 90

11. Click Go to Parent to return to the Gradient parameters. Copy the Particle Age map from the Color#2 slot to the Color #3 slot. Set the Particle age colors:
Color #1: Color = (R = 64, G = 64, B = 64), Age = 0
Color #2: Color = (R = 124, G = 124, B = 124), Age = 70
Color #3: Color = (R = 0, G = 0, B = 0), Age = 90

12. Apply the material to the Super Spray Steam particle system.

Create the Water Material

1. Select another unused slot and rename it **Water**. Set the following:
   Ambient = gray value of 229
   Diffuse = gray value of 253
   Specular = gray value of 255
   Filter = gray value of 235
   Shininess = 0
   Shin. Strength = 0
   Self-Illumination = 50

2. Click the Opacity map slot and set the Map Type to Particle Age. Set the Particle Age colors:
   Color #1: Color = (R = 255, G = 255, B = 255), Age = 0
   Color #2: Color = (R = 180, G = 180, B = 180), Age = 50
   Color #3: Color = (R= 0, G = 0, B = 0), Age = 90

3. Apply the material to the Super Spray Geyser particle system.

Now that you've got the correct textures on all of the scene objects you can move on to the last step.

Create the Lighting

Next, create the lighting effects for the scene (see Figure 7).

1. Create an omni light in the Front viewport at x = −197.897, y = −1.955, z = 143.64 with an RGB value of 255. Place it to the left and above the geyser relative to your camera's position.

2. Create a second omni light in the Front viewport with a value of 100. Place it to the right of the geyser at x = 135.833, y = −160.79, z = 56.107 about half as high off the ground plane as the first omni.

Like most of the effects in this book, the steps here should give you a solid base to expand the effect or change it for your own purposes. You can change the Wind parameters for dramatically different looking movement and you can adjust the color values for the Combustion effect to create everything from dust to flames.

You can find the final MAX file, geyser.max, in this project's Scene folder and the final AVI file in the Images folder.

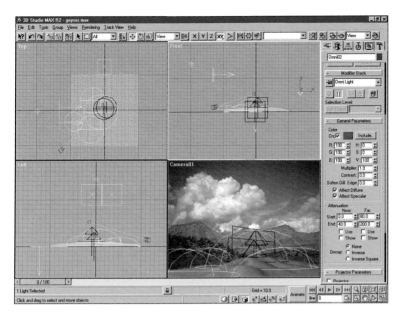

Figure 7
Placing the omni light.

PART II

Space Effects

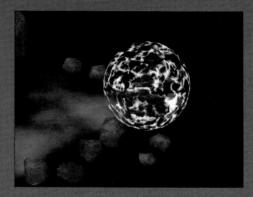

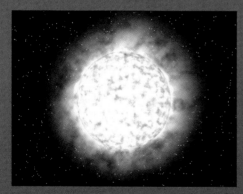

Normal Sun

by Greg Carbonaro

The sun is quite an interesting object to re-create. The basic description of the sun is a massive, glowing, hot, churning mass with a gaseous, wispy burning atmosphere. This surface presents interesting challenges to the animator. The solution, however, is quite simple. You can use a particle system to create the effect, but I don't recommend it. You can use Lens FX glow, but it's hard to make things glow without obscuring the detail of the object. The solution presented here is cleaner and simpler and works very well.

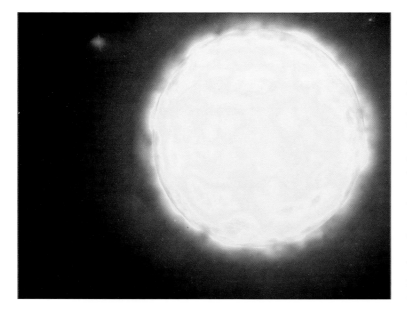

Note

All position and rotational information is based on absolute world coordinates. When creating objects, use keyboard entry where possible. When positioning objects use the Transform Type-In dialog box located in the Tools menu. These techniques ensure proper object placement and orientation.

Leave any settings that are not listed in the example at the MAX default values. Create objects in the Top viewport, unless otherwise indicated.

Preconfiguration

1. Copy the Normal Sun project map files from the accompanying CD-ROM to the MAX maps subdirectory.

2. Load the file Stars.max from the projects preload subdirectory on the CD-ROM. You should see a starfield background in your Perspective viewport. The animation length has been preset to 300 frames.

3. In the Material Editor, right-click any material slot and make sure Sample Windows are set to 3×2.

Modeling and Materials

In the following steps, you create the sphere that will be the sun object.

Sun Object Creation

1. Activate the Top viewport.

2. Create a standard primitive sphere in the Top viewport at approximately the center and then use the Transform Type-In dialog box to position it at x = −1.55, y = 3.61, z = 0. Set the following:
   Radius = 44
   Segments = 50
   Generate Mapping Coordinates = on

3. Name the object **Sun**.

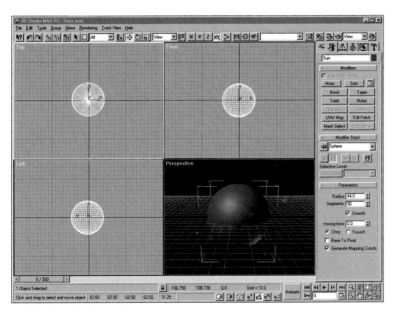

Figure 1
Create the object Sun in the Top viewport.

Creating the Sun Material

1. In the Material Editor, make material slot 1 active and set the Material Type to Standard.

2. Set the Basic Parameters as follows:
   Ambient = (R = 128, G = 128, B = 128)
   Diffuse = (R = 128,G = 128,B = 128)
   Specular = (R = 128,G = 128,B = 128)
   Shininess = 0
   Shin. Strength = 0
   Self-Illumination = 60

3. In the Maps area, set the amount for the Diffuse channel to 100. Click the Diffuse map channel and set the Type to Noise. Set the Noise Parameters as follows:
   Noise Type = Turbulence
   Size = 15
   Color1 = (R = 255, G = 246, B = 0)
   Color2 = (R = 255, G = 100, B = 0)

4. Animate the Coordinates Y Offset:
   Frame 0 (Keyframe 1) Y Offset = 0
   Frame 300 (Keyframe 2) Y Offset = −40

   After completing the animation, go back up to the parent level of the material.

5. Copy the Diffuse channel Noise to the Opacity channel as an Instance. Do this by dragging the Diffuse noise map to the Opacity map channel; when prompted with the Copy Map dialog box, select Copy as Instance.

6. Name the material **Sun Surface**.

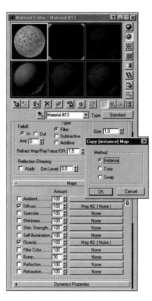

Figure 2
Copy the Diffuse channel Noise.

Space Ambiance

7. Apply the Sun Surface material to the sun object. Either drag and drop the material to the sun object or use the Assign Material to Selection button in the Material Editor.

So far, you have created the sun and its surface material.

Animation

Now create the burning gaseous turbulent atmosphere of the sun.

1. Create an omni light at approximately the center of the sun and then use the Transform Type-In dialog box to position it precisely at x = −1.55, y = 3.61, z = 0:
Color = (R = 255, G = 130, B = 0)
Multiplier = 6
Attenuation Far Use = on
Far Start = 38
Far End = 53.5

2. Name the omni light **SunGas Volume**.

3. In the Rendering Environment dialog box, add an Atmospheric effect Volume light with the following parameters:
Lights: Pick Light = SunGas Volume
Volume: Density = 5.5

4. Set the Noise Parameters:
Noise On = on
Amount = 0.85
Type = Turbulence
Link to Light = on

5. Set the Noise Threshold:
Uniformity = 0.5
Levels = 6
Size = 15

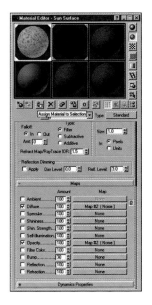

Figure 3
Creation of the sun's surface material. An animated noise was added to the material to create the illusion of burning gaseous internal combustion.

Figure 4
The Rendering Environment dialog box.

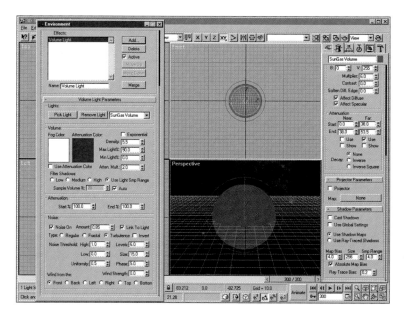

Figure 5
The Noise Threshold parameters.

Space Ambiance

6. Animate the Phase:
Frame 0 (Keyframe 1) phase = 0
Frame 300 (Keyframe 2) phase = 5

Now create another omni volume light. This one produces the glowing halo around the sun.

7. Create an omni light at approximately the center of the sun and then use the Transform Type-In dialog box to position it precisely at x = −1.55, y = 3.61, z = 0. Set the following:
Color = (R = 255, G = 225, B = 0)
Multiplier = 2
Attenuation Far Use = on
Far Start = 38
Far End = 100

8. Name the omni light **SunHalo Volume**.

9. In the Rendering Environment dialog box, add an Atmospheric effect Volume light with the following parameters:
Lights: Pick Light = SunHalo Volume
Volume: Density = 1

10. Set the Noise Parameters:
Noise On = on
Amount = 0.25
Type = Turbulence
Link to Light = on

11. Set the Noise Threshold:
Uniformity = 0.1
Levels = 6
Size = 20

12. Animate the Phase:
Frame 0 (Keyframe 1) phase = 0
Frame 300 (Keyframe 2) phase = 2

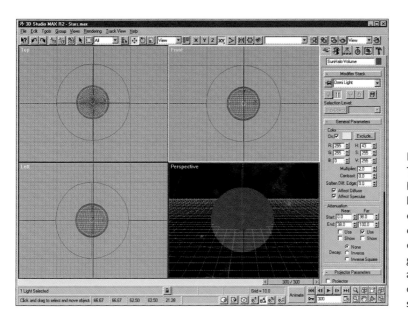

Figure 6
Two omni volume lights were created here, one directly on top of the other. One produces the sun's gaseous burning atmosphere; the other creates the sun's glowing halo.

Lighting Setup

Now that the effect light is complete, you can create some lights to illuminate the scene.

1. Create an omni light in the Top viewport in front of the sun and then use the Transform Type-In dialog box to position it at x = 111, y = −335, z = −149:
Color = (R = 180, G = 180, B = 180)
Multiplier = 1

2. Name the omni light **Under Light**.

3. Create an omni light in the Top viewport behind the sun and then use the Transform Type-In dialog box to position it at x = −136, y = 267, z = 23.

4. Name the omni light **Back Light**.

5. Create a target spotlight in the Top viewport just in front of the
   sun, pointing directly at it; then use the Transform Type-In dialog
   box to position the body at x = –183, y = –224, z = 122.
   Position the target at x = –27, y = –15, z = 0.

6. Name the target spotlight **Front Spot**.

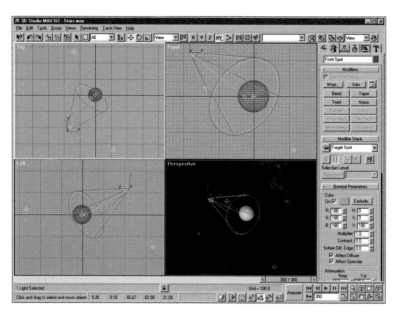

Figure 7
Position the target
spotlight Front
Spot.

Camera

Next, set up the camera through which you will view the finished effect.

1. Create the target camera in the Top viewport just in front of the
   sun and pointing directly at it; then use the Transform Type-In
   dialog box to position the body at x = –48, y = –307, z = –7.
   Position the target at x = –47, y = 3, z = 0.

Animating the Camera

1. Animate the camera body:
   Frame 0 (Keyframe 1) body position = (x = –48, Y = –307,
   z = –7)
   Frame 300 (Keyframe 2) body position = (x = –69.5, Y = 56,
   z = –7)

2. Switch the Perspective viewport to the camera view.

Note

*To animate the cam-
era body position,
turn Animate on and
at frame 0, set
x = –48, y = –307,
z = –7. Move the
Time Slider to frame
300 and set
x = –69.5, y = 56,
z = –7. Turn Animate
off.*

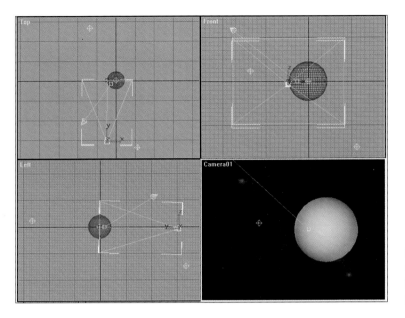

Figure 8
Completed
Normal Sun
animation.

Volumetric omni lights have a broad range of uses. Simple changes to the settings yield a variety of wispy gaseous effects—everything from the sun's turbulent, burning atmosphere to the cool mist of an evening swamp fog.

Star Field and Planet with Atmospheric Glow

S ometimes the most dramatic effects are achieved with the least expected techniques, and the Star Field and Planet effect is one such example. In this effect, you use some unexpected MAX features to create a dramatic space scene—a Noise material for a deep, rich star field complete with gaseous nebula, a combustion apparatus for fluffy, slow-moving clouds, and a volumetric omni light to produce a glowing atmospheric halo. These techniques represent unconventional approaches to common animation problems. The results speak for themselves. Don't be afraid to experiment and try the unconventional approach in your animations.

Note

All position and rotational information is based on absolute world coordinates. When creating objects, use keyboard entry where possible. When positioning objects, use the Transform Type-In dialog box located in the Tools menu. These techniques ensure proper object placement and orientation.

Leave any settings that are not listed in the example at the MAX default values. Create objects in the Top viewport, unless otherwise indicated.

Preconfiguration

1. Before beginning this effect, please either reset *or* restart MAX.

2. Copy the project map files from the accompanying CD-ROM to the MAX maps subdirectory.

3. Load the SunFlare.max file from the this project's Preload subdirectory on the CD-ROM. The animation length has been preset to 300 frames.

4. Open the Materials Editor; right-click any material slot and make sure Sample Windows are set to 5×3.

At this point, you should see a small spherical object in your scene. This small sphere uses a LenFX flare that shows up when the scene is rendered through Video Post.

Environment Setup

Now you create the basic environmental background map that serves as the basis for a star background.

1. In Rendering/Environment, set the Environment Map to Noise. Set the following:
   Use Map = on

2. In the Material Editor, copy (drag and drop an Instance) the Noise Environment Map from the Environment dialog box to slot 4 of the Material Editor.

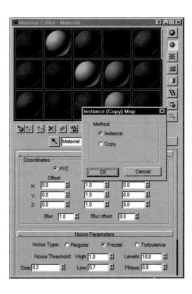

Figure 1
Make an Instance copy of the noise to material slot 4.

Star Field Material

1. In the Material Editor, make sure slot 4 is active. Set the Noise parameters:
   Noise Type = Fractal
   Size = 0.2
   Noise Threshold: Low = 0.7
   Levels = 10

2. Add a Noise sub map to Color #1. Set the Noise parameters as follows:
   Noise Type = Fractal
   Size = 15
   Noise Threshold: Low = 0.45
   Phase = 2
   Color #2 of the Noise sub map = (R = 67, G = 0, B = 114)

3. Return to the parent level and name the material **Star Field**.

4. Activate the Perspective viewport. In Views/Background Image, turn on both the Use Environment Background and Display Background check boxes.

You should now see a star field with a purple gaseous nebula.

Galaxy Backdrop

Next you add a distant spiral galaxy to your scene.

1. Activate the Front viewport.

2. In the Front viewport, create a standard primitive box at x = −31, y = 141, z = 78. Set the following:
   Length = 30
   Width = 60
   Height = 0

3. Apply a UVW Map modifier to the box. Set Mapping to Planar.

4. Name the object **GalaxyBackdrop**.

Galaxy Material Creation

1. In the Material Editor, make material slot 2 active and set the Material Type to Standard.

2. Set the Basic Parameters as follows:
   Shininess = 0
   Shin. Strength = 0
   Self-Illumination = 100

3. Set the Diffuse map slot to Bitmap, and select galaxy.bmp as the
   Bitmap. Turn on Show Map in Viewport. Copy an Instance of the
   Diffuse map channel to the Opacity map channel.

4. Name the material **Galaxy**.

5. Apply the Galaxy material to the GalaxyBackdrop object.

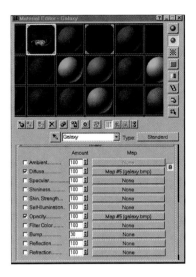

Figure 2
Creating and apply-
ing the spiral galaxy
material to apply
to your backdrop.

In your perspective view, you should now see a star field and small spiral
galaxy in the top-left quadrant of the viewport. Depending on your
monitor, the small square that the spiral galaxy is mapped on may be visible as well; this disappears when rendered.

Moon Creation

Now create the moon object.

1. Activate the Top viewport.

2. Create a standard primitive sphere at x = –72.7, y = 116.26,
   z = 53.49. Set the following:
   Radius =15
   Segments =30
   Smooth = On
   Generate Mapping = On

3. Name the object **Moon**.

Moon Material Creation

1. In the Material Editor, make material slot 3 active and set the Material Type to Standard.

2. Set the Basic Parameters as follows:
   Shininess = 0
   Shin. Strength =0
   Self-Illumination = 8

3. Set the Diffuse map slot to Bitmap, and select MOON.jpg as the Bitmap. Turn on Show Map in Viewport. Copy an instance of the Diffuse map channel to the Bump map channel. Set the Bump Amount to 100.

4. Name the material **Moon**.

5. Apply the Moon material to the Moon object.

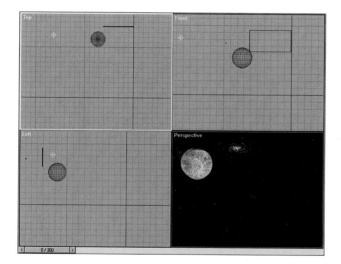

Figure 3
Creating the moon object and applying its material.

In your perspective view, you should now see a star field, spiral galaxy, and the completed moon object.

Earth Creation

Now you create the earth object.

1. Activate the Top viewport.

2. Create a standard primitive sphere at x = −1.55, y = 3.61, z = 0. Set the following:
   Radius = 44

Segments = 60
Smooth = On
Generate Mapping = On

3. Name the object **Earth**.

Earth Material

1. In the Material Editor, make material slot 1 active and set the
   Material Type to Standard.

2. Set the Basic parameters as follows:
   Shininess = 0
   Shin. Strength = 0

3. Set the Extended parameters as follows:
   Reflection Dimming: Apply = On
   Reflection Dimming: Refl Level = 2

4. Set the Diffuse map slot to Bitmap, and select EARTHY.jpg as
   the bitmap. Turn on Show Map in Viewport. Copy an instance of
   the Diffuse map channel to the Bump map channel. Set the
   Bump Amount to 6.

5. Set the Reflection map slot to Bitmap, and select CLOUD2.jpg
   as the Bitmap.

6. Name the material **EARTHandCLOUDS**.

7. Apply the EARTHandCLOUDS material to the earth object.

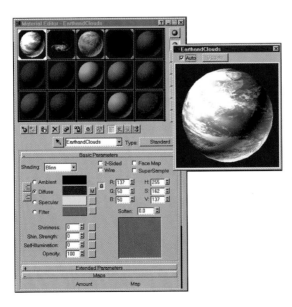

Figure 4
Creating an earth
material.

The earth object now fills up a major portion of the scene from the top to bottom-right area of the viewport.

Cloud Layer Creation

Next you add additional depth and character to your earth by generating three-dimensional clouds with Combustion and a SphereGizmo.

1. Create an atmospheric apparatus helper SphereGizmo at x = −1.55, y = 3.61, z = 0. Set the following:
   Radius = 45

2. Link the SphereGizmo01 to the earth object.

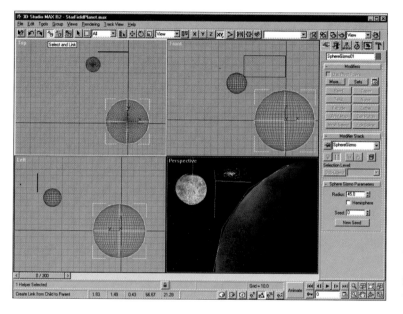

Figure 5
Creating and linking the combustion SphereGizmo to the earth object.

3. In Rendering/Environment, add an atmosphere Combustion effect. In the Combustion Parameters rollout, set the following:
   Gizmos: **Pick Gizmo** = SphereGizmo01

4. In the Colors section, set the following:
   Inner Color = (R = 215, G = 224, B = 252)
   Outer Color = (R = 132, G = 140, B =173)

5. In the Shape section, set the following:
   Shape = Fire Ball
   Regularity = 0.8

Note

This gizmo is center-aligned with the earth object. Instead of using the Transform Type-In dialog box for positioning, you can use the Alignment tool for precise alignment.

Space Ambiance

6. In the Characteristics section, set the following:
   Flame Size = 6
   Flame Detail = 5
   Density = 10,000
   Samples = 5

7. Now animate the cloud layer by animating its phase:
   Animate the Phase:
   Frame 0 (Keyframe 1) Phase = 0
   Frame 300 (Keyframe 2) Phase = 100

   When done animating close the Environment dialog box.

8. Now animate a slight rotation of the earth; the clouds follow this rotation because they are linked to the earth object.

   Animate the earth's z-axis Rotation in the top viewport:
   Frame 0 (Keyframe 1) z-axis rotation = 0 degrees
   Frame 300 (Keyframe 2) z-axis rotation = 15 degrees

You just created the combustion effect and set its values and characteristics so that it emulates a slow-moving cloud layer. This cloud layer is linked with the earth and will rotate with it.

Atmospheric Glow

You can create a rich Atmospheric glow using a volumetric omni light.

1. Create an omni light at x= −1.55, y = 3.61, z = 0. Set the following light parameters:
   Color = (R = 107, G = 124, B = 255)
   Multiplier = 8

2. Set the Attenuation parameters:
   Far Use = on
   Far Start = 45
   Far End = 55

3. Name the omni light **EarthGlow**.

4. In Rendering/Environment, add a Volume Light effect. Set the Volume Light parameters:
   Lights: Pick Light = EarthGlow
   Volume: Density = 1

5. Set the Noise parameters as follows:
   Noise On = on
   Amount = 0.25
   Type = Turbulence

Note

To animate the Phase, turn Animate on. At Frame 0, set Phase to 0. Move the Time Slider to Frame 300 and set the Phase to 100. Turn Animate off.

Note

To animate the earth's z-axis rotation, turn Animate on. At frame 0, set z-axis rotation to 0. Move the Time Slider to frame 300 and set the z-axis rotation to 15 degree. Turn Animate off.

Note

This omni light is center-aligned with the earth object. Instead of using the Transform Type-In dialog box for positioning, you can use the Alignment tool for precise alignment.

> **Link to Light** = on
> **Uniformity** = 1
> **Levels** = 6
> **Wind From the** = Back

6. Animate the Phase:
   Frame 0 (Keyframe 1) Phase = 0
   Frame 300(Keyframe 2) Phase = 2

The effect is almost finished. All the major elements are complete, including the earth's glowing atmosphere, which will be visible at render time.

Lighting

In this section, you create some additional lighting to properly illuminate the scene.

1. Create an omni light at −163.9, y = 124.1, z = 82.3. Set the following:
   Color = (R = 255, G = 255, B = 255)
   Multiplier = 1.5
   Cast Shadows = on

2. Name the omni light **Sun**.

Note

To animate the phase, turn Animate on. At frame 0, set phase to 0. Move the Time Slider to frame 300 and set the phase to 2. Turn Animate off.

Space Ambiance

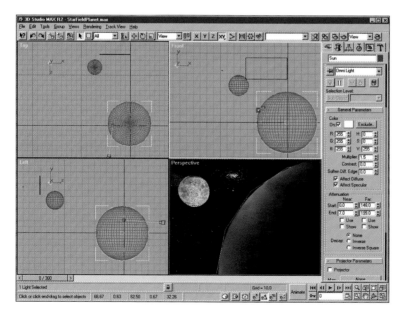

Figure 6
Creating the omni light that simulates the sun light.

Camera Setup

Next, set up the camera through which you can view the finished effect.

1. Create a target camera at x = –43.855, y = –65.356, z = 17.633.
   Position the target at x = –36.104, y = 0.315, z = 21.839.

Rendering

1. This scene must be rendered from Video Post for the sun flare to
   show up in the final output.

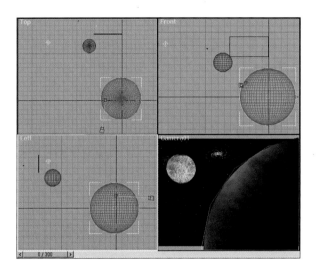

Figure 7
Completed star
field and planet
with Atmospheric
Glow effect.

You can create similar end results with MAX in many ways and each
approach has its own subtle nuances and unique, fine variations of control that can produce just what you want in the final output. Remember
that in animation, it's not how you do it, it's what it looks like when you
finish.

Asteroid Impact Explosion

by Frank Delise as written by Steve Alexander

This Asteroid Impact effect simulates the surface of an imaginary planet being bombarded by several asteroids. You can simulate the surface two ways: by the use of particle clouds for the sprayed impact material and Lens Effects Flare for the glow of the incoming asteroids and their resulting impact with the surface. An added camera movement timed with the impact will heighten the illusion.

Note

All position and rotational information is based on absolute world coordinates. When creating objects, use keyboard entry when possible. When positioning objects, use the Transform Type-In dialog box located in the Tools menu. These techniques ensure proper object placement and orientation.

Leave any settings that are not listed in the example at the MAX default values. Create objects in the Top viewport, unless otherwise indicated.

Preconfiguration

1. Before beginning this effect, please reset *or* restart MAX.

2. Open the file Asteroid.max from the project's Pre-load directory on the accompanying CD-ROM.

The scene consists of 3 asteroid setups each with a dummy parent, an oblong asteroid object, and a light all on a downward trajectory. All materials are standard map files included with MAX.

Objects and Materials

Ground Creation

1. Create a standard primitive box for the surface anywhere in the Top viewport and use the Transform Type-In dialog box to position it at x = –100, y = –50, z = 0. Set the following parameters:
Length = 700
Width = 1000
Height = 0
Length Segments = 128
Width Segments = 128
Generate Mapping Coord = checked

2. Add a Displace modifier. Set the following parameters:
Image: Bitmap = jupiter2.jpg
Strength = 50

3. Add an Affect Region modifier. Set the following parameter:
Falloff = 40

4. Add a Noise modifier. Set the following parameters:
Scale = 50
Fractal = checked
Strength: Z = 10

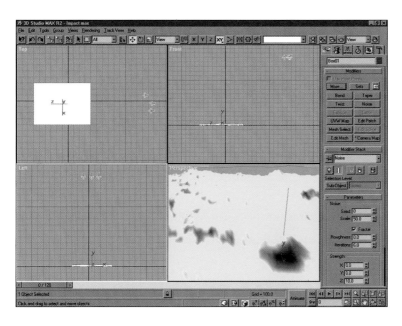

Figure 1
The surface object at the correct position.

The object you created will serve as the surface with which the asteroids will appear to impact. Play your animation in a shaded viewport to ascertain when each of the asteroids will impact with the surface. This information will be important later on. The frames for the impact are included in these later steps, but you must know how the frame numbers were obtained.

Ground Material

1. In the Material Editor, activate slot 2. Click the Diffuse slot and set the Map Type to Bitmap. Set the following Bitmap parameters:
   U Tiling = 8.0
   V Tiling = 8.0
   Bitmap = dirtgray.jpg
   Blur = 1

2. Go to Parent material, and set the Amount for the Bump channel to 400. Drag a copy of the Diffuse material to the Bump channel and set the following parameters:
   Blur = 5.0

3. Apply the material to the ground object.

Particle Systems

When the small asteroids impact with the surface, you'll simulate some of the surface material spraying up with a particle system for each of the asteroids.

1. Create a PCloud particle system anywhere in the Top viewport and position it at x = –98, y = –42, z = 6. Rotate the PCloud y = 22. Set the following parameters:
   Cylinder Emitter = checked
   Rad/Len = 32
   Height = 5.0

2. In the Particle Generation rollout, set the following parameters:
   Use Total = 500
   Speed = 10
   Particle Motion Variation = 100
   Enter Vector: x = 0.0, y=0.0, z = 1.0
   Variation = 20
   Emit Start = 40
   Emit Stop = 40
   Display Until = 100
   Life = 80
   Particle Timing Variation = 50
   Size = 2

3. In the Particle Type rollout, set the following parameters:
Standard Particles = Facing

4. In the Particle Rotation rollout, set the following parameters:
Direction of Travel Motion Blur = on
Stretch = 20

5. Right-click on the PCloud, choose Properties, and set the following parameters:
Motion Blur = Image
Multiplier = 2.0

6. Create 2 clones of the PCloud particle system. Position Pcloud02 at x = –225, y = 95, z = 6.
Position Pcloud03 at x = –120, y = –165, z = 6.

7. Set the PCloud02 Particle Timing parameters as follows:
Emit Start = 60
Emit Stop = 60
Display Until = 100

8. Set the PCloud03 Particle Timing parameters as follows:
Emit Start = 80
Emit Stop = 80
Display Until = 120

These steps stagger the burst of particles to coincide with the impact of the asteroid objects.

Gravity

1. Create a Gravity space warp anywhere in the Top viewport, and set the following parameter:
Strength = 0.2

2. Bind each of the PCloud particle systems to the Gravity space warp. The easiest way to do this is to select all of the PClouds, press the Bind to Space Warp button, press the Select By Name button and double click the Gravity selection.

Figure 2
The gravity warp binding dialog.

Particle Material

1. In the Material Editor, activate slot 3. Set the following Basic Parameters:
Face Map = checked
Diffuse = (R = 229, G = 229, B = 229)

2. Click the Opacity slot and set the Map Type to Gradient. Set the following Gradient parameters:
Gradient Type = Radial
Swap Color #1 and Color #3

3. Set the following parameters in the Noise section:
Amount = 0.5
Fractal = checked
Size = 10.0

4. Apply the material to all the particle systems.

This material will make the particles look like dirt spraying up.

Sky Background

In this section you'll create a sphere surrounding the area the camera will view, and you'll add a sky Bitmap to act as an environment. (See Figure 3.)

1. Create a standard primitive sphere anywhere in the Top viewport, and position it at x = –90, y = –60, z = 0. Set the following parameters:
Radius = 600
Segments = 32
Generate Mapping Coord = checked

2. Add a Normal modifier and check the Flip Normals checkbox.

3. In the Material Editor, select the first slot and name the material **Sky**.

4. Set the following Basic Parameters:
Self-Illumination = 100

5. Click the Diffuse slot and set the Map Type to Bitmap. Set the following Bitmap parameters:
Bitmap = sky.jpg

6. Apply the Sky material to the sphere.

7. Press the Show Map in Viewport button if you wish to see the map in the viewports.

Figure 3
The background sphere setup.

This sphere provides you with the necessary base object for your background. The normal modifier is an easy way to flip normals on objects.

Lighting Setup

Next, create the lighting effects for the scene.

1. Create an omni light anywhere in the Top viewport. Place it at x = –95, y = –60, z = 30. Set the General parameters as follows:
   Color = (R = 255, G = 190, B = 0)
   Multiplier = 0.001

2. Set the Attenuation parameters as follows:
   Far Range Use checkbox = checked
   Far Start = 65
   Far End =150

3. Make 2 copies of the light. Place copy #1 at x = –220, y = 75, z = 30 and copy #2 at x = –115, y = –185, z = 30.

   Later you will animate the Multipliers for these lights so that there is a flash when the asteroids hit the ground.

4. Create a target spotlight anywhere in the Top Viewport. Position the body at x = 700, y = –790, z = 775 and the target at x = –180, y = 35, z = 135. Set the following parameters:
   Color = (R = 255, G = 225, B = 180)
   Multiplier = 1.5
   Cast Shadows = checked

This light illuminates the terrain and casts some shadows from the hills.

Animating the Lights

1. Open the Track View and in the Multiplier track for Omni01, create keys using the impact start frames from the first asteroid object:
   Frame 40: Value = 0.001
   Frame 41: Value = 2.0
   Frame 50: Value = 1.0
   Frame 65: Value = 0

2. Create keys for the Multiplier track of Omni02 light, using the impact start frames from the second asteroid object:
   Frame 60: Value = 0.001
   Frame 61: Value = 2.0
   Frame 70: Value = 1.0
   Frame 85: Value = 0

3. Create keys for the Multiplier track of Omni03 light, using the impact start frame from the third asteroid object:
Frame 80: Value = 0.001
Frame 81: Value = 2.0
Frame 90: Value = 1.0
Frame 105: Value = 0

These lights with their animated multipliers will add a dramatic blast when the impacts occur.

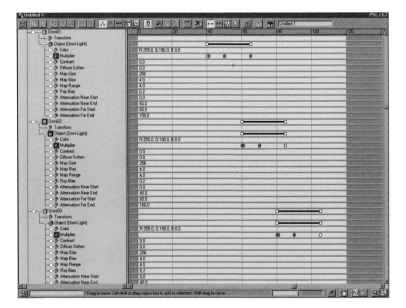

Figure 4
The Track View window with the correct settings for the omni light multipliers.

Environment

Add a fog to simulate a dusty looking planet surface which will cut the brightness of the sky background a bit.

1. Select Environment the Rendering menu.

2. Add a Fog atmospheric effect with the following setting:
Color = (R = 125, G = 100, B = 55)

Camera Setup

Now you will set up the camera through which you will view the finished effect. (See Figure 5.)

1. Create a target camera anywhere in the Top Viewport. Place the body at x = –600, y = –300, z = 70. Place the target at x = –170, y = –75, z = 95. Make the Perspective view the camera view.

2. Select the camera and set the Far Environmental range to 1170 in order to push the fog effect back far enough so that the background image will be slightly visible.

3. Select the camera target.

4. In the Track View, create a key at Frame 40 and one at Frame 41. Set the following:
   Frame 40: (x = –170, y = –75, z = 95)
   Frame 41: (x = –150, y = –75, z = 105)

5. Copy the Key at Frame 40 to frames 42, 44, and 46. Copy the Key at Frame 41 to frames 43 and 45. This will alternate the values of every other key, causing the camera target to shake at the moment of asteroid impact.

6. Change the Out tangent of the key at Frame 45 to the Square type. This will keep the camera target stationary after the asteroid impact.

7. Select all 7 keys and copy them to Frame 60 and again to Frame 80. This completes the shake of the camera for each impact.

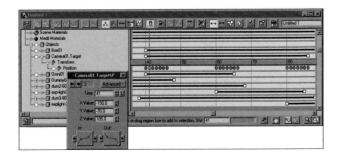

Figure 5
Copying the keys.

Shaking the camera at impact time heightens the effect.

Video Post Setup

In this section you'll add a Lens Effects Flare to give the asteroids a different-worldly look.

1. Open Video Post and add a Scene Event, choosing Camera01.

2. Add an Image Filter event, choosing the Lens Effects Glow filter. Click OK, double-click this entry in the queue and then click Setup (this is the best sequence for setting up VP filters).

3. In the Properties tab set the following:
   Source = Whole
   Filter: Bright = checked, Value = 150

Asteroid Impact Glow

1. Click on an empty space in the Video Post queue to deselect any items, and add a Lens Effects Flare filter. Set the label name to **Burst1** and click OK. Double-click this entry in the queue and then click Setup. In the Lens Flare Properties section, set the following parameters:
   Size = 30.0
   Intensity = 0.0001
   Squeeze = 0
   Node Source = Omni01

2. Turn on Animate. In the Lens Flare Properties section set the following:
   Frame 40: Intensity = 0
   Frame 42: Intensity = 100
   Frame 43: Intensity = 80
   Frame 49: Intensity = 50
   Frame 55: Intensity = 0

   Turn off Animate.

3. In the Prefs tab set the following parameters:
   Render = unchecked for all parts except Glow and Man Sec
   Squeeze = unchecked for all parts
   Occlusion = 50.0 for Glow and Man Sec

4. In the Glow tab set the following parameters:
   Size = 300
   Radial Color: Pos 0 key = (R = 255, G = 255, B = 255)
   Radial Color: Pos 100 key = (R = 255, G = 190, B = 0)
   Delete Radial Color Pos 93 key

Note

Set a gradient key by double-clicking the key indicator on the color bar. Delete a gradient key by right-clicking the key indicator and choosing Delete.

Space Ambiance

5. This has set up a bursting flare for the impact of the first asteroid on the ground. Add two more Lens Effects Flare filters to repeat this burst for the other two asteroids. Use the timing of the impact of the asteroids for the animation of the intensity setting. Set the Node Sources to the appropriate impact omni light (Omni02 and Omni03, respectively).

Asteroid Flare

1. Create another Lens Effects Flare entry for the effect on each of the asteroids. Name it **AstroFlare**. (See Figure 6.)

2. Click the Node Source button and choose all 3 lights named Astrolight. In the Lens Flare Properties section, set the following parameters:
   Size = 30.0
   Squeeze = 0

3. In the Prefs tab set the following parameters:
   Render = unchecked for all parts except Glow and Streak
   Off Scene = unchecked for all parts
   Squeeze = unchecked for all parts

4. In the Glow tab set the following parameters:
   Size = 45
   Radial Color: Pos 0 key = (R = 255, G = 255, B = 255)
   Radial Color: Pos 100 key = (R = 255, G = 190, B = 0)
   Delete Radial Color Pos 93 key

5. In the Streak tab set the following parameters:
   Size = 100
   Axial Align = checked
   Width = 10.0
   Sharp = 8.0
   Taper = 0.0

6. Delete all Radial Color gradient keys except the first and last. Set the following Radial Color keys:
   Radial Color: Pos 0 key = (R = 255, G = 255, B = 255)
   Radial Color: Pos 100 key = (R = 220, G = 135, B = 0)

7. Delete all Section Color gradient keys except the first and last. Set the following Section Color keys:
   Section Color: Pos 0 key = (R = 0, G = 0, B = 0)
   Section Color: Pos 25 key = (R = 220, G = 135, B = 0)
   Section Color: Pos 50 key = (R = 255, G = 255, B = 255)
   Section Color: Pos 75 key = (R = 220, G = 135, B = 0)
   Section Color: Pos 100 key = (R = 0, G = 0, B = 0)

8. Delete all Section Transparency gradient keys except the first, the last, and the Pos 50 key.

9. Add an image output event for an AVI and render your result.

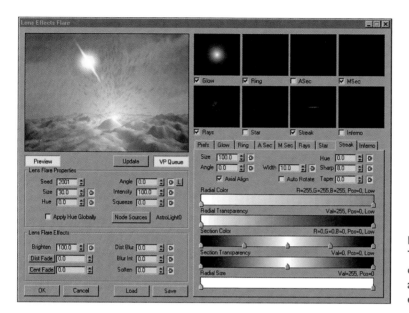

Figure 6
The Flare Streak color arrangement and the rendered effect at Frame 54.

The impacts of the asteroids timed with the shaking camera movement create a dramatic effect. This technique can be used in any animation that uses concussions.

You can find the final MAX file, AsteroidFinal.max, in this project's Preload folder and the final AVI file in the Scene folder.

Force Field

by Jay Kapadia

E very good science fiction story has force fields, so this is an important effect to add to your collection. You can use it with futuristic
detention centers or as a shield for ships. You can even take the material
and map it on facing particle systems to create electrical effects.
Fortunately, a force field is an easy effect to achieve. You can map it to
any piece of geometry, and you can create the effect entirely in the
Material Editor.

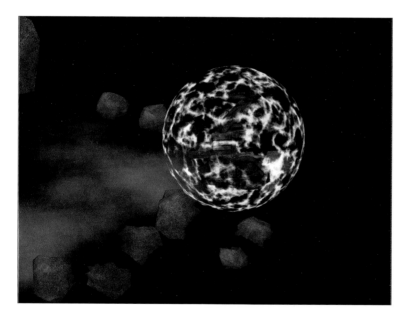

Note

*All position and rota-
tional information is
based on absolute
world coordinates.
When positioning
objects in your scene,
always use the
Transform Type-In
dialog box located in
the Tools menu. This
ensures proper object
orientation.*

Leave any settings that are not listed in the example at the MAX default
values. Most objects are created in the Top viewport, except where otherwise noted.

Preconfiguration

1. Before beginning this effect, either reset *or* restart MAX.

2. Open the file Force.max from the project's Preload directory on
the accompanying CD-ROM.

At this point, you should see a scene containing a spaceship, an asteroid field, and a large sphere, which is used for the environment. The animation length is preset to 90 frames.

Creating Objects and Materials

In this section, you create the basic geometry for the force field.

Creating the Force Field Object

1. Activate the Top viewport.

2. Create a standard primitive sphere. Place it so that the sphere encompasses the entire ship or use the Transform Type-In dialog box to position the sphere at x = −1030.1, y = 4190.7, z = 1226.1. Set the following:
   Radius = 357
   Segments = 40

3. Name the sphere **force field**.

4. Link the object force field to the group main body.

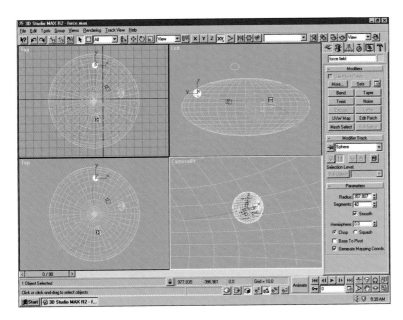

Figure 1
The parameters and location of the object force field.

Creating the Force Field Material

1. In the Material Editor, make material slot 2 active.

2. Set the Basic Parameters:
   Ambient = (R = 136, G = 217, B = 255)
   Diffuse = (R = 136, G = 217, B = 255)
   Specular = (R = 255, G = 255, B = 255)
   Filter = (R = 255, G = 255, B = 255)
   Shininess = 0
   Shin. Strength = 0
   Self-Illumination = 100
   Shading = Phong
   2-Sided = checked

3. Name the material **force field**.

4. Click the Opacity slot and assign Noise.

5. Set the Noise Parameters:
   Noise Threshold: High = 0.285, Levels = 10

6. Apply the force field material to the force field object.

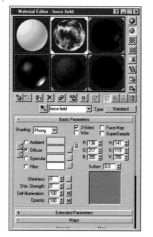

Figure 2
The basic creation parameters for the force field material.

At this point, you should see a spherically shaped electrostatic force field around a spaceship.

Animation

Next, you animate the force field so that it doesn't look so stagnant.

1. Turn Animate on. At frame 0, set Phase to 0. Move the Time Slider to 90 and set Phase to 10.

2. Copy the map to the Self-Illumination slot, click Instance, and turn Animate off.

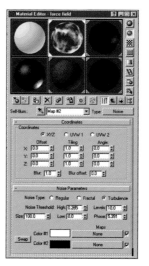

Note

The High value makes a majority of the material drop out. The higher the Levels value, the crisper the edge between the two colors.

Figure 3
The Noise Parameters of the force field material.

Sci-Fi Effects

3. In Track View, select MEdit Materials and then select force field. Next, select Maps, Self-Illum., Map #2. In Color#1, create a key at frame 15 and another key at frame 45.
Frame 15 = (R = 0, G = 0, B = 0)
Frame 45 = (R = 255, G = 255, B = 255)

This makes the force field seem to power up between frames 15 to 45.

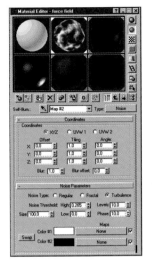

Note

To make the force field activate and deactivate, you have to animate the opacity over time. It automatically changes the Self-Illumination because it is an Instance.

Figure 4
Animating the phase of a material makes the noise move.

At this point, your spaceship should flip on its force field right before it enters the asteroid belt. If it doesn't, there's going to be a bumpy ride! You can find the final MAX file for this effect in the project's Scene directory as Final_Force.max.

Figure 5
This figure shows you how the keys for the force field material should look.

Beaming Effect

by Jay Kapedia

B "Beam me up, Scottie," as the saying goes. You can use this
Beaming effect to teleport items or as a weapon, such as a disinte-
gration ray. The effect, which you can easily achieve, relies on Video Post
and particle systems. In Video Post, the Lens Effect Glow makes the
beam come alive by producing a soft, yet bright edge. Particle systems are
a great way to create the illusion of molecules separating. They provide
movement and variations in color that catch the eye.

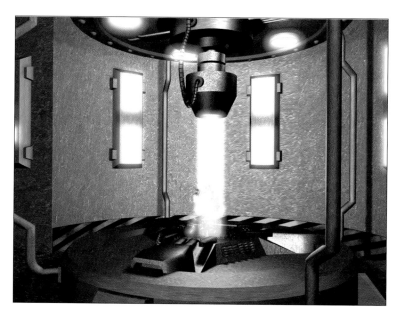

Leave any settings that are not listed in the example at the MAX default
values. Create objects in the Top viewport, unless otherwise indicated.

Preconfiguration

1. Before beginning this effect, please reset *or* restart MAX.

2. Copy the Beaming Effect project map files from the accompanying CD-ROM to the MAX maps subdirectory.

3. Load the file Beam.max from the accompanying CD-ROM.

Modeling and Materials

1. Create a standard primitive cylinder under the laser emitter at
    x = 0.18, y = −2.78, z = 227.46. Set the following:
    Radius = 15
    Height = 10
    Sides = 40

2. Name the cylinder **laser beam**. (See Figure 1.)

3. With object laser beam still selected, go into the Modifier Stack
    and choose FFD 2x2x2.

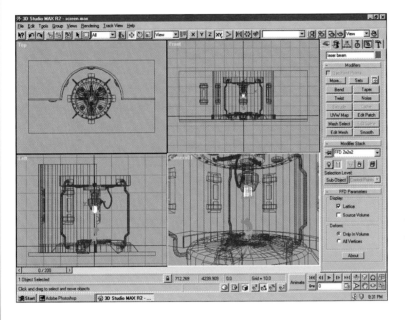

Figure 1
This figure shows
the position of the
laser beam and the
FFD 2x2x2
Modifier applied to
the object.

Creating the Beam Material

1. In the Materials Editor, activate slot 5, and create a material:
    Effects Channel = 1
    Shininess = 0
    Shin. Strength = 0
    Opacity = 30
    Diffuse = (R = 0, G = 0, B = 240)
    Filter = (R = 0, G = 0, B = 240)

2. Name the material **beam**.

3. Apply material beam to object laser beam.

4. Turn Animate on and move the Time Slider to Frame 17. Change the color of the omni light:
   Color = (R = 0, G = 0, B = 240)

5. Select the beam and go to the Modify command panel.

6. Click Sub-Object and move the four lower FFD control points straight down until they touch the object platform at coordinates x = 0.18, y = –2.78, z = 30.85.

7. Turn Animate off.

Figure 2
The bottom of the beam now touches the object platform.

At this point, the beam should shoot down and the room should turn blue.

Lighting Setup

In this section, you create the lighting effects for the scene. (See Figure 3.)

1. Create an omni light and position it in the center of the beam. Set the following:
   Color = (R = 0, G = 0, B = 0)

2. In the Attenuation box under Far, set the following:
   Use = On
   End = 500
   Cast Shadows = On

3. Click Exclude and select laser beam. You don't want the light to affect the laser beam.

4. Name the omni light **omni laser**.

Note
To make the object affected by the beam fade out, simply animate the visibility over time. Use a Super Spray to create the effect of the object molecules separating.

Sci-Fi Effects

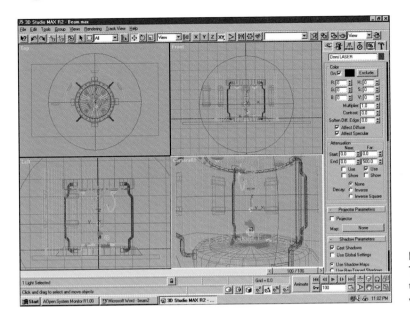

Figure 3
The lights positioned and all the variables set.

The light now fades as it moves further away from the beam.

Dissolving the Object

In this section, you are going to fade away the target object, which, in this case, is a flower. (See Figure 4.)

1. Open a Track View. Create a Visibility Track for object flower. Assign a Bezier float controller to the track.

2. Create a key at 37 and set the Value to 1. Create a second key at 64 and set the Value to 0.

3. Select the Visibility Track and copy it.

4. Create a Visibility Track for object flowerpot. Assign a Bezier float controller to the Visibility Track. Paste the keys from object flower. Close Track View.

   At this point, the flower should look normal until Frame 37, at which point it begins to fade away. By Frame 64, the flower should be completely dissolved.

5. To make it look like the molecules are dispersing, create a Spray particle system and place it in front of the flowers at x = 4.76, y = −11.76, z = 69.66. Set the following:

Drop Size = 2

Variation = 30

Render Box = Tetrahedron

Start = 40

Life = 25

Birth Rate = 4

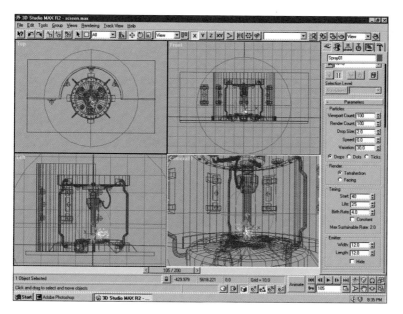

Figure 4
The particles start to move when the objects start to fade out.

6. In the Material Editor, activate slot 4, and create new material:

Diffuse = (R = 229, G = 229, B = 229)

Self-Illumination = 100

7. Name the new material **spray**.

8. Change the Effects Channel to 1 and apply material spray to object Spray01.

At this point, the beam shoots down and the flower fades away while the particles are moving about.

Sci-Fi Effects

Animating the Size of the Particles

In this section, you are going to make the particles fade out while they are wildly swirling.

1. Open up a Track View and go to object Spray01, Drop Size.

2. Create keys at 25, 60, and 75. Set the Value of the keys as follows:
   Key 25 = 2
   Key 60 = 2
   Key 75 = 0

3. To make the particles swirl about randomly, create a Gravity space warp at x = 17.53, y = –51.33, z = 64.82 and bind it to Spray01 (see Figure 5). Set the following:
   Strength = 60
   Shape = Spherical

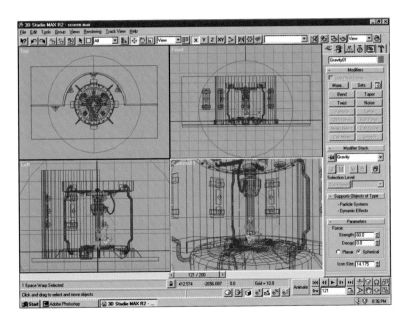

Figure 5
Placing the Gravity space warp directly in front of Spray01.

4. To make object laser beam go back up, select object laser beam in the Track View. Click Modified Object, FFD 2x2x2 and copy all the keys from 0 to 97. Then copy all the keys from 17 to 82.

5. Since the beam is going back up, the room should lose its blue tint. Click Omni Laser again in the Track View and copy all the keys from 2 to 97. Then copy all the keys from 17 to 82.

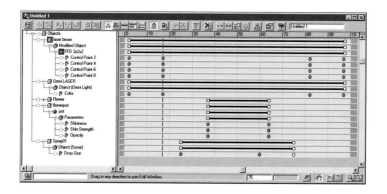

Figure 6
Placing the keys so that everything happens at the correct time.

The effect is essentially complete at this point. Go into Video Post to add glows, which will make this effect a good one.

Adding the Glow in Video Post

You are going to use Lens Effects glow to enhance this effect. The glow will produce a nice soft edge along the laser beam and the particles.

1. Click Scene Event and pick Camera01.

2. Click Add Image Filter Event and choose Lens Effects Glows.

3. Click Setup and then click Properties.

4. In the Source box, choose Material ID.

If you press Preview and VP Queue, Video Post will actually render out your scene with the effect, so you can preview your effect without actually rendering it. If you change any of the variables, Video Post automatically updates the Preview window.

5. Click Preferences and set the following:
Size = 2
Color Box = Gradient

Now you're all set to render your scene though Video Post and see what a difference the glow actually creates. You can find the final MAX file, BeamFinal.max, in this project's Scene folder and the final AVI in the Images folder.

Acme All-Purpose Freeze Ray Gun

by Steve Alexander

In the Freeze Ray effect, you will use animated splines to simulate arcing rays and a Target Directional light to add slight volumetric smoke around the arcs. You will create the frozen effect with a mesh object made from metaballs and scaled to surround the character in the scene. You'll also produce the frozen look from a raytraced refraction material with an icy color. In order to achieve a fiery electric look on the sparks, you'll use a Noise modifier and then glow the sparks with LensFX.

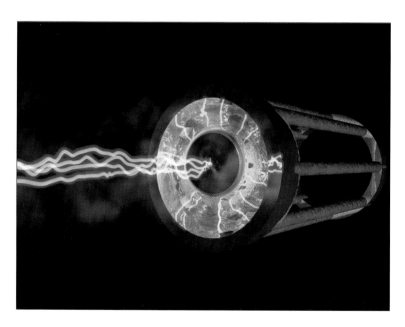

Note

All position and rotational information is based on absolute world coordinates. When creating objects, use keyboard entry when possible. When positioning objects, use the Transform Type-In dialog box located in the Tools menu. These techniques ensure proper object placement and orientation.

Leave any settings that are not listed in the example at the MAX default values. Create objects in the Top viewport, unless otherwise indicated.

Preconfiguration

1. Before beginning this effect, please either reset *or* restart MAX.

2. Load the Freeze.max file from this project's Pre-load folder on the accompanying CD-ROM.

This scene contains a model of the Acme all-purpose freeze ray machine and a duck, which will be frozen by the ray. There is an object inside the duck that will be scaled to emulate a solid frozen piece of ice. The animation is set to 300 frames.

Modeling and Materials

To begin this effect you'll create a set of splines that you will animate and rotate so that they appear to be sparks or arcs of electricity.

1. With the Top viewport active, create a spline by using the keyboard entry rollout and clicking Finish. Set the following:
Add Point at X = 0
Add Point at X = 15.00

2. Using the Transform Type-In dialog box, position the spline at x = 0, y = 0, z = 65.

3. Rotate the spline y = 90 degrees.

4. Modify on the segment level. Select the segment and then divide it by 10.

5. Come off the Sub-Object level and in the Rendering portion of the panel, set the following:
Renderable = Checked
Thickness = 0.7

6. Name the spline **Spark**.

7. Add a Noise modifier:
Fractal = Checked
Roughness = 0.37
Strength = (x = 15.0, y = 0, z = 15.0)
Animate Noise = Checked
Phase = 100 at Frame 300

8. Click the Select and Rotate Toolbar Button and the Use Transform Coordinate Center Button choice in the flyout. This is the last selection in the flyout.

9. Change the Reference Coordinate System drop-down list to Pick.

10. Select the RayGun Ball object and select the Restrict to Y button.

11. Hold the Shift key and rotate the Spark 30 degrees in the Camera viewport. Make 11 copies.

12. Select each copy and change the Seed number on the Noise modifier of each to add randomness to each spark.

13. Create a Freeze Ray spline. In the Creation Method Rollout, set the following:
Initial Type = Smooth
Drag Type = Smooth
Top Viewport = 180 units long, centered at the Raygun Ball

14. In the Modify panel, set the following:
Sub-Object: Segment: Divide = 10 divisions

15. Turn off Sub-Object and set the following (see Figure 1):
Renderable = Checked
Thickness = 1.0

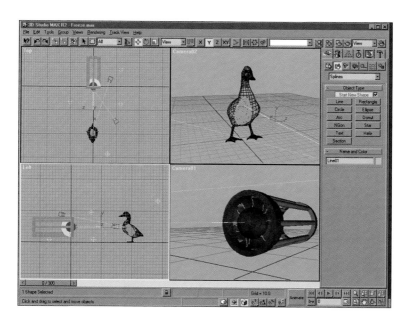

Figure 1
The spline for the main rays.

16. Add a Noise modifier:
Fractal = Checked
Roughness = 0.5
Strength: X, Y & Z = 10.0
Animate = Checked

Sci-Fi Effects

17. In the Hierarchy panel, check Affect Pivot Only and move the pivot in the Top viewport so that it is at the start of the spline.

18. Open the Material Editor. Choose the first material and set the following (see Figure 2):
Ambient = (R = 255, G = 255, B = 255)
Diffuse = (R = 255, G = 255, B = 255)
Shininess = 0
Shin. Strength = 0
Self-Illumination = 80
Opacity = 60
Material ID Channel = 1

19. Apply the material to the Raygun Line and the Sparks.

At this point your ray gun has the necessary spark objects for the initial part of the effect.

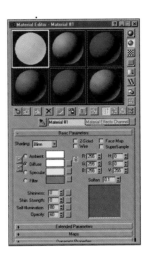

Figure 2
Material Editor
with the Ray mate-
rial.

Lighting Setup

The light you are about to create will serve as a volumetric effect to simulate smoke or frozen vapor surrounding the freeze rays.

1. Create a Target Directional light at x = 0, y = 0, z = 50. Position the target at x = 0, y = –180, z = 50. Set the following:
Far Attenuation: Start = 35, End=170.
Far Use = checked
Hotspot = 15
Falloff = 25

2. Name the light **RayGun Light**.

3. Create the Volume from the Rendering/Environment menu, Add Atmosphere, Volume Light (see Figure 3):
Light = Raygun Light
Fog Color = (R = 175, G = 215, B = 225)
Density = 15
Noise: On, Amount = 1, Noise Type = Fractal, Size = 9
Phase: Animate, Frame 300 Phase = 1
Wind Strength = 200
Wind From the = Back

This light effect enhances the look of the
freeze ray simulation. At this point you need
to work on the sparks.

Animation

You have created the sparks and ray objects
and now you must rotate them to give the
appearance of a buildup of electrical
charges.

Figure 3
The Volume light
settings for the
Raygun Light.

1. Select all the smaller sparks that surround the ball, and group them
   together. Set the Time Slider to
   Frame 300, turn on the Animate
   button, and rotate the group 360
   degrees.

2. Select the Longer Freeze Ray
   Spline. Go to Frame 120, right-click the Time Slider bar, and
   create a scale key.

3. Create scale keys at frames 150, 215, and 245.

4. For each separate spline, choose the Motion command panel.
   PRS Parameters: click the Scale button:
   Frame 120: Y = 0.1
   Frame 150: Y = 100
   Frame 215: Y = 100
   Frame 245: Y = 0.1

5. Make 3 copies and change the Noise Seed for each.

6. Animate Camera01. At Frame 0, x = 3.0, y = –18.5, z = 49.0. At
   Frame 60, x = 100, y = –150, z = 50. An easy way to do this is
   to use the move Transform Type-In dialog in conjunction with
   the animate button.

At this point, you have sparks rotating and rays shooting out toward your
unwitting subject. The camera move is used to enhance the overall look
of the animation. The camera starts at the ball of the machine, showing a
reflection of the duck, and moves out to reveal the machine and its
pending evil purpose (see Figure 4).

Sci-Fi Effects

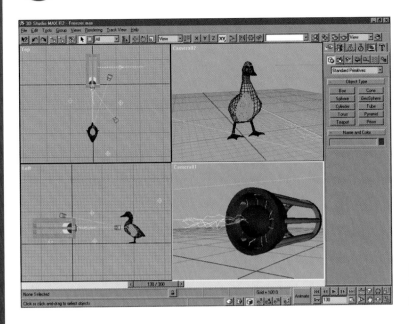

Figure 4
The final spark and
ray objects.

Video Post Setup

Completing the following steps in Video Post adds a glow to the sparks
and rays to create that electric feel.

1. Create Camera01 and Camera02 scene events. Set the following:
   Camera01:VP Start = 0, End = 135
   Camera02:VP Start = 136, End = 300

2. Create a Lens Effects Glow filter event. Set the following:
   VP Start = 59
   VP End = 245

3. Click the Properties tab, and set the following: **Material ID** = 1

4. Click the Preferences tab, and set the following: **Effect Size** = 1

5. Set the Color:
   User = 0, 10, 135
   Intensity = 50

6. Set up an image output event for an AVI file (see Figure 5).

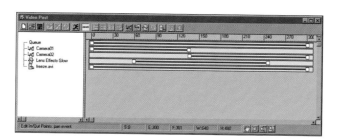

Figure 5
The Video Post queue for the glow effects and AVI output.

This completes the glows for the arcs.

Duck's Ice Pack

Here you will scale the object hidden inside the duck to make it appear as though ice is forming around the duck as the rays touch him.

1. Select the Frozen Layer object. This object was made with a metaball modeler and was scaled so that it fit inside the duck. As the effect unfolds, you'll scale the ice ball so that it encompasses the whole duck.

2. Go to Frame 150 and right-click the Time Slider. Create a scale key. Create another scale key at Frame 300.

3. At Frame 300, go to the Motion Command Panel and set the X, Y, and Z Values for scale to 100.

Ice Material

1. In the Material editor, select slot 2. Change the Material Type to a Blend. Discard the old material. Set the Mix Amount to 20.

2. Set the Basic Parameters for material 1:
Shininess = 85
Shin. Strength = 100

3. Set the Extended Parameters for material 1:
Refract Map/RayTrace IOR = 1.25

4. Name the material **ICE**.

5. In the Maps rollout, set the Refraction Map to RayTrace.

6. Set the Basic Parameters for material 2:
Ambient = (R = 25, G = 25, B = 235)
Diffuse = (R = 25, G = 215, B = 235)

7. Apply to the Frozen Layer object (see Figure 6).

Note

Because this method of changing values is equivalent to working in the Track View, there is no need to use the Animate button to create the animation of the scale.

Sci-Fi Effects

To further enhance the look of this simulation, you might want to add some sur-
roundings for the effect—maybe a factory
setting or room with other machinery.

You can find the final MAX file,
Freezer.max, in this project's Scene folder
and the final AVI in the Images folder.

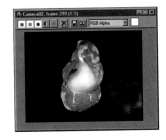

Figure 6
The frozen duck.

Alien Sun Effect

by Jeff Abouaf

An Alien Sun requires an animated gaseous effect. As a first step, you need to create a multilayered animated Noise material by using different colors ranging from red to orange to white. The next step is to apply a series of animated glow effects. By layering several glow effects you can create the complex animated glowing surface, radiating lighting effects and physical flares. Unlike the alien planet example in which a Displacement modifier on the geometry is helpful in portraying the textured surface, a burning star requires no geometric deformation. If your shot involves a close up, you might add particle systems with combustion and/or glow effects (see the Warhead Explosion example for adding burning particle effects to the scene). Keep track of your color tones by using the Color Clipboard—both for creating the material and for Lens Effects Glow gradient settings.

Note

All position and rotational information is based on absolute world coordinates. When creating objects, use keyboard entry when possible. When positioning objects, use the Transform Type-In dialog box located in the Tools menu. These techniques ensure proper object placement and orientation.

Leave any settings that are not listed in the example at the MAX default values. Create objects in the Top viewport, unless otherwise indicated.

Preconfiguration

1. Before beginning this effect, please reset *or* restart MAX.

2. Load the alien_sun.max file from this project's Pre-load directory on the accompanying CD-ROM.

This file consists of a highly segmented sphere, two omni lights, and a camera. Increase the sphere segments as necessary for high-detail rendering.

Create Materials

The sun surface consists of an self-illuminated animated material, to which you will add glows later. The material contains Noise maps (procedural materials) in the Diffuse and Self-Illumination channels, which prevents pixelation if the camera moves in.

1. In the Material Editor, create a Standard material. Click the Diffuse map slot and set the Map Type to Noise. Set the following Noise parameters:
Noise Type = Fractal
Size = 10
Low = 0.215
Levels = 10
Phase = 25.0

2. Turn Animate on, advance to Frame 100 and increase Phase to 30. Turn Animate off and return to Frame 0.

3. Click the Color#1 Maps slot and set the Map Type to Noise. Set the following Noise parameters:
Noise Type = Fractal
Size = 15.0
Levels = 3.0
Phase = 0.0

4. Turn Animate on, advance to Frame 100, and increase Phase to 5. Turn Animate off and return to Frame 0. Set the following:
Color#1 = (H = 5, S = 230, V = 103)
Color#2 = (H = 24, S = 238, V = 228)

5. Go up one level and copy the Color#1 Noise map created in Step 3 to Color#2 (not as an Instance). Click the Color#2 Noise map button. Set the following:
Color#1 = (H = 26, S = 26, V = 248)
Color#2 = (H = 37, S = 122, V = 255)

6. Return to the top level and set the Basic Parameters:
Self-Illumination = 100
Diffuse = (H = 25, S = 146, V = 235)

7. In the Maps rollout, copy the Diffuse map button as an Instance to the Self-Illumination Map channel:
Amount = 33

8. Select the Sun object in the scene and apply the material to it.

9. Apply a Displace modifier to object Sun. Drag the Noise Map material from the Diffuse map channel in the Material Editor to the Displace modifier map button, copying as an Instance. Set the following:
Strength = 2.0
Decay = 0.1
Luminance Center = Checked
Center = 0.5
Map = Spherical

This slightly deforms the sun surface, which will animate in sync
with the noise material (see Figure 1).

Video Post Setup

The next step is to apply filters in Video
Post to create the Sun's radiation. (Note, all
of following filter settings are saved with the
final MAX file and as separate LZG files on
the accompanying CD.)

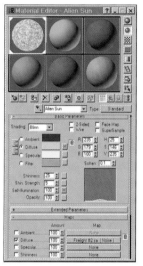

Figure I
The final sun mate-
rial structure.

1. Select object sun, right-click on it, select Properties, and set the following:
Object Channel = 1

2. In Video Post, add a Scene Event, choosing Camera01. Highlight the Camera01 entry and add an Image Filter event. Label it **LE Glow Sun** and select the Lens Effects Glow filter. Click OK, double-click this entry in the queue and then click Setup (this is the best sequence for setting up VP filters).

3. Click the Preview and VP Queue buttons. In Properties, set the following:
Source: Object ID = 1
Filter: Bright = Checked, **Value** = 90

4. In Preferences, set the following:
Scene: Affect Alpha = Checked
Scene: Affect Z Buffer = Checked
Distance Fade: Lock = Checked
Bright and **Size** = Activated, **Value** = 900.0
Effect: Size = 4.0
Color = Gradient
Softness = 50.0

5. Under the Gradients tab, set Radial Color to progress from yellow on the left to red on the right:

6. Fade the Radial Transparency from white at left and very light gray at right:
White = (R = 255, G = 255, B = 181)
Light Gray = (R = 226, G = 226, B = 226)

7. Set Circular Color left to right as follows:
White = (R = 255, G = 25, B = 181)
Light Orange = (R = 250, G = 101, B = 38)
Red = (R = 235, G = 30, B = 30)
Light Orange = (R = 250, G = 101, B = 38)
White = (R = 255, G = 255, B = 181)

8. Set Circular Transparency black at left and right and white close to the left (see Figure 2):
Black = (R = 0, G = 0, B = 0)
White = (R − 255, G = 255, B = 181)

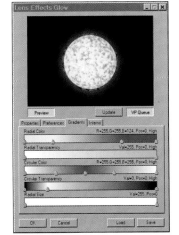

9. Under the Inferno Tab, choose Gaseous. Set the following:
Red, **Green**, **Blue** = Checked
Motion = 5.0
Quality = 8
Size = 2.0
Speed = 5.0
Base = 70
Bias = 55.0
Edge = 75.0

Figure 2
The Lens Effects Glow Gradients settings for the Sun.

10. Highlight the LE Glow Sun event in the VP queue and add another LE Glow filter. Label it **LE Glow Corona**. Enter Setup for this filter. Under Properties, set the following:
Filter: Perimeter Alpha = Checked

11. Under Preferences tab, set the following:
Scene: Affect Alpha = Checked
Scene: Affect Z Buffer = Checked
Distance Fade: Lock = Checked
Bright and **Size** = Activated, **Value** = 2000.0
Effect: Size = 25.0
Color = Gradient
Softness = 70.0

12. Click the Gradients tab. Under Radial Color, insert 3 more flags between the left and right gradient flags. Make colors left to right as follows:
Yellow = (R = 255, G = 255, B = 124
White = (R = 255, G = 255, B = 181)
Red = (R = 235, G = 30, B = 30)
Light Red = (R = 235, G = 30, B = 30)
Blue = (R = 0, G = 0, B = 255)

13. Fade the Radial Transparency Gradient from light gray to black as follows:
Light Gray = (R = 226, G = 226, B = 226)
Black = (R = 0, G = 0, B = 0)

14. Add 3 or 4 interior flags to the Circular Color Gradient, and choose colors that progress left to right as follows:
White = (R = 255, G = 255, B = 255)
Orange = (R = 250, G = 101, B = 38)
Light Red = (R = 235, G = 30, B = 30)
Orange = (R = 250, G = 101, B = 38)
Light Gray = (R = 195, G = 195, B = 195)

15. Set the Circular Transparency Gradient to Black. Set the Radial Size Gradient from White (left) to Light Gray (right) as follows:
White = (R = 255, G = 255, B = 255)
Light Gray = (R = 195, G = 195, B = 195)

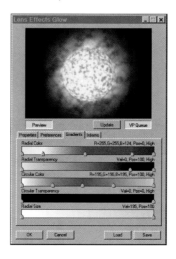

Figure 3
The Gradients setup for the sun's corona.

Sci-Fi Effects

16. Under the Inferno tab, choose Gaseous and set the following:
Red, **Green**, **Blue** = Checked
Motion = 10.0
Quality = 3.0
Size = 8.0
Speed = 10.0
Base = 40.0
Bias = 60.0
Edge = 50.0

17. Fade the Radial Density from white at left to black at right. Save the file to LE_Glow_Corona.lzg Click OK.

18. With the LE Glow Corona highlighted, add a Starfield Blur Image Event Filter. Go into Setup and make sure it is set to Camera01—this plug-in only renders the camera view. Leave the settings at the default.

Figure 4
The Starfield Blur Video Post Filter Interface—the filter works only with a camera view.

19. With the Starfield event highlighted, add another Lens Effects Glow Filter event. Label it **LE Glow Detail**.

20. In the LE Glow Detail Properties setup, set the following:
Filter: Perimeter Alpha = Checked

21. Under Preferences, set the following:
Affect Alpha and **Affect Z Buffer** = Checked
Size = 2.0
Color = Gradient
Softness = 5.0

22. Under the Gradients tab, from left to right, set Radial Color to medium-yellow orange, red, red brown; Radial Transparency to even white to black; Circular Color to black, red brown, black; Circular Transparency and Radial Size medium gray to black.

23. Under Inferno, choose Fiery and set the following:
   Red, Green, Blue = Checked
   Motion = 5.0
   Quality = 3
   Size = 10.0
   Base = 100.0
   Bias = 50.0

24. Save the settings as LE_Glow_Detail.lzg. This and the other Lens Effects glow file settings are included on the accompanying CD.

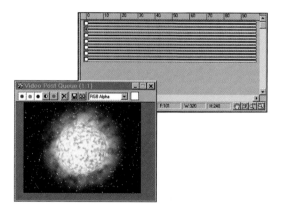

Figure 5
The final Video Post Queue and render for the Alien Sun effect.

This effect uses a single sphere with three glow effects. To make the sun appear more gaseous and complex, consider cloning the sphere, expanding it about 1½ percent in size, and applying a second set of noise materials, varying color, noise size, and phase settings. If you use the same object ID, the glows from the foregoing exercise will apply to it. Try additional glows to one or both.

You can find the final MAX file, aliensun_final.max, in this project's Scene folder and the final AVI file in the Images folder.

Alien Planetary Sky

by Steve Alexander

I n this example of an Alien Sky, you will make use of the combustion atmospheric effect to create gaseous clouds surrounding a small moon overlooking a planetary arrangement. There is a lake of unknown substance on the small moon that reflects the scene. The view also shows an interesting sun that has an eerie effect when viewed through the cloud. You will achieve the Sun effect with the Lens Effects plug-in.

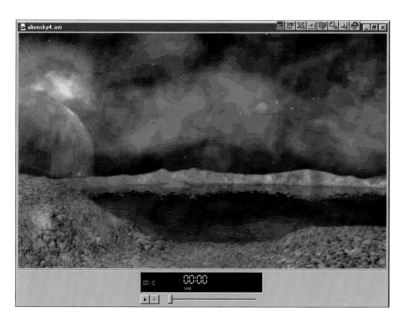

Note

All position and rotational information is based on absolute world coordinates. When creating objects, use keyboard entry when possible. When positioning objects, use the Transform Type-In dialog box located in the Tools menu. These techniques ensure proper object placement and orientation.

Leave any settings that are not listed in the example at the MAX default values. Create objects in the Top viewport, unless otherwise indicated.

Preconfiguration

1. Before beginning this effect, please reset *or* restart MAX.

2. Open the AlienSky.max file from this project's Pre-load folder on the accompanying CD-ROM.

3. Open the Material Editor. Right click in any material slot and make sure Sample Windows are set to 3×2.

The scene is an arrangement of geometry, lights, and a camera. There is a point helper object that you will use as the origin of the Lens Effects sun.

Material Creation

In this section you will create the Starfield background and materials for the various planets (see Figure 1).

Create the Starfield Material

1. In the Material Editor select the first slot. This will be the starfield for the background. Name the material **Stars**.

2. Set the Amount for the Diffuse map slot to 100. Click the Diffuse map slot and set the Map Type to Noise. Set the following Noise parameters:
   Noise Type = Fractal
   Noise Threshold: High = 0.2
   Size = 0.1
   Output Amount = 3.0

3. Swap Color#1 and Color#2.

4. Go to the parent material and open the Rendering Environment drop-down menu. Drag the Diffuse map slot to the Environment map slot and make it an Instance when prompted. Close the Environment dialog box.

Figure 1
The Starfield background material Noise settings.

Create the Moon Material

1. In the Material Editor activate slot 2. This material will be used for the moon. Name the material **Moon** (see Figure 2). Set the Basic Parameters as follows:
   Shininess = 0
   Shin. Strength = 0

2. Set the Amount for the Diffuse map slot to 100. Click the Diffuse map slot and set the Map Type to Bitmap. Set the following Bitmap parameters:
   Mapping = Planar from Object XYZ
   U Tiling = 12
   V Tiling = 12.0
   Blur = 0.6
   Bitmap = dirtgray.jpg

3. Go to the parent material and drag an Instance of the Diffuse material to the Bump map channel. Set the following parameter:
Bump Amount = 100

4. Apply this material to the Asteroid Crater object.

5. In the Material Editor, activate slot 3. This material will be used for the lake on the small moon. Name the material **Mirror Lake**. Set the Basic Parameters as follows:
Ambient = (R = 0, G = 0, B = 0)
Diffuse = (R = 0, G = 0, B = 0)
Specular = (R = 154, G = 154, B = 154)
Shininess = 45
Shin. Strength = 65

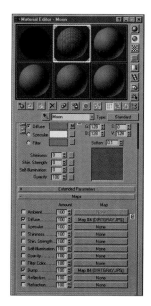

6. Set the Amount for the Bump map slot to 5. Click the Bump map slot and set the Map Type to Noise. Set the following Noise parameters:
Noise Type = Fractal
Size = 15

Figure 2
The Moon material.

7. Go to the parent material and set the Amount for the Reflection map slot to 100. Click the Reflection map slot and set the Map Type to Raytrace.

8. Apply this material to the Lake object.

Create the Large Planet Material

1. In the Material Editor, activate slot 4. This material will be used for the large planet. Name the material **Big Planet** (see Figure 3).

2. Set the Amount for the Diffuse map slot to 100. Click the Diffuse map slot and set the Map Type to Bitmap. Set the following Bitmap parameters:
Bitmap = salmnskn.tga
Blur = 0.01
Angle: U = 0.5, V = 10.0

3. Apply this material to the Big Planet object.

Create the Small Planet Material

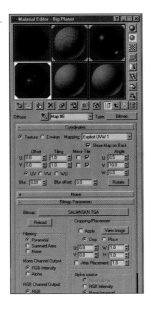

Figure 3
The Big Planet material.

1. In the Material Editor, activate slot 5. This material will be used for the small planet. Name the material **Small planet**. Bitmaps override any color for a material. Leave this out.

2. Set the Amount for the Diffuse map slot to 70. Click the Diffuse map slot and set the Map Type to Bitmap. Set the following Bitmap parameter:
   Bitmap = Jupiter2.jpg

3. Apply this material to the Planet object. Then close the material editor.

You placed the materials and can now begin the alien cloud formations.

Create Gaseous Clouds

Next you will create a SphereGizmo that will act as a container for the atmospheric clouds (see Figure 4).

1. Create a SphereGizmo anywhere in the Top viewport, and position it at x = 233.977, y = 60.428, z = –145.484. Set the following parameters:
   Radius = 2353.153
   Seed = 0
   Hemisphere = Checked

2. In Rendering/Environment, create a Combustion effect and change its name to Combustion01. Set the following parameters:
   Pick Gizmo = SphereGizmo01
   Flame Type = Tendril
   Stretch = 1.0
   Regularity = 0.1
   Inner Color = (R = 250, G = 225, B = 125)
   Outer Color = (R = 165, G = 0, B = 0)
   Samples = 2.0
   Flame Size = 500
   Flame Detail = 5.0
   Density = 0.05

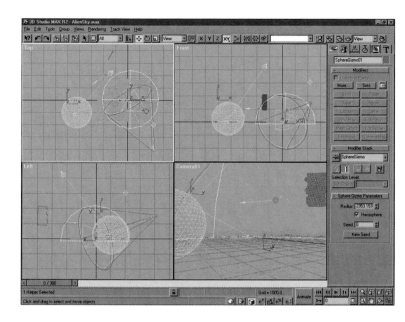

Figure 4
The SphereGizmo in the correct position.

3. Move the Time Slider to Frame 150. Turn Animate on and set the following:
Flame Size = 600
Density = 0.07
Phase = 3.0
Drift = 5.0

4. Advance the Time Slider to Frame 300, set the following parameters, and turn Animate off.
Flame Size = 700
Density = 0.05
Phase = 15.0
Drift = 10.0

5. Create a clone of the SphereGizmo. Change the Seed to 32196.

6. Add another Combustion effect and change its name to Combustion02 (see Figure 5). Set the following parameters:
Pick Gizmo = SphereGizmo02
Inner Color = (R = 250, G = 225, B = 125)
Outer Color = (R = 235, G = 145, B = 0)
Flame Type = Fire Ball
Stretch = 1.0
Regularity = 0.1

7. At Frame 0, set the following:
Flame Size = 500
Density = 0.05
Flame Detail = 5.0
Samples = 2.0
Phase = 15.0
Drift = 0

8. Turn Animate on, advance to Frame 150, and set the following:
Flame Size = 600
Density = 0.07
Phase = 0
Drift = 5.0

9. Advance to Frame 300, set the following, and then turn Animate off:
Flame Size = 700
Density = 0.05
Phase = 0
Drift = 10.0

Figure 5
The Environment dialog for the atmospheric gizmos.

10. Add a Volume Fog effect and set the following parameters:
Pick Gizmo = SphereGizmo01
Volume Color = (R = 135, G = 100, B = 130)
Exponential = Checked
Density = 0.5

11. Set the Noise parameters:
Noise Type = Fractal
Size = 300

12. Select the Volume Fog in the Environment window (see Figure 6). Use the Move Up button until the Fog is the first item in the window. Make sure the order is as follows:
Volume Fog (SphereGizmo01)
Combustion01 (SphereGizmo01)
Combustion02 (SphereGizmo02)

Create the Sun

The last effect is the sun with a nebula–like appearance. Accomplish this with the Lens

Figure 6
The final settings for the Environment dialog.

Effects plug-in, using the Inferno feature for a gaseous effect surrounding
the light of the Lens Flare.

I. Open the Video Post window from the Rendering menu.

2. Click Add Scene Event, and choose Camera01. Click OK.

3. Click Add Image Filter Event and choose Lens Effects Flare.
Click on OK.

4. Double-click the Lens Effects Flare entry and click Setup.

5. Load the included Aliensky.lzf file (see Figure 7). This is a completed Lens Effects settings file.

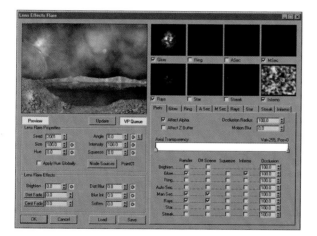

Figure 7
The main panel for
the Lens Effects
dialog.

Look over the settings in this Lens Effects dialog. You will find settings
that will give this scene that extra 'flare'; pardon the pun!

Alien Planetary Surfaces

by Jeff Abouaf

To create the Alien Planet effect you use a complex procedural material to achieve rich color and complex texture, with some of the maps applied with a Displace modifier to enhance the textured effect. Then you will clone the planet sphere (without the Displace modifier), expand it slightly, and map it with transparent Noise to create the cloud atmospherics. Finally, you will apply Lens Effects Glow and Flare to enhance the clouds and complete the image. By using a procedural material on the planet you avoid pixelation, which can occur if the camera gets too close to an object mapped with a low-resolution bitmap.

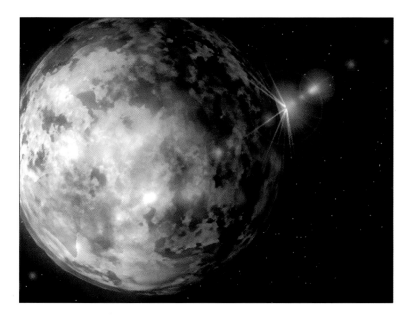

Note

All position and rotational information is based on absolute world coordinates. When creating objects, use keyboard entry when possible. When positioning objects, use the Transform Type-In dialog box located in the Tools menu. These techniques ensure proper object placement and orientation.

Leave any settings that are not listed in the example at the MAX default values. Create objects in the Top viewport, unless otherwise indicated.

Preconfiguration

1. Before beginning this effect, please reset *or* restart MAX.

2. Copy the project map files from the accompanying CD-ROM to the MAX maps subdirectory.

3. Load the Planet.max file from this project's Pre-load folder on the accompanying CD-ROM.

This scene consists of two concentric spheres. The smaller is the planet object, and the larger object is the cloud layer. There are also two omni lights and one camera.

Create the Planet

The first step is to create an earth-type planet texture map by using a Planet map.

1. In the Material Editor, select an empty slot and set the Material Type to Standard.

2. Click the Diffuse map slot and set the Map Type to Planet. Set the following parameter:
Colors = dark blues and medium browns

A color clipboard file (planet.ccb) is included as an example of the color scheme. While not realistic at this point, the planet map helps create a general water-continent layout. Leave Blend Water/Land unchecked.

3. In the Material Editor, uncheck the Show End Result button. While at the Planet map level in the material tree, right-click the slot containing the planet and select Render Map. Render a single-frame targa file 640×640.

4. Name the Planet map (not the material) **Planet** for later referencing.

5. If you have an image editor such as Photoshop, open the rendered map in a separate image editor. Convert the image to grayscale. Add a Noise filter for texture. Selectively lighten areas in the continent which will be your higher elevations and darken the ocean areas away from land.

6. Save the altered file (if you don't have an image editor, use planet2a.tga on the accompanying CD-ROM). This file serves as a mask for the Blend material.

You now have a textured grayscale pattern resembling the planet map used in the material (see Figure 1).

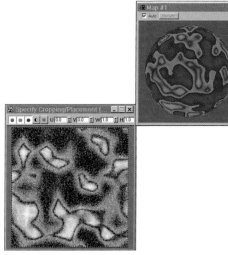

Figure 1
Examples of the
rendered planet
map and edited
grayscale version
for use as a com-
ponent of the final
material.

Sci-Fi Effects

Creating Colors and Patterns

The next several steps involve creating colors and patterns within patterns.

1. In the Material Editor, select an empty slot. Click the Type button and set the Material Type to Blend.

2. Click the Mask map slot and set the Map Type to Bitmap. Click
   Bitmap and assign the planet2a.tga file.

3. Return to the Blend material and click the Material 1 map slot.
   Click the Diffuse map slot and set the Map Type to Noise. Set
   the Noise parameters:
   Noise Type = Fractal
   Size = 35.0
   High = 0.75
   Low = 0.2
   Levels = 10

4. Click the Color #1 Maps slot and set the Map Type to Gradient.
   In the Noise Rollout, set the following:
   On = Checked
   Amount = 0.001
   Levels = 7
   Size = 2

Note
*For the next several
steps, open the
Material/Map
Navigator Window—
it helps you keep
track of which level
in the tree you're
working in. Also, you
might want to keep
the Show End Result
button unchecked to
see what you're doing
at each level.*

5. In the Gradient Parameters rollout, set the following:
Color 2 Position = 0.45
Gradient Type = Radial

6. In the second Noise section, set the following:
Noise Amount = 0.1
Size = 1.0
Noise Type = Fractal
Levels = 6.0

7. Click the Color #1 Maps slot and set the Map Type to Noise (you are now four levels down). Set the Noise parameters:
Noise Type = Fractal
Size = 5.0
High =0.9
Low = 0.225
Levels = 6.0

8. Move up two levels to the Diffuse map level. Under Noise Parameters, click the Color #2 Maps slot and set the Map Type to Mask. Click the Map slot and set the Map Type to Gradient.

9. From your color clipboard (or planet.ccb), select a medium blue for Color #1, a medium sand for Color #2, and a deep blue for Color #3.

10. In the Gradient Parameters rollout, set the following:
Gradient Type = Radial
Noise Amount = 0.1
Size = 1.0
Fractal = Checked
Levels = 4.0
Low = 0.33
High = 1.0

11. Move up one level to the Mask level. Check the Invert Mask box. Click the Mask slot and set the Map Type to Cellular. Set the following:
Cell Color = Light beige
Variation = 20.0
Division Colors = Neutral gray and dark blue
Cell Characteristics = Chips
Fractal = Checked
Size = 10.0
Spread = 0.5
Iterations = 3.0
Adaptive = Checked
Roughness = 0.1
Thresholds: Low = 0.0, Mid = 0.29, and High = 0.81

12. Go up three levels to Material 1 Standard.

13. Copy the Diffuse Map button (Noise) as an Instance to the Specular. Under the Basic Parameters rollout, set the following:
Shininess = 8
Shin. Strength = 5

14. Copy the Diffuse Map slot (Noise) NOT as an Instance to the Bump Map slot. Set the Bump Amount to 80.

15. Return to the top level (Blend material).

16. Click the Material 2 map slot. Click the Diffuse Map slot and choose the Planet (Planet) map created earlier. Specify to Copy the map.

17. Return to the top level (Blend material) and name the material **Alien Planet1**. Assign the completed material to object planet.

18. If not selected, select the Planet sphere. Open the Modify command panel and apply a Displace modifier.

19. In Material Editor, click the Material 1 (Standard) slot. Drag-copy the Diffuse map slot to the Parameters/Image/Map button in the Displace modifier rollout. Specify to Instance the map.

20. Set the following Displace parameters:
Spherical Map = Checked
Displacement Strength = 2.0
Decay = 0.1
Luminance Center = Checked

This slightly deforms the planet geometry consistent with the applied material. The planet without cloud cover appears on the accompanying CD as alien_planet_bare.tga (see Figure 2).

This recipe is an approach only. You want patterns within patterns with unique colors and distinctive, non-repetitive features. In this case, the goal was to create a planet that might sustain life as we know it, but one which clearly is not Earth. So I used familiar color combinations with unfamiliar texture formations.

Sci-Fi Effects

Figure 2
Planet without
cloud cover.

Create the Cloud Layer

Next, create the cloud layer.

1. In the Material Editor, select an empty slot and name it **Cloud Atmosphere**.

2. Click the Diffuse map slot and set the Map Type to Noise. Set the Noise parameters:
   Type = Fractal
   Size = 60.0
   Levels = 3.0

3. Click the Color #2 map slot and set the Map Type to Gradient. Set the following parameters:
   Color #1 = (H = 0, S = 0,V = 205)
   Color #2 = (H = 0, S = 0,V = 126)
   Color #3 = (H = 0, S = 0,V = 205)
   Gradient Type = Radial

4. In the Noise section of the Gradient Parameters, set the following:
   Noise Amount = 0.7
   Size = 1.4
   Fractal = Checked
   Levels = 6.0
   Low = 0.135
   High = 0.775
   Smooth = 0.335

5. Return to the top level and set the following:
   Shininess = 0
   Shin. Strength = 0

6. Copy the Diffuse (Noise) slot to the Opacity and to the Bump map slots as a Copy. Set Bump Amount to 100.

7. Click the Bump slot and drag the Color #1 slot to the Color #2 slot.

8. Select object cloud layer and assign the Cloud Atmosphere material to it.

9. Apply a Displace modifier to object cloud layer. Return to the Cloud Material in the Material Editor and drag the Diffuse Map slot (Noise) to the Displace modifier Map button in the Command/Modify panel. Set the following Displace parameters:
   Displacement Strength = 10.0
   Decay = 0.50
   Luminance Center = Checked, 0.2
   Map = Spherical

   This deforms the Cloud geometry synchronized with the Cloud material.

10. For high-resolution rendering, increase the cloud layer sphere segments to 164 or higher. As an optional touch, apply a Noise modifier and set the following parameters:
    Seed = 100
    Scale = 0.2
    Strength = (X = 2.0, Y = 2.0, Z = 1.0)

    A Left view of the planet together with the cloud layer is included on the CD as alien_planet2.tga (see Figure 3).

Sci-Fi Effects

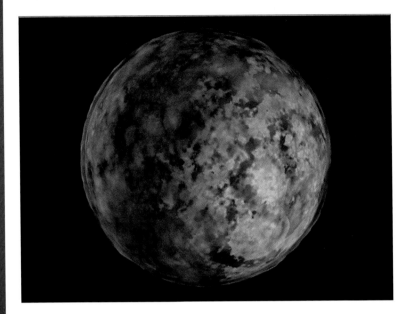

Figure 3
Planet with cloud layer.

You now have the completed planet with atmosphere. The last step is to smooth the atmosphere and place the planet in context.

Video Post Setup

At this point, you're ready to finish the scene by refining the cloud illumination with a soft glow (the glow becomes part of the atmosphere), using a starfield filter to generate the backdrop and Lens Effects Flare to add the effect of back lighting from a star.

1. In Video Post, click the Add Scene Event icon and choose Camera01. Click OK.

2. Highlight the Camera01 scene event in the VP queue and click the Add Image Filter Event icon. From the drop-down menu, select Lens Effects Glow and click OK.

3. Highlight Lens Effects Glow in the queue, click Add Image Filter Event, and select Starfield filter. Click Setup to initialize the Source Camera for the Starfield filter and click OK to exit the Setup dialog. Click OK to exit the Add Image Filter Event dialog.

4. Highlight the Starfield filter event, click Add Image Filter Event, and select Lens Effects Flare. Click OK (see Figure 4).

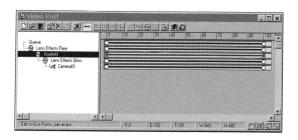

Sci-Fi Effects

Figure 4
The Video Post Queue set up with Lens Effects Glow, the Starfield filter, and Lens Effects Flare.

5. Double-click the Lens Effects Glow entry and then Setup. Click on Preview and VP Queue. The planet renders in the Lens Effects Glow dialog.

6. Load a_planet1.lzg from the accompanying CD. Note the settings:
   Source = Object ID, value = 1
   Filter = Bright, value = 70

7. Under the Preferences tab:
   Effect Size = 50.0
   Softness = 70.0
   Bright = On, value = 1000.0
   Size = On, value = 1000.0
   Color = Gradient

8. The Cloud effects come from the Inferno Settings:
   Gaseous = Checked
   Size = 50.0
   Speed = 1.0
   Base = 45.0
   Bias = 55.0

9. In the Gradients tab, the Radial Color gradient goes from white to blue, while the Circular Color gradient goes from black to dark blue. Radial Size goes from a value of 255 to a value of 0.

10. The Starfield filter ships with MAX R2 and is left at its default settings.

11. Highlight the Lens Effects Flare entry in the VP queue. Load a_planet3.lzf from the accompanying CD (see Figure 5).

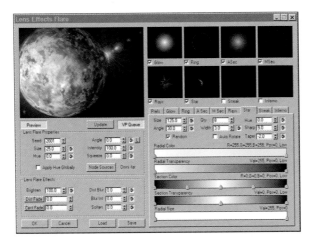

Figure 5
The Lens Effects Flare dialog lets you combine up to eight different types of effects at once, with multiple effects available from within the Automatic and Secondary effect options. This example uses the far omni light as the node source. The light is strategically positioned so the flare peeks from behind the planet.

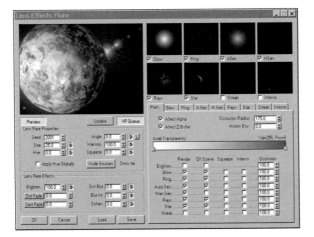

Figure 6
The most dramatic part of the flare comes from the Star effect. Note the precise settings from the file.

Most of this scene derives from procedural maps, so you avoid most scaling problems and can animate the atmosphere and certain surface phenomena. You can also make the planet look more "alien" simply by adjusting some of the gradient and planet color swatches (see Figure 6).

You can find the final MAX file, PlanetFinal.max, in this project's Scene folder and the final AVI file in the Images folder.

PART III

Atmospheric and Terrestrial Realism

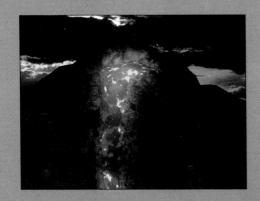

Snow Blizzard

by Greg Carbonaro

A blizzard is an elegant cacophony of particle motion. At first glance, you might assume it's an easy effect to re-create. But as is true with all things in nature, the look is unmistakably unique. To mimic the subtle nuances and feel of this winter storm, you must use two particle systems and a Volume Fog with some unique settings.

Note

All position and rotational information is based on absolute world coordinates. When creating objects, use keyboard entry where possible. When positioning objects, use the Transform Type-In dialog box located in the Tools menu. These techniques ensure proper object placement and orientation.

Leave any settings that are not listed in the example at the MAX default values. Create objects in the Top viewport, unless otherwise noted.

Preconfiguration

1. Before beginning this effect, please either reset *or* restart MAX.

2. Copy the project map files from the accompanying CD-ROM to the MAX maps subdirectory.

3. Load the file SnowScene.max from this project's Preload subdirectory on the CD-ROM. The animation length has been preset to 300 frames.

4. In the Material Editor, right-click in any material slot and make sure Sample Windows are set to 5×3.

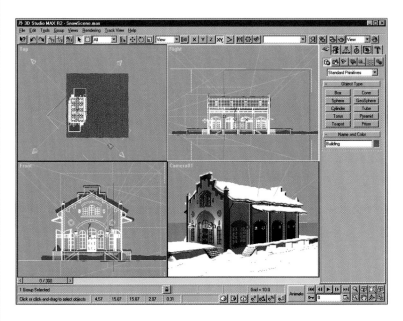

Figure 1
The viewports show a building covered in snow.

When you load the file, you should see a building covered in a blanket of snow in your viewports (see Figure 1).

Environment Setup

Now you can create the haze and windblown wisps of snow that hug the ground.

1. In Rendering/Environment, add an Atmosphere Fog effect. Set the Fog Parameters:
Fog Color = (R = 58, G = 58, B = 58)

2. Create an atmospheric apparatus helper BoxGizmo at x = 4,940, y = 569, z = −807. Set the following:
Length = 15,000
Width = 15,000
Height = 1,000

3. Name the BoxGizmo **SnowBlowing**.

4. In Rendering/Environment, add a Volume Fog effect. Set the Volume Fog Parameters:
Gizmos: Pick Gizmo = SnowBlowing
Gizmos: Soften Gizmo Edges = 1
Volume: Density = 0.2
Volume: Max Steps = 40

5. Set the Noise Parameters as follows:
   Noise Type = Fractal
   Noise Threshold: High = 0.3, Low = 0.2
   Levels = 6
   Size = 1,000
   Wind Strength = 500
   Wind from the = Back

6. Animate the Noise Phase:
   Frame 0 (Keyframe 1) Noise Phase = 0
   Frame 300 (Keyframe 2) Noise Phase = 7

You have just added an Atmospheric apparatus for the windblown wisps of snow (see Figure 2).

Snow Animation

Now you can create the first snow-generating particle system.

1. Create a Snow particle system in the Top viewport roughly centered over the ground and then use the Transform Type-In dialog box to position it at x = 1021, y = 324, z = 5658. Click the Select and Rotate button and use the Transform Type-In dialog box to set rotation of the particle system to x = –20. Set the following:
   Render Count = 60,000
   Flake Size = 15
   Speed = 85
   Variation = 60
   Tumble = 1
   Tumble Rate = 2
   Render = Facing
   Start = -200
   Life = 300
   Emitter: Width = 16,450, Length = 14204

2. Use the default name **Snow01**.

3. Create a Wind space warp in the Front viewport roughly in the center and then use the Transform Type-In dialog box to position it at = x = 1312, y = 8905, z = 1475. Click the Select and

Note

In Step 6, to animate the Noise Phase, turn Animate on. At Frame 0, set Phase to 0. Move the Time Slider to Frame 300 and set the Phase to 7. Turn Animate off.

Figure 2
Adding the Volume Fog to simulate windblown snow.

Weather Conditions

Rotate button and use the Transform Type-In dialog box to set rotation of the Wind to x = 90. Set the Force Parameters as follows:
Strength = 10

4. Set the Wind Parameters as follows:
   Turbulence = 20
   Frequency = 1,000
   Icon Size = 1,000

5. Use the default name **Wind01**.

6. Bind the Wind01 space warp to the Snow01 particle system.

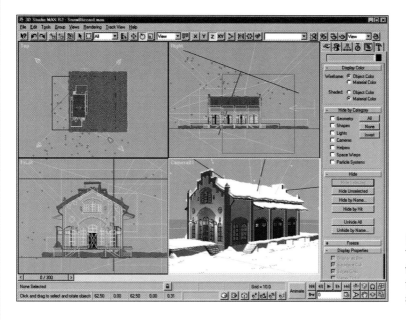

Figure 3
The creation of the first particle system snow emitter and blowing wind.

You have just completed the creation of the first snow emitter that will produce the fiercely blowing snow (refer to Figure 3).

Snow Material

Next, you produce a puffy snowflake material.

1. In the Material Editor, activate material slot 10 and set the Material Type to Standard.

2. Set the Basic Parameters as follows:
Ambient = (R = 0, G = 0, B = 0)
Diffuse = (R = 255, G = 255, B = 255)
Specular = (R = 255, G = 255, B = 255)
Filter = (R = 255, G = 255, B = 255)
Shininess = 0
Shin. **Strength** = 0
Self Illumination = 50

3. Click the Diffuse map slot and set the Map Type to Noise. Swap Color#1 with Color#2 and set the Noise Parameters as follows:
Noise Type = Fractal
Size = 50

4. Set Noise's Output parameters as follows:
RGB Offset = 1

5. Go back to the parent level of the material and copy the Diffuse map channel as an Instance to the Bump map channel. Set the Bump Amount to 999.

6. Click the Opacity map slot and set the Map Type to Mask.

7. Click the Mask's map slot and set the Map Type to Noise. Swap Color#1 with Color#2 and set the Noise Parameters as follows:
Noise Type = Fractal
Size = 25
Noise Threshold: High = 0.7, Low = 0.4

8. Click the Mask's Mask slot and set the Map Type to Gradient. Swap Color#1 with Color#3 and set the Gradient Parameters as follows:
Color#2 = (R = 55, G = 55, B = 55)
Gradient Type = Radial

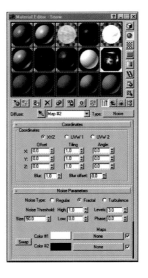

Figure 4
Adding some noise to create a snowflake material.

Figure 5
In Steps 7 and 8, you must first be at the Opacity channels Mask level to select the Map slot in Step 7 and then the Mask slot in Step 8.

9. Go back up to the parent level and name the material **Snow**.

10. Apply the Snow material to the Snow01 particle system.

You have just created the snow material and applied it to the first particle system.

More Snow Animation

Now you can create the second snow-generating particle system that will produce the stream of snow particles that will fall directly to the ground; these will not be affected by the wind.

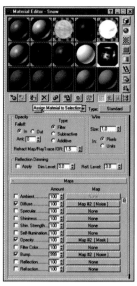

Figure 6
Creating a snowy material.

1. Create a Snow particle system in the Top viewport roughly centered over the ground and then use the Transform Type-In dialog box to position it at x = 1021, y = 324, z = 5658. Set the following:
Render Count = 40,000
Flake Size = 12
Speed = 85
Variation = 35
Tumble = 1
Tumble Rate = 5
Render = Facing
Start = –200
Life = 300
Emitter: Width = 16,450, Length = 14,204

2. Use the default name **Snow02**.

3. Apply the Snow material to the Snow02 particle system.

The scene is now complete. You should have a beautiful snow-covered winter scene with lots of snowflakes emanating from the particle system emitters (see Figure 7). You can find the final MAX file, SnowBlizzard.max, in the Scene subdirectory for this effect.

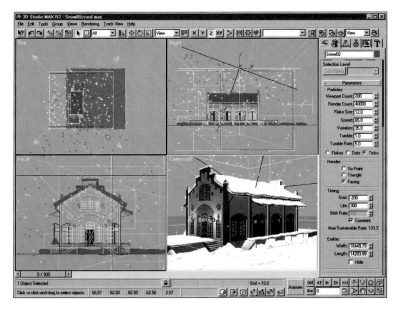

Figure 7
Completed Snow Blizzard effect.

Rolling Graveyard Fog

by Greg Carbonaro

Y ou can accomplish the same effects in MAX in various ways—
some more complex than others. However, as you will see in the
effect presented here, the simple solution is sometimes the more elegant
choice, especially when you consider processing power and rendering
time. The challenge in this effect is to create a slow moving, rolling fog
that hugs the ground and wraps itself around the obstacles that it
encounters in its path. The obvious solution is to use a particle system
with many UDeflectors and collision detection. This approach, however,
is very processor-intensive. The solution presented in this example is
much simpler and renders much more quickly.

Leave any settings that are not listed in the example at MAX default values. Create objects in the Top viewport, unless otherwise indicated.

Preconfiguration

1. Before beginning this effect, either reset *or* restart MAX.

2. Copy the Graveyard Fog project map files from the accompanying CD-ROM to the MAX maps subdirectory.

3. Load the file Graveyard.max from the projects preload subdirectory on the accompanying CD-ROM. The animation length has been preset to 1600 frames. This is the time it takes for the fog to move from the back of the graveyard up and out the front gate because you want the fog to creep.

4. In the Material Editor, right-click any material slot and make sure Sample Windows is set to 3×2.

At this point, you should see a complete graveyard in your viewports. This serves as the backdrop for the rolling fog.

Environment Setup

You can now add an environmental fog that serves as a backdrop background for the real rolling fog.

1. Add a Rendering Environment Fog atmosphere effect:
   Color = (R = 83, G = 98, B = 116)
   Fog Background = on
   Layered = on
   Layered = Top = 2, Bottom = 0
   Horizon Noise = on (size = 20)
   Falloff = Top

2. Animate the Horizon Noise Phase:
   Frame 0 (Keyframe 1) noise phase = 0
   Frame 1600 (Keyframe 2) noise phase = 32

Note

To animate the noise phase, turn Animate on. At frame 0, set phase animation to 0. Move the Time Slider to frame 1600 and set the phase animation to 32. Turn Animate off.

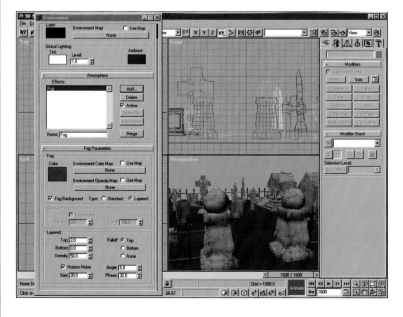

Figure 1

This atmospheric fog provides a backdrop for the rolling fog, giving it an apparent point of origin.

Animation

Now you can create the rolling fog for the scene.

Fog Particle System Creation

1. Create a Spray particle system in the Front viewport roughly centered in the graveyard and then use the Transform Type-In dialog box to position it at x = 3100, y = 5392, z = 89. Next, click the Select and Rotate button and use the Transform Type-In dialog box to set rotation of the spray icon at x = −90, y = 0, z = −11. Set the following:

   Render Count = 300
   Drop Size = 400
   Speed = 12
   Variation = 1
   Particles = Drops
   Render = Facing
   Life = 1601
   Emitter: width = 5958, length = 195

2. Name the Spray **Fog Emitter**.

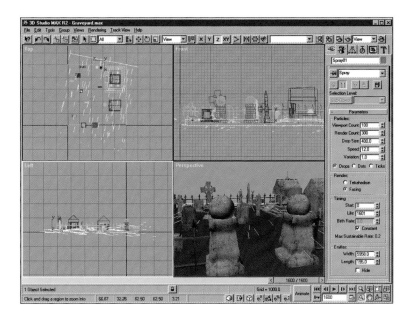

Figure 2
Slow moving particles set the mood for the scene.

If you move the Time Slider to frame 1600, you should see a stream of particles emanating from the emitter at the back of the graveyard.

Fog Particle System Material

Now create the material that turns these ordinary particles into a wispy fog.

1. In the Material Editor, make material slot 3 active.

2. Set the Basic Parameters as follows:
   Ambient = (R = 29, G = 29, B = 29)
   Diffuse = (R = 128, G = 128, B = 128)
   Filter =(R = 170, G = 170, B = 170)
   Shininess = 0
   Shin. Strength = 0
   Soften = 1

3. Set the Extended Parameters as follows:
   Opacity Falloff = Out (amount = 100)

4. In the Maps area, set the Amount for the Diffuse channel to 100. Click the Diffuse map channel and set the Map type to Noise.

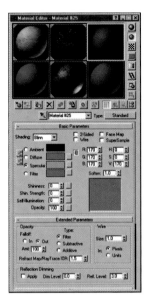

Figure 3
Set the Basic and Extended Parameters in the Material Editor.

5. Click the noise channel and set the Noise Parameters as follows:
   Noise Type = Fractal
   Size = 400

6. Animate the Noise Phase:
   Frame 0 (Keyframe 1) phase = 0
   Frame 1600 (Keyframe 2) phase = 8

When done animating, return to the parent level of the material.

7. In the Maps area, click the Opacity map channel and set the Map type to Mask.

Figure 4
Set the Maps parameters in the Material Editor.

8. Click the Opacity channel and then when you are on the Mask level of the material, set the Map type to Noise.

9. Click the Noise channel of the mask and set the Noise Parameters as follows:
   Noise Type = Fractal
   Size = 400

10. Animate the Noise Phase:
    Frame 0 (Keyframe 1) phase = 0
    Frame 1600 (Keyframe 2) phase = 8

    When done animating, go up one level back to the Mask level of the material.

11. At the Mask level of the material, click the Mask channel, and set the Type to Gradient. Drag Color #1 over Color #3 and specify to swap the colors. Set the Gradient Type to Radial.

12. Return to the parent level of the material and name the material **Foggy**.

13. Apply the Foggy material to the Fog Emitter object. Either drag and drop the material to the sun object or use the Assign Material to Selection button in the Material Editor.

Figure 5
Set the Map type of the Opacity map channel.

Figure 6
Set the Map type to Noise.

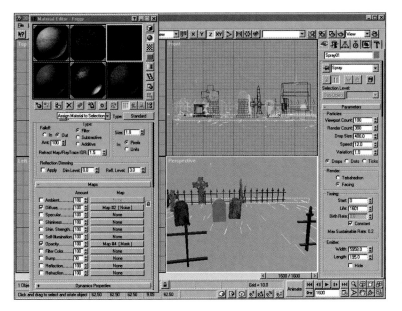

Figure 7
Creating a subtle enough fog material requires a fine balance of settings.

Lighting Setup

Next, illuminate the graveyard.

1. Create a target spotlight in the Front viewport, pointing down toward the graveyard and then use the Transform Type-In dialog box to position it at x = 7344, y = –3369, z = 6266. Position the target at x = 1473, y = 2385, z = 272. Set the following:
   Color = (R = 40, G = 59, B = 117)
   Hotspot = 1, falloff = 127
   Cast Shadows = on
   Use Global Settings = on

2. Name the target spot **Shadow Spot**.

3. Create an omni light in the Top viewport in the center of the graveyard and then use the Transform Type-In dialog box to position it at x = –881, y = 81, z = 975. Set the following:
   Color = (R = 36, G = 63, B = 94)
   Multiplier = 1.5

4. Name the omni light **Fill Light**.

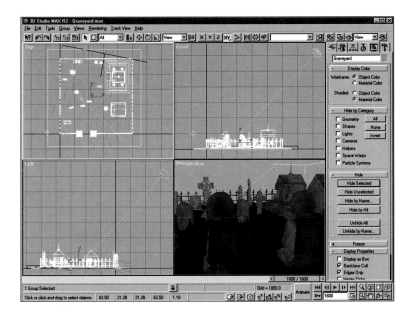

Figure 8
Position the omni light in your scene.

Camera Setup

The final step is to set up the camera through which you will view the finished effect.

> Create a target camera in the Top viewport, pointing at the graveyard and then use the Transform Type-In dialog box to position it at x = 1185, y = −1925, z = 1062. Position the target at x = 1930, y = 1108, z = 413.

The 1600-frame length of this animation is directly dictated by the speed of the rolling fog. To create a slow, creeping movement, slow particle motion is required.

Weather Conditions

Hot Lava Flow

by Greg Carbonaro

Y ou can simulate the Molten Lava effects with a series of particle systems. Universal Deflectors and Gravity help move and channel the particles, and Image Motion Blur and Lens Effects Glow meld them into what appears to be a flowing liquid. Smoke and steam appear to emanate from the hot material via a Volume Fog and the associated atmospheric apparatus to which they are attached.

Note

All position and rotational information is based on absolute world coordinates. When creating objects, use keyboard entry when possible. When positioning objects, use the Transform Type-In dialog box located in the Tools menu. These techniques ensure proper object placement and orientation.

Leave any settings that are not listed in the example at the MAX default values. Create objects in the Top viewport, unless otherwise indicated

Preconfiguration

1. Before beginning this effect, please either reset *or* restart MAX.

2. Copy the Hot Lava project map files from the accompanying CD-ROM to your MAX maps subdirectory.

3. Load the Mountain scene from the project pre-load directory on the CD-ROM. The animation length is preset to 300 frames.

4. Open the Material Editor. Right-click in any material slot and make sure Sample Windows are set to 3×2.

You should see blue mountain and sky backdrop in your perspective viewport.

Modeling and Materials

The first thing you are going to do is create a rocky material for the mountain.

Creating the Mountain Material

1. In the Material Editor, make the material slot 2 active and set the Material Type to Standard.

2. Set the Basic Parameters as follows:
   Ambient = (R = 26, G = 26, B = 26)
   Diffuse = (R = 0, G = 0, B = 0)
   Specular = (R = 128, G = 128, B = 128)
   Shininess = 0
   Shin. Strength = 0
   Soften = 0.01

3. Set the Amount for the Diffuse slot to 100. Click on the Diffuse map slot and set the map Type to Mix. Set the Mix parameters as follows:
   Mix Parameters: mix amount = 0.15

4. Click on the Color 1 map slot and set the map Type to Bitmap. Set the Bitmap parameters as follows:
   Bitmap = Sponge.jpg
   Coordinates: Texture = On, U Tiling = 7, V Tiling = 7
   Output: RGB Offset = −0.5

5. Return to the Mix map, click on the Color 2 map slot and set the map Type to Noise. Set the Noise parameters as follows:
   Noise Type = Fractal
   Size = 6
   Noise Threshold: High = 0.61, Low = 0.175

6. Swap Color #1 and Color #2.

7. Return to the top of the material definition, set the Bump amount to 100, click the Bump map slot and set the map Type to Cellular. Set the Cellular parameters as follows:
   Cell Characteristics: Chips = on, Fractal = on, Size = 6

8. Return to the Mask map, click on the Mask slot and set the map Type to Gradient. Drag Color #1 over Color #2 and specify to swap the colors. Set the Gradient Type to Radial.

9. Return to the top of the material definition and name the material **Mountain Rock**.

10. Apply the Mountain Rock material to the Mountain object.

The material that you just created should now appear on the mountain. The mountain is now starting to look a little more realistic.

Creating the Lava Dome

1. Activate the Top viewport.

2. Create a standard primitive sphere roughly centered in the hole on the top of the mountain, then use the Transform Type-In to position it precisely at x = −1.32, y = 1.44, z = 25.69. Set the following:
Radius = 10
Segments = 25

3. Scale the sphere on the Z axis 62 percent.

4. Add a Noise modifier (see Figure 1):
Noise: Scale = 3, Fractal = Checked
Strength: x = 2, y = 2, z = 2
Animate Noise = On
Frequency = 0.04

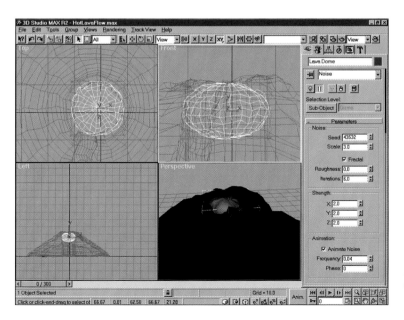

Figure 1
Creating and placing the modified sphere object that will serve as the lava dome.

Natural Disasters

5. Add a UVW Mapping modifier to the sphere. Set Mapping to Spherical.

6. Name the object **Lava Dome**.

Creating the Lava Material

1. In the Material Editor, make the material slot 3 active.

2. Set the Material Type to Standard material.

3. Set the Basic Parameters as follows:
   Ambient = (R = 18, G = 18, B = 18)
   Diffuse = (R = 164, G = 0, B = 0)
   Specular = (R = 255, G = 224, B = 0)
   Shininess = 12
   Shin. Strength = 62
   Soften = 0

4. Set the Amount for the Bump slot to 500. Click the Bump map slot and set the map Type to Noise. Set the Noise parameters as follows:
   Noise Type = Fractal
   Size = 5

5. Animate the Noise Coordinate Z Offset. Animate the z coordinate as follows:
   Frame 0 (Keyframe 1) Z = 0
   Frame 300 (Keyframe 2) Z = –10

6. Name the material **Hot Lava**.

7. Apply Hot Lava material to the Lava Dome object.

Next you are going to create a hazy smoke atmosphere around the lava dome.

Creating the Dome Smoke Apparatus

1. Activate the Top viewport.

2. Create atmospheric apparatus helper SphereGizmo roughly centered around the Lava Dome object, then use the Transform Type-In to position it precisely at x = –1.36, y = 0.38, z = 28. Set the following:
   Radius = 13

3. Name the SphereGizmo **Dome Smoke Gizmo**.

Note

To animate the z coordinate, turn Animate on. At Frame 0, set z to 0. Move the Time Slider to Frame 300 and set z to –10. Turn Animate off.

4. In the Rendering drop-down menu click Environment to open the Environment dialog box and then add a Volume Fog (see Figure 2):
   Gizmos: Pick Gizmo = Dome Smoke Gizmo
   Volume: Color (R = 152, G = 152, B = 152), Density = 90
   Noise: Type = Fractal, Threshold Low = 0.05, Size = 2.5, Wind Strength = 0.3
   Wind From the = Bottom

5. Animate the Noise Phase as follows:
   Frame 0 (Keyframe 1)
   Phase = 0
   Frame 300 (Keyframe 2)
   Phase = 5

At this point the scene should include the Mountain, Lava Dome, and a SphereGizmo.

Lava Bubble Particles

Now you are going to create some boiling lava particles that will periodically shoot up from the top of the lava dome.

1. Activate the Top viewport.

2. Create a PCloud roughly centered on the Lava Dome object, then use the Transform Type-In to position it at x = −1.44, y = 2.7, z = 27.34. Set the following:
   Particle Formation = Cylinder Emitter
   Display Icon: Rad/Len = 17, Height = 6
   Viewport Display: Percentage of Particles = 10%
   Particle Generation: Use Total = 25
   Particle Motion: Speed = 0.2, Variation = 15%
   Enter Vector: (x = 0, y = 0, z = 1), variation = 10%
   Particle Timing: Emit Stop = 301, Display Until = 301, Life = 301, Variation = 150
   Particle Size: Size = 1.5, Variation = 50%

3. Set the Particle Type parameters:
   Standard Particles = Constant

4. Name the PCloud **Lava Bubble Particles** (see Figure 3).

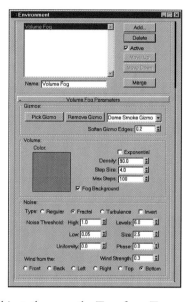

Note

To animate Phase, turn Animate on. At Frame 0, set Phase to 0. Move the Time Slider to Frame 300 and set Phase to 5. Turn Animate off.

Figure 2
Adding the Volume Fog to the Lava Dome SphereGizmo.

Natural Disasters

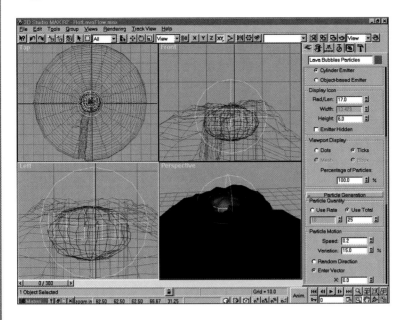

Figure 3
Creating the Lava Bubbles particle emitter.

5. Apply the Hot Lava material to the Lava Bubble Particles.

6. Set the object properties as follows:
Motion Blur = Image
G-Buffer Object Channel = 1

7. Add a Gravity space warp at x = –66, y = –37, z = 0. Set the following:
Parameters Force Strength = 0.003
Planar = On (downward)
Icon Size = 4

8. Bind the Gravity space warp to the PCloud Lava Bubble Particles.

Once you bind the Gravity to the Lava Bubble Particles, their trajectories change. During the course of the animation they will shoot upward slightly and then fall back into the lava dome.

Lava Stream Particles

1. Create a PCloud roughly centered at the top of the trough that runs down the side of the mountain, then use the Transform Type-In to position it at x = –5.3, y = –8.79, z = 30.62. Once positioned, use the Transform Type-In to rotate it precisely to x = 118.856, y = 11.851, z = –20.441. Set the following:
   Particle Formation = Cylinder Emitter
   Display Icon: Rad/Len = 5, Height = 2
   Viewport Display: Percentage of Particles = 10%

2. Set the Particle Generation parameters:
   Use Rate = 100
   Particle Timing: Emit Stop = 301, Display Until = 301, Life = 301
   Particle Size: Size = 4, Variation = 100%

3. Set the Particle Type parameters:
   Standard Particles = constant

4. Name the PCloud **Lava Stream Particles**.

5. Apply the Hot Lava material to the Lava Stream Particles.

6. Set the object properties as follows:
   Motion Blur = Image
   G–Buffer Object Channel = 1

7. Bind the Gravity space warp to the PCloud Lava Stream Particles.

8. Add a UDeflector space warp at x = –80.0, y = –37.0, z = 0 Set the following:
   Pick Object = Mountain
   Icon Size = 8

9. Set the Particle Bounce parameters:
   Bounce = 0.75
   Variation = 10%
   Chaos = 10%

10. Bind the Lava Stream Particles to the UDeflector.

Now the lava stream emitter is located at the top of the mountain, ready to flow.

Next you will add some smoke to the flow. This will help give the look of extreme heat.

Lava Stream Smoke Apparatus

1. Create an atmospheric apparatus helper Cylgizmo roughly centered at the top of the trough that runs down the side of the mountain, then use the Transform Type-In to position it at x = –2.83, y = –2.57, z = 33.1. Set the following:
   Radius = 7
   Height = 0.001

2. Once the Cylgizmo is positioned, use the Transform Type-In to rotate it to x = 56.23, y = –175.71, z = –6.16.

3. Animate the Cylgizmo's Height:
   Frame 0 (Keyframe 1) Height = 0.001
   Frame 300 (Keyframe 2) Height = 70

4. Name the Cylgizmo **Lava Stream Smoke Gizmo**.

5. In the Rendering drop-down menu click Environment to open the Environment dialog box and add Volume Fog:
   Gizmos: Pick Gizmo = Lava Stream Smoke Gizmo

6. Set the Volume Parameters:
   Color = (R = 152, G = 152, B = 152)
   Density = 90

7. Set the Noise parameters:
   Noise Type = Fractal
   Threshold Low = 0.05
   Size = 2.5
   Wind Strength = 0.3
   Wind from the = Bottom

8. Animate the Noise Phase:
   Frame 0 (Keyframe 1) Phase = 0
   Frame 300 (Keyframe 2) Phase = 5

All of the necessary particle systems and atmospheric gizmos are now in place.

Note

To animate the Height, turn Animate on. At Frame 0, set Height to 0.001. Move the Time Slider to Frame 300 and set Height to 70. Turn Animate off.

Note

To animate Phase, turn Animate on. At Frame 0, set Phase to 0. Move the Time Slider to Frame 300 and set Phase to 5. Turn Animate off.

Camera Setup

Set up the camera through which you will view the effect.

1. Activate the Top viewport.

2. Create a target camera in front of and pointing at the mountain, then use the Transform Type-In to position the body at x = –8.33, y = –62.53, z = 57.27. Position the target at x = –0.28, y = 3.28, z = 20.51.

Creating Glows in Video Post

1. Use the Rendering drop-down menu and click Video Post to open the Video Post dialog box.

2. Add Scene Event: Camera01.

3. Add an Image Filter event: Add Lens Effects Glow.

4. Set the Glow Properties:
   Source = Object ID#1
   Filter = Brightness

5. Set the Glow preferences:
   Effect Size = 9
   Color = Pixel
   Intensity = 60

6. Add an Image Output event and select AVI as the output file type. Use the Cinepak codec by Radius with Compression quality set to 100%. Uncheck the "Key Frame Every" checkbox to get the best quality.

Lighting Setup

Next, add some colored lights to illuminate the mountain in a color the agrees with the sky.

1. Activate the Top viewport.

2. Create a target spot light in front of and pointing at the mountain and use the Transform Type-In to position the body at x = –72, y = –108, z = 107. Position the target at x = –4, y = –4, z = 31. Set the following:
   Color = (R = 253,G = 139, B = 81)
   Cast Shadows = On
   Shadow Map Size = 1024

3. Click the Exclude button and exclude the following objects from Both (Shadow Casting and Illumination):
Lava Bubbles Particles, Lava Dome, Lava Stream Particles.

4. Name the target light **Mountain Spot.**

5. Create a target spot light in front of and pointing at the mountain, then use the Transform Type-In to position the body precisely at x = –63, y = –107, z = 107. Position the target at x = –4, y = –4, z = 31. Set the following:
Color = (R = 253, G = 139, B = 81)
Multiplier = 3
Cast Shadows = On
Shadow Map Size = 1024

6. Click the Exclude button and exclude the Mountain object from Both (Shadow Casting and Illumination).

7. Name the target light **Lava Spot** (see Figure 4).

Figure 4
Final Video Post
Lens Effects glow
settings.

One of the things you will find surprising about this effect is that the liquid-like flow of the particles does not require the use of metaparticles. You achieve the smooth contiguous liquid look of the lava stream with the right combination of settings and a basic glow.

You can find the final MAX file, HotLavaFlow.max, in this project's Scene folder and the final AVI file in the Images folder.

Rock Slide

by Kim Lee

I n this effect, you will create a rock slide on a canyon wall. The Rock Slide effect relies heavily on what I consider procedural animation—animation that doesn't require the artist to hand animate the motion of the key objects in the scene. Two classic categories of procedural animation are particle systems and solid dynamics, both of which you will use to achieve this effect. Due to the somewhat unpredictable nature of solid dynamics in general, regardless of software platform, I urge the reader to read through this effect in its entirety while examining the original scene file before attempting to re-create the results.

Note

All position and rotational information is based on absolute world coordinates. When positioning objects in your scene, always use the Transform Type-In dialog box located in the Tools menu. This ensures proper object orientation.

Leave any settings that are not listed in the example at the MAX default values.

Preconfiguration

1. Copy the Rock Slide project map files from the accompanying CD-ROM to the MAX maps subdirectory.

Create the Environment Objects

1. In the Top viewport, create a standard primitive box at
   x = 13.494, y = -4.337, z = -46.446. Set the following
   parameters:
   Length = 600
   Width = 500
   Height = 4
   Length Segments = 50
   Width Segments = 50
   Height Segments = 1

2. Rename the object **Land**.

3. In the Left viewport, rotate the land object clockwise, 42.5
   degrees around its local X axis.

4. Apply a Displace modifier to the stack. Set the following parameters:
   Strength = 50.

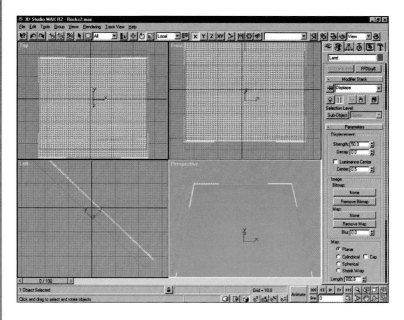

Figure 1
Applying a
Displace modifier.

5. Enable the Sub-Object button and rotate the gizmo 42.5 degrees
   counterclockwise in the Left viewport. Under Alignment, click
   the Fit button.

6. Disable the Sub-Object button. In the Image area under Map,
   click the button labeled None and select a Noise map.

7. In the Material Editor, click and drag the button now labeled Map#1 (Noise) to an empty slot in the Material Editor. Select method Instance. Set the following parameters:
   Noise Type = Fractal
   Size = 121

8. Rename the material **Land Displace**.

9. Using the Move tool, make a copy of the Land object and name it **Land2**. Go down the Modifier Stack to Box, and set the following parameters:
   Length = 140
   Width = 650

10. Rotate and move Land2 to x = 13.494, y = 234.3, z = 201.69.

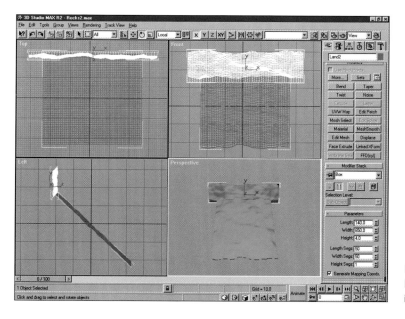

Figure 2
Rotating and moving Land.

11. Go up the Modifier Stack to the Displace modifier and click the Fit button under Alignment.

12. Create a target camera in the Left viewport near the lower-right end of the Land object directed up toward the Land2 object. The camera should be at x = 0, y = –272.605, z = –203.807 and the target object should be at x = 0, y = –188.107, z = –138.843. Change the Perspective viewport to a Camera viewport.

13. In the Front viewport, create a QuadPatch object at x = 38.931, y = 209.335, z = 479.875. Set the following:
Length = 505
Width = 820

14. Use the Move and Rotate tools to position the QuadPatch so that it is parallel with the camera view and extends beyond the frame in all directions (see Figure 3).

15. Rename the object **Sky**.

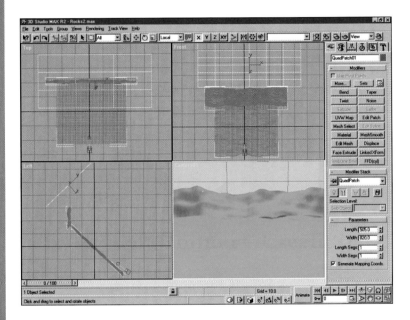

Figure 3
Positioning the QuadPatch.

Land Material Creation

1. In the Material Editor, select an unused slot. Rename the material **Land**.

2. Click the Diffuse map slot and set the map Type to Bitmap. Choose Rocks002.jpg as your map and set the following parameters:
U Tiling = 4
V Tiling = 4

3. Turn on the Show Map in Viewport button. Instance copy this Diffuse map to the Bump channel and set the bump amount to 100.

4. Apply the material to the Land object.

5. Copy the Land material to an unused slot and name it **Land2**.

6. Go to the Diffuse map channel and change the following settings:
   U Tiling = 2
   V Tiling = 0.5

7. Apply this material to the Land2 object.

8. Select an unused slot in the Material Editor and set the following parameters:
   Self-Illumination = 100

9. Click the Diffuse map slot and set the map Type to Bitmap. Choose Cloud2.jpg as your map. Turn on the Show Map in Viewport button.

10. Apply the material to the Sky object.

Render a still and you should now see a rocky cliff and a blue sky behind it.

Rock Geometry Creation

In this section you will create the large rocks that will come crashing down the cliff walls.

1. Create a Geosphere with the following parameters:
   Radius = 11
   Segments = 8

2. Rename the object **Rock01**.

3. Apply a Noise modifier:
   Scale = 10
   X Strength = 10
   Y Strength = 10
   Z Strength = 6

Natural Disasters

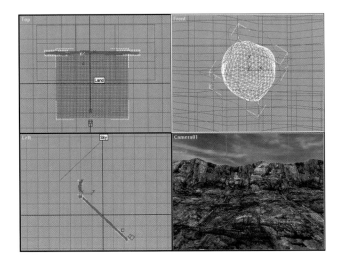

Figure 4
Applying a Noise modifier to Rock01.

4. Position the Rock01 object near the top of the Land object and just in front of the Land2 object. Constrained to the X axis make 5 copies of the Rock01 object in the Camera viewport. Use the following absolute world coordinates for each rock:
   Rock01: (x = -55.814, y = 199.1, z = 190.113)
   Rock02: (x = 0.183, y = 199.1, z = 193.402)
   Rock03: (x = 25.224, y = 199.1, z = 184.493)
   Rock04: (x = 50.265, y = 199.1, z = 178.684)
   Rock05: (x = 75.306, y = 199.1, z = 178.913)
   Rock06: (x = 100.347, y = 199.1, z = 198.054)

5. Vary the radius of each copy. This effect uses a range between 5 and 13.

6. Vary the Noise effect of each rock by changing the Seed value for each rock's Noise modifier (see Figure 5).

7. In the Material Editor copy the Land material into an unused slot.

8. In the Diffuse map channel, set the following:
   U Tiling = 1
   V Tiling = 1
   Show Map in Viewport = on

9. Rename the material **Rocks**.

10. Apply the material to all 6 rocks.

Note

Every value will give you a different result which might or might not look right, so experiment with the Noise modifier. For example, notice that I incremented each rock's Seed number by one but didn't use 4 because it didn't look right.

Figure 5
Varying the Noise effect.

You should now have six random-looking rocks sitting precariously at the top of the cliff with texture maps applied.

Animate with Dynamics

In this section apply the rigid dynamics to the rock objects, causing them to crash realistically down the cliff wall.

1. Create a Gravity space warp in the Top viewport (see Figure 6).

2. Open the Utilities tab in the command column. Select Dynamics to open the Dynamics control panel. Click the New button to create a new simulation.

3. Press the Edit Object List button. Highlight Rock01 through Rock06 and the Land object in the left-hand column. Click the arrow pointing right to move them into the right column. This makes the objects active in the simulation. Click OK.

4. Click the Edit Object button. From the Object rollout menu and select the Land object.

5. In the Misc. Dynamics Controls area check the box next to This Object is Immovable. Select Mesh in the Collision Test area.

6. Click on the Assign Object Collisions button and select all Rock objects in the left column. Move them all to the right column and click OK (see Figure 7).

Natural Disasters

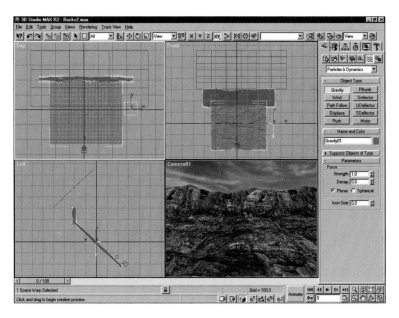

Figure 6
Creating a Gravity
space warp.

7. From the Object rollout menu select the Rock01 object.

8. Select Sphere in the Collision Test area and Bounding Sphere in the Physical Properties area.

9. Click the Assign Object Effects button and move Gravity into the right column.

10. Click the Assign Object Collisions button and select the Rock02 and Land objects in the left column. Move them to the right column and click OK.

11. Repeat steps 7-10 for Rock02 through Rock06. The only variance will be in step 10. All Rocks will collide with the Land, but the rocks assigned to the collision list will vary:
Rock02 collides with Rocks 1 and 3
Rock03 collides with 2 and 4
Rock04 collides with 3 and 5
Rock04 collides with 3 and 5
Rock05 collides with 4 and 6
Rock06 collides with Rock05

12. Set the following Timing and Simulation parameters (see Figure 8):
Start Time = 10
End Time = 100
Calc Intervals Per Frame = 2

Note

You will use Sphere instead of Mesh as the Collision Type because it speeds up calculations and produces more predictable results. Considering that the rocks will be rolling rather quickly, it is better that the motion look realistic than be technically accurate. Selecting Mesh would increase calculation time to the point where the visual pay-off isn't worth the effort.

13. In the Material Editor, select the Land material. Open the Dynamics Properties rollout and set all values to 0.0.

14. Select the Rocks material. Open the Dynamics Properties rollout and set the following:
Bounce Coefficient = 0.0
Static = 0.5
Sliding Friction = 0.5

Figure 7
The Assign Object Collisions dialog box.

Optionally, you can check the Update Display w/ Solve to see the results of the dynamics solution as it calculates. This is good if you are unsure whether your settings are close to what they should be on complicated scenes that take a while to calculate. In either case, click the Solve button and wait for the calculations to finish. You might find it useful to set up the simulation to calculate only one or two rocks at a time so that you can focus on tweaking the motion of individual rocks without. Once you get motion that you are happy with for one rock, you can remove that rock from the simulation and add another. The motion for the rock that was removed will not be deleted. This way, you can gradually build your scene in a controlled manner.

Note

You will only calculate collisions for objects that have a high probability of colliding. If you find other rocks colliding with ones you did not account for, add them to the collision list and recalculate.

Figure 8
Setting the Timing and Simulation parameters.

15. Play back the animation in wire frame (or shaded mode if your computer can handle it) to see if the motion looks right.

You should now see the six main rocks barreling down the cliff towards the camera.

Particle System Creation

Use various particle systems to fill out the rest of the effect. First, add large numbers of smaller rocks and pebbles to roll down the canyon wall.

1. Select the Land object and in the Front viewport, use Shift to move along the Y axis to create a copy slightly above the original.

2. Name this object **Emitter**.

Natural Disasters

3. In the Material Editor, select an unused slot and toggle on the Wire check box. Apply the material to Emitter. This allows you to see the Land object under the Emitter when in shaded mode.

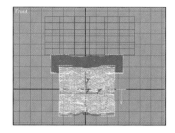

Figure 9
Moving the Land object.

4. Create a Geosphere somewhere out of camera view:
Radius = 2
Segments = 3

5. Name the object **Rock Particle Master**.

6. Add a Noise modifier:
Scale = 3
X Strength = 10
Y Strength = 5
Z Strength = 0

7. Apply the Rocks material to this object.

8. In the Creation tab, select Particle Systems and click PArray. Create a PArray in the Top viewport

9. Rename the PArray **Small Rocks**.

10. In the Modifiers panel under Basic Parameters click the Pick Object button and select the Emitter object. Under Particle Formation, set the following:
At Distinct Points = 20
Viewport Display = Mesh, 100%

11. In the Particle Generation rollout, set the following:
Use Rate = 10
Speed = 2
Divergence = 50
Emit Start = 50
Emit Stop = 70
Display Until = 100
Life = 100
Size = 0.75
Variation = 50
Grow For = 2
Fade For = 0

12. In the Particle Type rollout, select Instanced Geometry. Click the Pick Object button and pick the Rock Particle Master object.

13. In the Particle Rotation rollout, set the following:
    Spin Time = 30
    Variation = 50
    Phase = 60
    Variation = 50
    Spin Axis Controls: **User Defined**: X axis = 1, Y axis = 0,
    Z axis = 0
    Variation = 30

14. Bind the PArray icon to the Gravity space warp. Scrub the Time
    Slider and you should see many small rocks falling through the
    Land object.

Figure 10
The rocks fall
through the Land
object.

15. In the Creation tab, select Space Warps and create a UDeflector
    in the Top viewport.

16. In the Modifiers tab, click the Pick Object button and select the
    Land object. Set the following parameters:
    Bounce = 0.75

17. Bind the PArray icon to the UDeflector space warp. Scrub the
    Time Slider to see many of the small rocks rolling and bouncing
    down the canyon wall.

18. Hide the Rock Particle Master and Emitter objects.

At this point we have almost all our elements in place. There should be
a group of smaller rocks tumbling down with the big rocks.

Dust Creation

Now you need to add some dust to the scene. First create dust trailing off the larger rocks as they tumble down the canyon.

Dust Trail Creation

1. Create a PArray in the Top viewport.

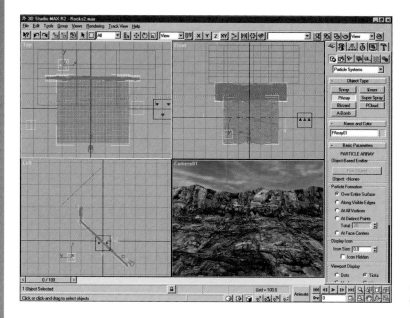

Figure 11
Creating a PArray.

2. In the Modifiers panel, under Basic Parameters, click the Pick Object button and select the Rock01 object. Under Particle Formation, set the following:
   Over Entire Surface = on
   Viewport Display = Dots, 100%

3. In the Particle Generation rollout, set the following:
   Use rate = 5
   Speed: 1
   Divergence = 10
   Emit Start = 27
   Emit Stop = 100
   Display Until = 100
   Life = 50
   Size = 20
   Variation = 25
   Grow For = 0
   Fade For = 0

4. In the Particle Type rollout, set the following:
    Standard Particles = Facing

5. In the Object Motion Inheritance rollout, set the following:
    Influence = 3.0

6. In the Top Viewport, make 5 copies of this PArray.

7. In the Modifier panel, edit each PArray so that they each use a different Rock as an emitter.

8. Select the six PArrays just created, right-click one of them, select Properties and toggle off Cast Shadows and Receive Shadows.

Now you should have plumes of dust coming off of the main rocks as they careen down the cliff.

Dust Puffs Creation

As a last touch, add small puffs of dust where the rocks impact the ground as they roll down the slope. Before beginning, select all the PArray objects and hide them to increase responsiveness during the following steps. You will reveal them once you are finished.

1. In the Top viewport, create a Super Spray particle system and rename it **Impact Dust 01**. Scrub through the animation to see where Rock01 impacts the ground and move the Impact Dust 01 object to that point.

2. Set the Basic Parameters as follows:
    Off Axis Spread = 85
    Off Plane Spread = 180

3. Set the Particle Generation parameters as follows:
    Use Rate = 10
    Speed = 4
    Emit Start = 56 (depending on the frame in which the impact occurs)
    Emit Stop = 58 (depending on the frame in which the impact occurs)
    Display Until = 100
    Life = 15
    Size = 20
    Variation = 3%
    Grow For = 1
    Fade For = 0

4. In the Particle Type rollout, set the following:
    Standard Particles: Facing

5. In the Particle Rotation rollout, set the following:
   Variation = 50%

6. Make as many copies of this particle system as necessary and place them wherever a rock looks as if it is impacting the ground with significant force. Be sure to adjust the Emit Start and Emit End times accordingly for each one.

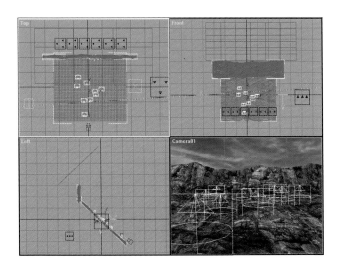

Figure 12
Copying and placing the rocks.

Dust Material Creation

1. In the Material Editor, select an unused slot.

2. Set the Basic Parameters as follows:
   Ambient = (R = 223 G = 211 B = 189)
   Diffuse = (R = 229 G = 218 B = 205)
   Specular = (R = 229 G = 216 B = 201)
   Filter = (R = 219 G = 215 B = 211)
   Face Map = on

3. Rename the material **Dust**.

4. Click the Opacity Map slot and set the Map Type to Gradient.
   Set the Gradient Parameters as follows:
   Color #1 = (R = 0, G = 0, B = 0)
   Color #2 = (R = 0, G = 0, B = 0)
   Color #3 = (R = 255, G = 255, B = 255)
   Gradient Type = Radial
   Noise Type = Fractal
   Amount = 0.59
   Size = 8.29

5. Click the Map button next to Color#3 and set the Map Type to Particle Age. This will allow you to gradually fade out the dust particles as they reach the end of their life cycle. Set the following color information:
Color #1: Age = 0, **Color** = (R = 150 G = 150 B = 150)
Color #2: Age = 50, **Color** = (R = 100 G = 100 B = 100)
Color #3: Age = 100, **Color** = (R = 0 G = 0 B = 0)

6. Apply the completed material to all of the Dust Impact particle systems and to the 6 PArray systems.

There should be quite a bit of dust in the air, accentuating the violent nature of our rock slide and adding a greater sense of realism.

Lighting Setup

In this final section, you create the lighting for the scene.

1. In the Left viewport, create a Target Directional light perpendicular to the Land object. Set the following:
Value = 255
Hotspot = 487
Cast Shadows = on

2. In the Left viewport, create an omni light and place it at x = –2.698, y = –404.815, z = –151.814, near the lower-right end of the Land Object. Set the following:
Value = 100

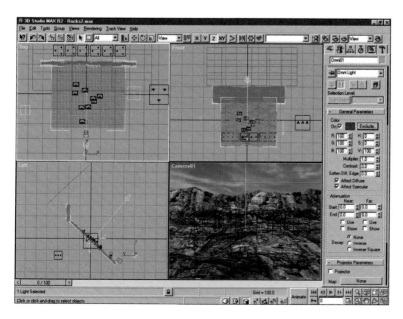

Figure 13
Creating an omni light.

Natural Disasters

3. Click the Exclude button and select Rock01 through Rock06. Move them to the right column and turn Include on.

4. Create one more omni Light and position it near the first omni light at x = -2.698, y = -444.769, z = -205.858. Set the following:
   Value = 25

5. Repeat step 3, but this time keep the Exclude button selected.

6. Rename the light **Dust Light**.

7. Select all the rock objects and right click on them. Select Properties and enable Image Motion Blur.

Like many other effects, this one is highly dependent upon the scale of a scene. So, be prepared to experiment when creating your own scenes. Due to the computationally intense nature of solid dynamics, you might find that it is faster to break your scene into multiple simulations, especially when you know that objects in one will never interact with objects in another. Another tip to keep in mind is that the dynamics engine tends to give better results when calculating collisions of actual box object geometry rather than using an objects bounding box. In these cases, you might be able to get away with creating stand-in box versions of your geometry and link the geometry to these boxes. More than in any other technique, animating with dynamics almost demands that you do extensive experimentation with parameters. Chances are you won't have many physicists watching you work, so your only concern is that the effect looks good, not that it is mathematically correct.

Dust Cloud

by Greg Carbonaro

I n the Dust Cloud effect you will be demolishing a Skyscraper. Yes that's right—complete and utter "Tower" annihilation. You'll begin the effect by destroying the building's support structure with a series of timed explosions. Then you'll watch in amazed delight as a giant dust cloud explodes from the base and the building collapses under its own weight. You've seen the real thing on TV and now you can do the same thing in the comfort of your own living room.

Note

All position and rotational information is based on absolute world coordinates. When creating objects, use keyboard entry when possible. When positioning objects, use the Transform Type-In dialog box located in the Tools menu. These techniques ensure proper object placement and orientation.

Leave any settings that are not listed in the example at the MAX default values. Create objects in the Top viewport, unless otherwise indicated.

Preconfiguration

1. Before beginning this effect, please reset *or* restart MAX.

2. Copy the project map files from the accompanying CD-ROM to the MAX maps subdirectory.

3. Load the City.max file located in the project Pre-load subdirectory on the accompanying CD-ROM.

4. Open the Material Editor. Right-click in any material slot and make sure Sample Windows are set to 5×3.

This file includes a building animation sequence that works in conjunction with this effect. The animation length has been pre-set to 300 frames.

Animating the Building Demolition

In this section, the particle system used to model the explosion on the first floor of the building is created. Similar particle systems will then be used for the explosions on the remaining floors.

1. Create a Super Spray particle system located at the center of the TheBuilding object at ground level. Use the Transform Type-In to position it at x = 1547, y = 24883, z = 40.

2. In the Particle Formation section of the Basic Parameters, set the following parameters:
   Off Axis = 75
   Off Axis Spread = 2
   Off Plane Spread = 180

3. In the Display Icon section, set the following parameters:
   Size = 300

4. In the Particle Quantity section of the Particle Generation rollout, set the following parameters:
   Use Rate = 300

5. In the Particle Motion section, set the following parameters:
   Speed = 400
   Variation = 10

6. In the Particle Timing section, set the following parameters:
   Emit Start = 10
   Emit Stop = 12
   Display Until = 300
   Life = 18
   Variation = 5

7. In the Particle Size section, set the following parameters:
   Size = 350
   Variation = 25
   Grow For = 0
   Fade For = 7

8. In the Particle Type rollout, set the following parameters:
   Standard Particles = Facing

9. Link the Super Spray to the object TheBuilding.

10. Name the particle system **Super SprayFL01**.

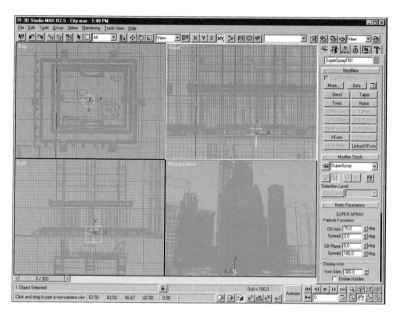

Figure I
Placement of the first explosion particle system at the center of the bottom floor of the building.

This is the first of seven Super Sprays with almost identical properties. Each will be used on a different floor of the building. After the material is created and a space warp is added, this particle system will be cloned six times in a subsequent step.

Explosion Material

In this section, you create the material used on the particle systems modeling the explosions on each floor.

1. In the Material Editor, activate material slot 3 and set the Material Type to Standard.

2. Set the following Basic Parameters:
   Face Map = Checked
   Ambient = (R = 231, G = 231, B = 231)
   Diffuse = (R = 243, G = 243, B = 243)
   Specular = (R = 255, G = 255, B = 255)
   Filter = (R = 200, G = 200, B = 200)
   Shininess = 0
   Shin. Strength = 0

Natural Disasters

3. Set the Amount for the Diffuse slot to 85. Click the Diffuse map slot and set the Map Type to Noise. Set the following Noise Parameters:
Noise Type = Fractal
Size = 150
Color #2 = (R = 170, G = 170, B = 170)

4. Swap Color #1 with Color #2.

5. Set the Amount for the Opacity slot to 100. Click the Opacity map slot and set the Map Type to Mask.

6. Click the Map slot and set the Map Type to Noise. Set the Noise parameters:
Noise Type = Fractal
Size = 150
Color #2 = (R = 170, G = 170, B = 170)

7. Swap Color #1 with Color #2.

8. Return to the Mask map level. Click the Mask map slot and set the Map Type to Gradient. Set the Gradient Parameters:
Gradient Type = Radial

9. Swap Color #1 with Color #3.

10. Name the material **ExplodeFL1**.

11. Apply the ExplodeFL1 material to the Super SprayFL01 particle system.

12. Open Track View and expand the hierarchy tree to display the Transparency Falloff track for material ExplodeFL1. Create the following animation keys (see Figure 2):
Frame 0 (Keyframe 1) Value = 20
    In tangent = Linear, Out tangent = Linear
Frame 25 (Keyframe 2) Value = 20
    In tangent = Linear, Out tangent = Linear
Frame 30 (Keyframe 3) Value = 92
    In tangent = Slow, Out tangent = Linear
Frame 34 (Keyframe 4) Value = 100
    In tangent = Linear, Out tangent = Linear

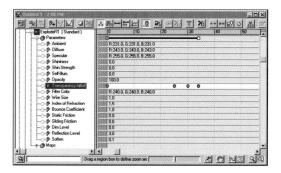

Figure 2
By increasing the Transparency Falloff over time, the explosion smoke becomes less dense.

This is the first of seven "Explode" materials with almost identical properties. Each will be used on a different Super Spray for each of the floors of the building. The only difference between the materials will be a slightly different animation for the Transparency Falloff. This material will be cloned six times in a subsequent section.

Animation

In this section, a Wind space warp will be created to slow down the explosion particles over time.

1. Create a Particles and Dynamics Wind space warp located at the same location as Super SprayFL01. Use the Transform Type-In to position the space warp at x = 1547, y = 24883, z = 40. Set the following parameters:
   Strength = –12
   Spherical = on
   Icon Size = 500

2. Bind Wind to the Super SprayFL01.

3. Link Wind to the object TheBuilding.

4. Name the space warp **WindFL01** (see Figure 3).

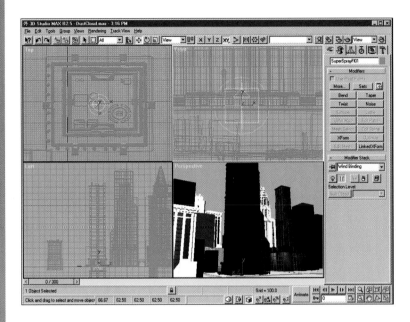

Figure 3
Creating the first of seven building destruction systems.

Create the Clones

In this section, you will copy the explosion particle system and Wind space warp to several floors of the building. Also, you will adjust the timing of the particle systems to create a cascading series of explosions.

Clone 1

1. Select Super SprayFL01 and WindFL01 and then copy them up to the third floor of TheBuilding at x = 1547, y = 24883, z = 2368.

2. Accept the default names Super SprayFL02 and WindFL02.

3. Edit the Super Spray. In the Particle Timing section of the Particle Generation rollout, set the following:
Emit Start = 15
Emit Stop = 17

4. In the Material Editor, copy the slot 3 material, ExplodeFL1, to slot 6.

5. Name the material **ExplodeFL2**.

6. Apply the ExplodeFL2 material to the Super SprayFL02 particle system.

7. Open Track View and expand the hierarchy tree to display the Transparency Falloff track for material ExplodeFL2. Select and drag the last 3 keys 5 frames to the right.

Clone 2

1. Select Super SprayFL01 and WindFL01 and then copy them up to the seventh floor of TheBuilding at x = 1547, y = 24883, z = 4382.

2. Accept the default names Super SprayFL03 and WindFL03.

3. Edit the Super Spray. In the Particle Timing section of the Particle Generation rollout, set the following:
   Emit Start = 20
   Emit Stop = 22

4. In the Material Editor, copy the slot 6 material ExplodeFL2 to slot 7.

5. Name the material **ExplodeFL3**.

6. Apply the ExplodeFL3 material to the Super SprayFL03 particle system.

7. Open Track View and expand the hierarchy tree to display the Transparency Falloff track for material ExplodeFL3. Select and drag the last 3 keys 5 frames to the right.

Clone 3

1. Select Super SprayFL01 and WindFL01 and then copy them up to the tenth floor of TheBuilding at x = 1547, y = 24883, z = 6305.

2. Accept the default names Super SprayFL04 and WindFL04.

3. Edit the Super Spray. In the Particle Timing section of the Particle Generation rollout, set the following:
   Emit Start = 25
   Emit Stop = 27

4. In the Material Editor, copy slot 7 material ExplodeFL3 to slot 8.

5. Name the material **ExplodeFL4**.

6. Apply the ExplodeFL4 material to the Super SprayFL04 particle system.

7. Open Track View and expand the hierarchy tree to display the Transparency Falloff track for material ExplodeFL4. Select and drag the last 3 keys 5 frames to the right.

Natural Disasters

Clone 4

1. Select Super SprayFL01 and WindFL01 and then copy them up to the thirteenth floor of TheBuilding at x = 1547, y = 24883, z = 8254.

2. Accept the default names Super SprayFL05 and WindFL05.

3. Edit the Super Spray. In the Particle Timing section of the Particle Generation rollout, set the following:
   Emit Start = 30
   Emit Stop = 32

4. In the Material Editor, copy the slot 8 material ExplodeFL4 to slot 9.

5. Name the material **ExplodeFL5**.

6. Apply the ExplodeFL5 material to the Super SprayFL05 particle system.

7. Open Track View and expand the hierarchy tree to display the Transparency Falloff track for material ExplodeFL5. Select and drag the last 3 keys 5 frames to the right.

Clone 5

1. Select Super SprayFL01 and WindFL01 and then copy them up to the sixteenth floor of TheBuilding at x = 1547, y = 24883, z = 10175.

2. Accept the default names Super SprayFL06 and WindFL06.

3. Edit the Super Spray. In the Particle Timing section of the Particle Generation rollout, set the following:
   Emit Start = 35
   Emit Stop = 37

4. In the Material Editor, copy slot 9 material ExplodeFL5 to slot 10.

5. Name the material **ExplodeFL6**.

6. Apply the ExplodeFL6 material to the Super SprayFL06 particle system.

7. Open Track View and expand the hierarchy tree to display the Transparency Falloff track for material ExplodeFL6. Select and drag the last 3 keys 5 frames to the right.

Clone 6

1. Select Super SprayFL01 and WindFL01 and then copy them up to the nineteenth floor of TheBuilding at x = 1547, y = 24883, z = 12092.

2. Accept the default names Super SprayFL07 and WindFL07.

3. Edit the Super Spray. In the Particle Timing section of the Particle Generation rollout, set the following:
   Emit Start = 40
   Emit Stop = 42

4. In the Material Editor, copy the slot 10 material ExplodeFL6 to slot 11.

5. Name the material **ExplodeFL7**.

6. Apply the ExplodeFL7 material to the Super SprayFL07 particle system.

7. Open Track View and expand the hierarchy tree to display the Transparency Falloff track for material ExplodeFL7. Select and drag the last 3 keys 5 frames to the right.

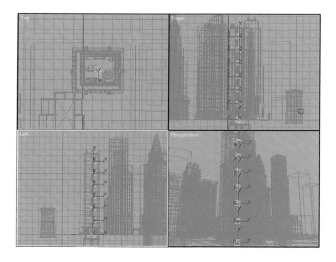

Figure 4
The Building with the seven Super Spray particle systems that will simulate successive explosions to destroy the structure.

Natural Disasters

Dust Cloud Creation

In this section, a particle system is created to model the cloud of dust at the base of the building as the building collapses.

1. Create a Super Spray particle system located at the center of the TheBuilding object just below ground level at x = 1513, y = 24996, z = −1846.

2. In the Particle Formation section of the Basic Parameters, set the following:
   Off Axis = 55
   Off Axis Spread = 20
   Off Plane Spread = 180

3. In the Display Icon section, set the following:
   Size = 1700

4. In the Particle Quantity section of the Particle Generation roll-out, set the following:
   Use Total = 2500

5. In the Particle Motion section, set the following: **Speed** = 100
   Variation = 5

6. In the Particle Timing section of the Particle Generation rollout, set the following:
   Emit Start = −10
   Emit Stop = 300
   Display Until = 300
   Life = 300

7. In the Particle Size section, set the following:
   Size = 1500
   Variation = 25
   Grow For = 30
   Fade For = 0

8. In the Particle Type rollout, set the following:
   Standard Particles = Facing

9. In the Particle Rotation rollout, set the following:
   Spin Time = 60
   Spin Variation = 33
   Phase = 180
   Phase Variation = 100

10. In the Bubble Motion rollout, set the following:
    Amplitude = 1.6
    Amplitude Variation = 20
    Period = 8
    Period variation = 40
    Phase = 180
    Phase Variation = 100

11. Name the Particles **DustCloud**.

12. Open Track View and expand the hierarchy tree to display the Speed track for object DustCloud. Set the following particle speed animation keys:
    Frame 0 (Keyframe 1) Speed = 100
    In tangent = Smooth, Out tangent = Slow
    Frame 130 (Keyframe 2) Speed = 1
    In tangent = Fast, Out tangent = Smooth

13. Create a Particles and Dynamics Gravity space warp located by the side of TheBuilding at x = –3900, y = 26600, z = 0.
    Set the following parameters:
    Icon Size = 700
    Strength = 0.25

14. Bind the Gravity space warp to the DustCloud Super Spray.

15. Select DustCloud, right-click on it, and choose Properties.
    Set the Object Properties:
    Cast Shadows = off

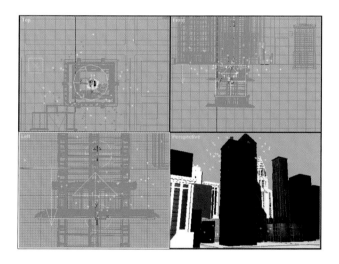

Figure 5
The DustCloud particle system is used to create a cloud of dust at the base of the building.

Dust Material

1. In the Material Editor, make material slot 4 active and set the Material Type to Standard.

2. Set the Basic Parameters:
   Face Map = checked
   Ambient = (R = 0, G = 0, B = 0)
   Diffuse = (R = 0, G = 0, B = 0)
   Specular = (R = 255, G = 255, B = 255)
   Filter = (R = 12, G = 7, B = 0)
   Shininess = 0
   Shin. Strength = 0

3. Set the Amount for the Diffuse slot to 100. Click the Diffuse map slot and set the Map Type to Noise. Set the Noise Parameters:
   Noise Type = Fractal
   Size = 600
   Color #1 = (R = 205, G = 189, B = 165)
   Color #2 = (R = 76, G = 56, B = 50)

4. Set the Amount for the Opacity slot to 100. Click the Opacity map slot and set the Map Type to Mask.

5. Click the Opacity map slot and set the Map Type to Noise. Set the Noise Parameters:
   Noise Type = Fractal
   Size = 25

6. Return to the Mask map level. Click the Mask map slot and set the Map Type to Gradient. Set the Gradient Parameters:
   Gradient Type = Radial

7. Swap Color #1 with Color #3.

8. Name the material **Dust**.

9. Assign the Dust material to the DustCloud Super Spray.

At this point, the scene contains the particle systems used to simulate a cascading sequence of explosions and the cloud of dust at the base of the building.

Lighting Setup

In this section, you will create the lighting effects for the scene.

1. Create an omni light to the right of and above the buildings at x = 18889, y = 8174, z = 85534. Set the following:
   Color = (R = 170, G = 180, B = 190)
   Multiplier = 5
   Cast Shadows = on
   Shadow Map Size = 2048

2. Name the omni light **Sun**.

3. Create an omni light at the top-right corner of the Ground object at x = 16122, y = 51511, z = 6323. Set the following:
   Color = (R = 170, G = 180, B = 190)
   Multiplier = 2.25
   Cast Shadows = on
   Shadow Map Size = 2048
   Smp Range = 8

4. Name the omni light **Shadow Light**.

5. Create an omni light at the same location as Shadow Light, x = 16122, y = 51511, z = 6323. Set the following:
   Color = (R = 170, G = 180, B = 190)
   Multiplier = 0.5

6. Click the Exclude button and select Both (Illumination and Shadow Casting). Select the following for exclusion: Super SprayFL01, Super SprayFL02, Super SprayFL03, Super SprayFL04, Super SprayFL05, Super SprayFL06, Super SprayFL07

7. Name the omni light **NoShadow Light**.

At this point particle systems, materials, and lighting have been created.

Camera Setup

The final step is to set up the camera through which you will view the finished effect.

1. Create a Free camera at the top-right corner of the Ground object. Position the body at x = 10798, y = 43737, z = 1272. Rotate to x = −77, y = −180, z = −28 (see Figure 6).

Natural Disasters

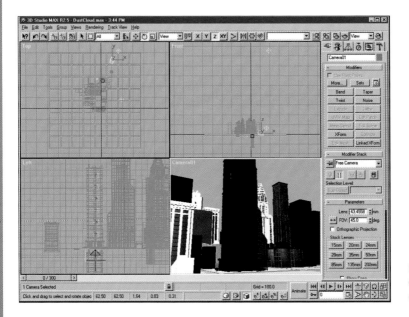

Figure 6
Completed Dust
Cloud effect.

You can find the final MAX file, DustCloud.max, in this project's Scene folder and the final AVI in the Images folder.

PART IV

Explosions and Pyrotechnics

Warhead Explosion

by Jeff Abouaf

To explode a warhead, you must consider how the missile flies, how it collides with the target, how it comes apart at collision, and the pyrotechnic reaction. 3D Studio MAX R2 ships with a Combustion atmospheric effect. We should thank Blur Studios and Peter Watje, two great assets to the MAX community, for writing variations to the Combustion plug-in: Blur Fire - Ver. 3.03 and Particle Combustion. Both are free plug-ins and are included on the accompanying CD-ROM.

This exercise uses all three, plus the Gravity and UDeflector space warps and the Blizzard and PArray particle systems. In R1, you could use Facing particles, with noise mapped onto each particle to simulate smoke and strategic lighting to show a fireball. Often, however, as Facing particles pass through MAX's atmospheric effects (especially Combustion), the square edges on the Facing particles appear, regardless of masking technique. Here, the entire sequence is created with atmospherics and particles.

Note

All position and rotational information is based on absolute world coordinates. When creating objects, use keyboard entry where possible. When positioning objects, use the Transform Type-In dialog box located in the Tools menu. These techniques ensure proper object placement and orientation.

Leave any settings that are not listed in the example at the MAX default values. Create objects in the Top viewport, unless otherwise indicated.

Preconfiguration

1. Before beginning this effect, either reset *or* restart MAX.

2. Load Blur Fire, ver. 3.03 and Particle Combustion from the accompanying CD-ROM.

3. Load warhead.max from this project's Preload folder on the CD-ROM. This scene contains a missile colliding with a wall.

Creating the Warhead

In this section, you create a SphereGizmo and then scale it into an ellipsoid shape for the warhead.

1. Create an atmospheric helper SphereGizmo behind the missile at x = –195, y = 2040, z = 289. Set the following:
Radius = 50

2. Nonuniformly scale the gizmo into an ellipsoid shape (use Scale Transform Type-In values of x = 54, y = 54, Z = 240). The length should equal approximately one-third of the missile length and diameter just larger than the missile body. Position the gizmo along the y-axis as the missile so about one-third of the gizmo is inside the missile. Link this SphereGizmo as a child of the missile and label it **SphereGizmo – Exhaust**.

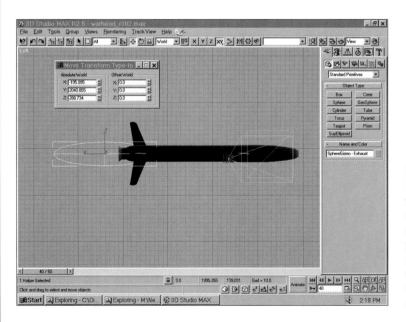

Figure I
Nonuniform scale the gizmo into an ellipsoidal, align it along the missile's y-axis, and position it so about one-third of the gizmo is inside the missile.

3. On the surface of the wall facing the missile and centered on the point of impact, create a SphereGizmo. Use the Transform Type-In dialog box to position the SphereGizmo at x = –200, y = –290, z = 285. Set the following:

Initial Radius = 0
Hemisphere = checked

4. Name it **SphereGizmo - Explode**.

As seen from the Top viewport, you should see a hemisphere resting atop the wall surface.

Animate the Warhead

1. Select SphereGizmo - Explode, turn Animate on, and set the following:
Frame 50: Radius = 0
Frame 60: Radius = 300
Frame 80: Radius = 600

2. At Frame 60, nonuniform scale away from the wall to 120% absolute (the local z-axis); advance to Frame 100 and NU scale to 160%. Turn off Animate.

Two combustion effects will be applied to the SphereGizmo. Animating the gizmo size gives the effect to the explosion radiating outward.

Create Particle Systems and Space Warps

1. On the wall surface facing the missile, create a Blizzard particle system emitter:
Initial Size = 100×100

2. Create a Particle Array (PArray) particle system. Under Basic Parameters, click Pick Object and select the missile at the Object-Based Emitter. Under the Particle Generation rollout, set the following:
Variation = 25%
Divergence = 90 degrees
Emit Start = 51
Display Until = 100
Life = 100

3. Turn Animate on. At Frame 40, set Speed to 5. Advance to Frame 100 and set Speed to 1. Turn Animate off.

4. Under the Particle Type rollout, select Object Fragments and in Object Fragment Controls, set the following:
Thickness = 10.0
Number of Chunks Minimum = 20

5. In the material mapping and source section, set the following and then press the Get Material From button:
Picked Emitter = checked

6. Create a Gravity space warp at the center of SphereGizmo - Explode at x = –206, y = –197, z = 282. Set the following:
   Spherical = checked
   Icon Size = 130

   Position the space warp at the point of impact, just in front of the wall. This space warp effects both the flame effect as well as the missile fragments.

7. Bind the Blizzard particle system to this space warp.

8. Bind the PArray particle system to the Gravity space warp twice. (The PArray modifier stack should have two Gravity Binding entries.) This draws the missile fragments to the wall, where they collide and burst outward.

9. Create a UDeflector space warp. Click Pick Object and select the wall. Set the following:
   Bounce = 0.15
   Chaos = 100%
   Friction = 10
   Inherit Velocity = 50%

10. Bind both the Blizzard and PArray particle systems to this space warp.

11. Create a particle bomb (PBomb) space warp:
    Blast Symmetry = Cylindrical
    Start Time = 55
    Duration = 10
    Strength = 0.05
    Range = 200

12. Bind this space warp to the PArray particle system. This disburses the debris.

Note

Space warp bindings are additive. Binding Gravity twice to PArray and once to Blizzard results in different gravitational effects applied to each system. But the overall effect is that the two particle systems intermingle better. Alternatively, you can bind PArray to a second animated Gravity space warp with different settings to achieve a similar result, although this approach requires greater attention to synchronicity.

At this point, you have a gizmo in place for the exhaust and one in place for the main part of the explosion. You have a Blizzard particle system to shoot additional flame and smoke from the POI, and a PArray system to break the missile into fragments. Both particle systems are collision-aware with the wall. Spherical gravity adds turbulence to the Blizzard particles and prevent them from disbursing too quickly.

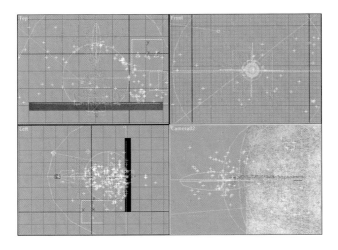

Figure 2
The two particle systems overlap as the fire (particle combustion) and the debris (missile fragments) are drawn in and blow out from the wall.

Adding Atmospheric Objects

Now you are ready to add Atmospheric Objects to your scene.

1. In the Environment dialog box, click Add under the Atmosphere Effects rollout and select Blur Fire - Ver. 3.03.

2. Name the effect **Blur Fire - Exhaust**.

3. Under the Fire Parameters, click Pick Object, and select SphereGizmo - Exhaust from the scene. Set the following:
    Fire Parameters/Type = Filament
    Density = 50
    Samples = 20

4. Return to the Atmosphere Effects rollout and add another Blur Fire. Name the Blur Fire **Impact** and set the following:
    Type = Regular fire

5. Click Pick Object and select SphereGizmo Explode from the scene. Under Flame Detail, set the following:
    Flame Size = 30

6. In the Atmosphere Effects rollout, add a Particle Combustion object. Name it **Particle Comb. - fire**. Click Pick Object and select the Blizzard particle system in the scene:
    Light Sources: sort = checked
    Inner Color = (R = 234, G = 135, B = 36)
    Check inner and outer based on Track View graph.

7. Under Shape, click Tendril Flame Type. Set the following:
Flame Detail = 10
Samples = 10
Density = 10
Use Track View Graph = checked
Explosion: Explosion = checked, Smoke = checked

8. Click Setup Explosion and set the following:
Start Time = 50
End Time = 100

9. Under Motion, set the following:
Drift = 100
Particle Size = 30
Use Track View Graph = checked
Localize Explosion = Particle life

10. In the Atmosphere Effects rollout, add another Particle
Combustion object. Name it **Particle Comb. – smoke**. Click
Pick Object and select the Blizzard particle system in the scene.
Under Light Sources, set the following:
Illuminate = checked
Tendril = checked
Flame Size = 50
Flame Detail = 5
Samples = 5
Motion/Drift = 100
Particle Size = 30
Seed = 500
Localize Explosion = Particle life

11. In the Atmosphere Effects rollout, add another Particle
Combustion object. Label it **Particle Combustion – frag**.
Click Pick Object and select the PArray01 in the scene. Set the
following:
Inner Color = (R = 212, G = 15, B = 0)
Tendril = checked
Explosion = checked
Smoke = checked
Flame Size = 10
Flame Detail = 6
Density = 15
Sample = 5
Fury = 50

12. Click Setup Explosion and set the following:
Start Time = 50
End Time = 100

All objects are in place, particle systems are linked to their respective space warps, and combustion objects referenced to the correct gizmo or particle system.

Animation

The next step is to animate the various systems and effects so that they move in harmony and to hide the missile and exhaust flame after they collide with the wall.

Figure 3
The Environment dialog box contains the five combustion objects, which you can animate in the main interface or in Track View.

1. Go to Frame 40 and select the Gravity space warp. Set the following:
   Decay = 0.004

2. Turn on Animate and set the following:
   Frame 50: Strength = –0.6
   Frame 53: Strength = 1
   Frame 57: Strength = 3
   Frame 63: Strength = –2
   Frame 66: Strength = 0
   Frame 80: Strength = –1
   Frame 100: Decay = 0

3. Select the Blizzard particle system and with Animate on, set the following:
   Frame 40: Speed = 10
   Frame 51: Speed = 6
   Frame 70: Speed = 3
   Frame 0: Emitter Length = 100, Emitter Width = 100
   Frame 60: Emitter Length = 300, Emitter Width = 300
   Frame 40: Birth Rate = 25
   Frame 51: Birth Rate = 25
   Frame 60: Birth Rate = 8

4. Select the PArray particle system and with Animate on, set the following:
   Frame 40: Speed = 5
   Frame 100: Speed = 1

5. Open Track View. Highlight the missile object and add a Visibility Track by clicking the Eye icon on the toolbar and then clicking the Create Key icon. Place a keyframe in the blue Visibility Track at Frame 53.

   This makes the original missile object disappear, just as PArray blows it apart.

6. In the Environment dialog/Atmospheric Effects, select Blur Fire - Exhaust and with Animate on, set the following:
   Frame 40: Density = 50
   Frame 60: Density = 0

7. Open Track View, find this Density track, and right-click the first key frame to bring up key attributes. Set each key to on/off. This leaves the rocket motor running through Frame 60, at which time it disappears.

8. In the Environment dialog/Atmospheric Effects, select Blur Fire - Impact and with Animate on, set the following:
   Frame 40: Density = 0
   Frame 51: Density = 50
   Frame 100: Density = 0

9. Set the In key attributes to on/off as in the previous step. This makes the combustion effect first appear at Frame 51.

10. In the Environment dialog/Atmospheric Effects, select Particle Comp - Fire and with Animate on, set the following:
    Frame 51: phase = 0
    Frame 100: phase = 50

11. In the Environment dialog/Atmospheric Effects, select Particle Comp - Smoke and with Animate on, set the following:
    Frame 40: Density = 1
    Frame 80: Density = 5
    Frame 100: Density = 1
    Frame 51: Phase = 0
    Frame 100: Phase = 50
    Frame 40: Particle Size = 30
    Frame 80: Particle Size = 30
    Frame 100: Particle Size = 60

12. In the Environment dialog/Atmospheric Effects, select Particle Combustion - Frag and with Animate on, set the following:
    Frame 51: Phase = 0
    Frame 100: Phase = 300

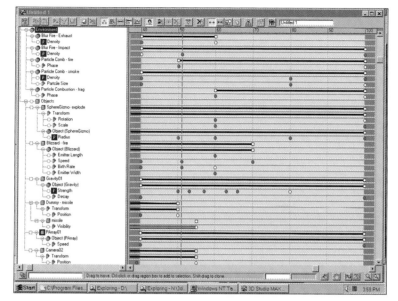

Figure 4
Track View filtered
to display only the
animated tracks.

13. Select PArray in the scene. Right-click and select Properties:
Object ID = 2

14. Select Blizzard – Fire in the scene and set the following:
Object ID = 1

The Blur Fire and Particle Combustion plug-ins are not identical in pattern or color. A glow effect can work to make the two appear as one reaction.

Adding Glows in Video Post

1. Open Video Post. Click the Add Scene Event icon and select Camera02. Highlight Camera02 in the VP Queue and click the Add Filter Event icon.

2. From the drop-down menu, choose Lens Effects – Glow. Click OK. Double-click the Lens Effect Glow entry in the queue, and then click Setup. Click Load and load explode.lzg from the accompanying CD-ROM. Advance to Frame 70 in the main interface.

3. Click Update in the Lens Effects Glow dialog box. The interactive renderer shows the glow applied to the particles.

4. Click the white area in the VP queue to deselect all events. Click the Add Image Output Event dialog box and Files to specify an AVI file. Click the Runner icon in VP and render Range 40–100.

Play the animation in the viewports. Note the symmetry of the particle systems and placement of gizmos and space warps. You have two particle systems moving differently, but in a complimentary way, and the space warps vary the rhythm of the blast. You can easily vary this recipe; because of its complexity, it can take some time to render, but it demonstrates how many objects can layer a combustion effect. The final version is included in this project's Scene folder on the accompanying CD-ROM as warhead_final.max.

Note

Lens Effects can take some time to render its interactive viewport.

Note

Although beyond the scope of this text, commercial plug-ins are available for creating volumetric and pyrotechnic effects, notably, UltraShock (a volumetric shader) and Pandora (a particle system to reflect aged particles), from Digimation, and Afterburn, a competing product not available at the time of this writing (see details on Afterburn at www.max3d.com).

Atomic Bomb Mushroom Cloud

by Greg Carbonaro

The atomic bomb mushroom cloud is an ominously distinctive and highly recognizable image, the awesome power of which is not easy to capture or duplicate in any form, including CGI. But through the clever use of particle systems, a good smoky material, and a custom-designed Universal Deflector, it becomes possible. The only limitation to a highly believable effect is the horsepower of the machine the effect is rendered on—the more particles the better. The ideal particle generation rate is about 12 for superior detail. The samples here were generated on a dual 333MHz Pentium at a particle generation rate of 6, and the final frames took approximately 11 minutes each at 320×240.

Note

All position and rotational information is based on absolute world coordinates. When creating objects, use keyboard entry when possible. When positioning objects, use the Transform Type-In dialog box located in the Tools menu. These techniques ensure proper object placement and orientation.

Leave any settings that are not listed in the example at the MAX default values. Create objects in the Top viewport, unless otherwise indicated.

Preconfiguration

1. Before beginning this effect, please reset *or* restart MAX.

2. Copy the Mushroom Cloud project map files from the accompanying CD-ROM to the MAX maps subdirectory.

3. Load the file Background.max from the projects pre-load subdirectory on the CD-ROM.

4. Open the Material Editor. Right-click in any material slot and make sure Sample Windows are set to 3×2.

Only the background image is defined in this scene, and no geometry is present. The animation length is set to 360 frames.

Environment Setup

In this section, you will create a volume fog that will fade out the ground object on the horizon. You will use an atmospheric apparatus with volume fog to create a depth cue, because standard camera distance cue techniques do not work well with the partially transparent materials used to simulate smoke.

1. Create an atmospheric apparatus helper BoxGizmo. Set the following:
   Length = 1840
   Width = 2500
   Height = 200
   Position = (x = –60, y = 1650, z = –77)

2. Name the BoxGizmo **Falloff**.

3. Open the Environment dialog (Rendering/Environment) and add a Volume Fog effect. Set the following parameters:
   Pick Gizmo = Falloff
   Color = (R = 240, G = 84, B = 53)
   Density = 0.5
   Uniformity = 1

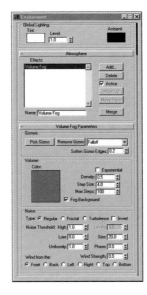

At this point the scene consists of the BoxGizmo referenced by the Volume Fog.

Figure 1
The volume fog will hide the ground object as it reaches the horizon.

Objects and Materials

In this section you will create the ground objects, and the geometry used as the particle emitter for the ground level explosion will be created. The object used as the deflector for the mushroom cloud will be imported. Materials will be created for each of these objects and the particle systems.

Ground Object

1. Create a standard primitive box centered slightly below the BoxGizmo center. Set the following parameters:
   Length = 2500
   Width = 2500
   Height = 2
   Length Segments = 15
   Width Segments = 15
   Height Segments = 2
   Generate Mapping Coordinates = on
   Position = (x = −48.5, y = 1117, z = 0)

2. Name the object **Ground**.

Ground Material

1. In the Material Editor, make material slot 3 active and set the Material Type to Standard.

2. Set the Basic Parameters as follows:
   Ambient = (R = 31, G = 31, B = 22)
   Diffuse = (R = 167, G = 109, B = 104)
   Specular = (R = 240, G = 240, B = 240)
   Shininess = 8
   Shin. Strength = 6
   Soften = 0.8

4. Set the amount for the Diffuse map slot to 60. Click the Diffuse slot and set the Map Type to Bitmap. Click Bitmap and select Dirtgray.jpg. Turn on Show Map in Viewport.

5. Drag the Diffuse map slot to the Bump map slot, choosing method Instance. Set the Amount for the Bump map slot to 250.

6. Name the material **Dirt Gray**.

7. Apply the Dirt Gray material to the Ground object.

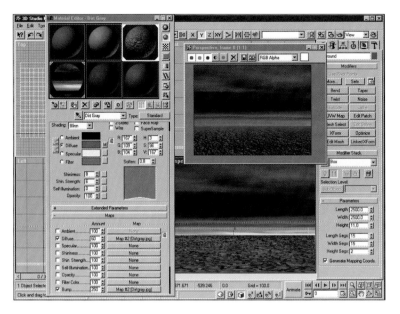

Figure 2
The ground plane becomes hazier in the distance due to the use of a volume fog effect.

At this point, the scene consists of the ground plane and the volume fog.

Explosion Base Object

1. Create a standard primitive torus at the lower center edge of the ground object. Set the following parameters:
    Radius 1 = 10
    Radius 2 = 4
    Position = (x = 12, y = 1, z = 11)

2. Name the object **Explosion Base**.

Explosion Base Material

1. In the Material Editor, make material slot 2 active and set the Material Type to Standard.

2. Set the Basic Parameters:
    Face Map = on
    Shininess = 0
    Shin. Strength = 0
    Self-Illumination = 100

3. Set the Extended parameters:
    Opacity Falloff = out
    Amt = 100

4. Set the Amount for the Diffuse map slot to 100. Click the Diffuse slot and set the Map Type to Noise. Set the Noise parameters:
Noise Type = Fractal
Size = 33
Color #2 = (R = 255, G = 240, B = 240)

5. Set the Amount for the Opacity map slot to 100. Click the Opacity slot and set the Map Type to Mask.

6. Click the Map map slot and set the Map Type to Noise. Set the Noise parameters:
Noise Type = Fractal
Size = 33

7. Return to the Mask map, click the Mask map slot and set the Map Type to Gradient. Set the Gradient parameters:
Gradient Type = Radial

8. Swap Color #1 with Color #3

9. Name the material **Smoke**.

10. Apply the Smoke material to the Explosion Base object.

At this point, the scene consists of the ground plane and the Explosion Base object, which will act as the particle emitter for the ground level blast.

Mushroom Cloud Deflector

1. Merge file Mushroom Cloud deflector.max into the scene from the project pre-load directory on the accompanying CD.

Mushroom Cloud Deflector Material

1. In the Material Editor, make material slot 1 active and set the Material Type to Standard.

2. Set the Basic Parameters:
Shininess = 0
Shin. Strength = 0
Opacity = 0

3. Name the material **Invisible**.

4. Apply the Invisible material to the Mushroom Cloud deflector object.

At this point, the scene consists of the ground plane, the Explosion Base object, and the Mushroom Cloud deflector object. Material has been created for these objects.

Animation Technique

In this section, Explosion Base object's size will be animated to simulate the expanding ground blast ring. The Mushroom Cloud deflector object's size and position will be animated to contain the expanding and rising mushroom cloud. Particle systems will be created to provide the actual blast ring and mushroom cloud.

Explosion Base Animation

1. Select object Explosion Base and turn Animate on. Advance to frame 360 and set the following parameters:
   Radius 1 = 60
   Radius 2 = 40

   Turn Animate off.

Explosion Base Particle System

1. Create a PArray next to object Explosion Base. The exact position and size do not matter. Set the following Basic parameters:
   Pick Object = Explosion Base
   Percentage of Particles = 20

2. Set the following Particle Generation parameters:
   Use Rate = 6
   Speed = 1
   Speed Variation = 50
   Divergence = 0
   Emit Stop = 400
   Display Until = 400
   Life = 250
   Size = 15
   Size Variation = 50

3. Set the Particle Type parameters:
   Standard Particles = Facing

4. In the Mat'l Mapping and Source section of the Particle Type rollout, Turn on Picked Emitter and click Get Material From.

5. Name the PArray **Explosion Base Particles**.

6. Create a Gravity space warp next to object Explosion Base. The exact position and size do not matter. Set the following:
Strength = 0.01
Force = Planar (downward)

7. Bind the Gravity space warp to the PArray Explosion Base Particles.

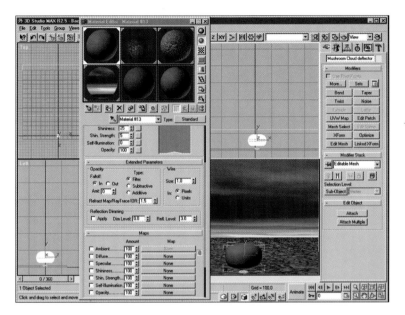

Figure 3
Explosion Base torus is used as the particle emitter for the ground level explosion.

At this point, the modeling of the ground blast ring is complete.

Mushroom Cloud Deflector Animation

1. Select object Mushroom Cloud deflector and apply an XForm modifier.

2. Turn on Animate. At frame 0, decrease the Gizmos' scale to 50%. Advance to frame 360 and increase the Gizmos' scale to 200%. Turn off Sub-Object mode, but leave Animate on and remain at frame 360.

3. Animate the position of the Mushroom Cloud deflector by moving it straight up in the Front view.
Position = (x = 12.9, y = 0, z = 258)

4. Turn Animate off.

Note

Do not use the Scale Transform Type-In dialog for the following step. Set the scale based on the XYZ scaling factors displayed at the bottom of the MAX window. Use Snap Percent to ensure accurate scaling.

Mass Destruction

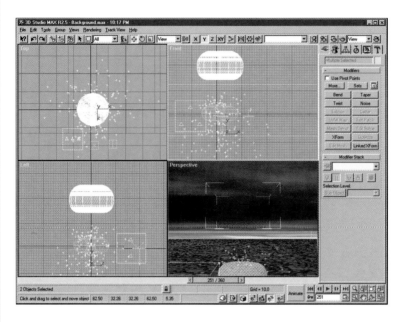

Figure 4
Explosion Base particle system and Mushroom Cloud deflector scaling animation.

Mushroom Cloud Particle System

1. Create a PCloud located at the center of object Explosion Base. Set the following Basic Parameters:
   Particle Formation = Cylinder Emitter
   Rad/Len = 29
   Height = 20
   Position = (x = 12, y = 1, z = 11)
   Percentage of Particles = 20

2. Set the Particle Generation Quantity parameters:
   Use Rate = 6
   Speed = 2
   Speed Variation = 50
   Enter Vector = (x = 0, y = 0, z = 1)
   Life = 400
   Size = 15
   Size Variation =50

3. Set the Particle Type parameters:
   Standard Particles = Facing

4. Name the PCloud **Mushroom Cloud Particles**.

5. Advance to frame 360 and turn Animate on. In the Basic Parameters rollout, set the following:
Rad/Len = 58

Turn Animate off.

6. Open Material Editor and apply material Smoke to the particle system.

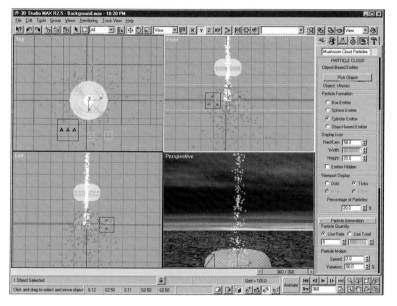

Figure 5
PCloud emitter radius animation to increase the scale of particle emission as the Mushroom cloud grows.

7. Create a UDeflector space warp next to object Explosion Base. The exact position and size do not matter. Set the following parameters:
Pick Object = Mushroom Cloud deflector
Particle Bounce = 0.6
Inherit Vel = 100

8. Bind the UDeflector space warp to the PCloud Mushroom Cloud particles.

At this point the modeling of the ground blast ring and mushroom cloud is complete.

Mass Destruction

Lighting Setup

In this section, you will create the lighting effects for the scene.

1. Create a target spot light located to the right of and above the ground object in the Left viewport. Position the target above the Mushroom Cloud deflector. Set the following parameters:
   Color = (R = 180, G = 180, B = 180)
   Multiplier = 3
   Hotspot = 73.2
   Falloff = 126.8
   Cast Shadows = on
   Body Position = (at x = −200, y = −633, z = 584)
   Target Position = (x = −25, y = −16, z = 201)

Camera Setup

The final step is to set up the camera through which you will view the finished effect.

1. Create a target camera below the target light level with the light target. Position the camera target at the light target.
   Body Position = (x = 12.7, y = −546.5 , z = 135.9)
   Target Position = (x = 12.7, y = −26.4, z = 170.6)

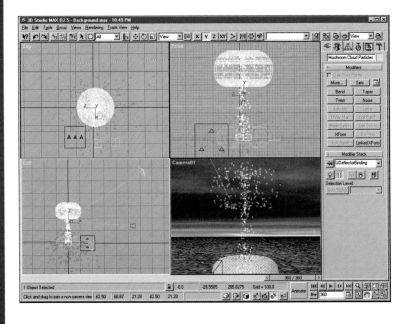

Figure 6
Completed Atomic bomb Mushroom cloud animation sequence.

You can find the final MAX file, AbombMushroomCloud.max, in this project's Scene folder and the final AVI file in the Images folder.

Shattering Geometry

by Jay Kapadia

Y ou can apply this all-purpose Shatter effect to any animation in
which you want an object to shatter, and you can shatter just
about anything you can create. A glass window breaking, a bomb blowing up a car—the examples are endless. The PArray is the key to this
effect. This technique works well when the geometry of the shattering
object is not too dense. If there are too many faces and vertices, the
objects tend to break apart and look less than convincing. You can add
thickness to the fragments of the exploding object when you use
PArray—something you cannot do with the Bomb space warp. The
thickness makes the fragments look like they have mass. Another advan-
tage to using PArray is that you can use all Particle Dynamic space warps
to manipulate the fragments.

Note

*All position and rota-
tional information is
based on absolute
world coordinates.
When creating
objects, use keyboard
entry where possible.
When positioning
objects, use the
Transform Type-In
dialog box located in
the Tools menu. These
techniques ensure
proper object place-
ment and orientation.*

Leave any settings that are not listed in the example at the MAX default
values. Create objects in the Top viewport, unless otherwise indicated.

Preconfiguration

1. Before beginning this effect, please either reset *or* restart MAX.

2. Copy the Shatter project map files from the accompanying CD-ROM to your MAX maps subdirectory.

3. Load the Shatter.max file from this project's Pre-load folder on the CD-ROM.

At this point, you should see a scene containing a floor, wall, and a plate. The animation is preset to 80 frames.

Creating the Materials

In this section you are going to create a PArray that will create the fragments of the plate shattering.

Particle System Creation

1. Create a Particle Array, which is found with the rest of the particle systems. Position it at x = −2.85, y = 0.0, z = 400 with an Icon Size of 77.

2. In the Basic Parameters rollout, click the Pick Object button and choose object plate. In the Viewport Display box choose Mesh.

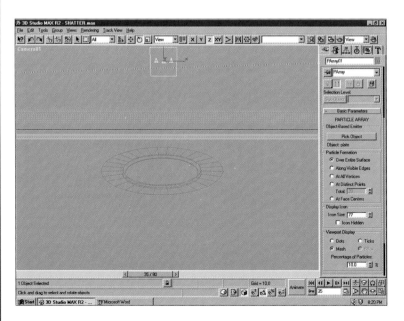

Figure 1

Assigning the plate to the PArray.

3. In the Particle Generation rollout, set the Particle Motion para-
   meters:
   Speed = 30
   Variation = 0
   Divergence = 50

4. Still in the Particles Generation rollout, set the **Particle Timing**
   parameters:
   Emit Start =15
   Display Until = 100
   Life = 100
   Variation = 0

5. In the Particle Types section of the Particle Type rollout, turn on
   Object Fragments.

6. In the Objects Fragments Controls section of the Particle Type
   rollout, set the following:
   Thickness = 6
   Number of Chunks = 20

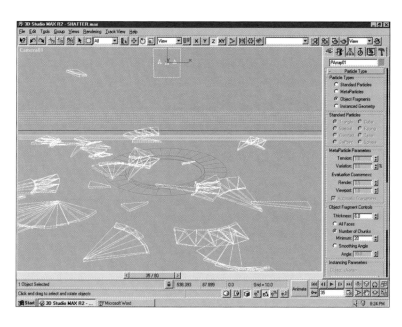

Figure 2
Pieces of the plate
that the PArray will
produce.

7. In the Mat'l Mapping and Source section of the Particle Type
   rollout, turn on Picked Emitter and then click the Get Material
   From button. This takes the material from the plate and applies it
   to the PArray.

8. Right-click the PArray and move the mouse down to Properties. Click Image Motion Blur with Multiplier set to 0.75.

At this point, you will notice that in any frame after 15, shattered pieces of the plate are flying all over.

Creating Deflectors

In this section, you are going to create Deflectors for the fragments to bounce off.

1. Create a Deflector that covers the entire floor and position it at x = 43.43, y = –37.51, z = 0.04. Set the following: **Bounce** = 0.7

2. Bind Deflector01 to object PArray01.

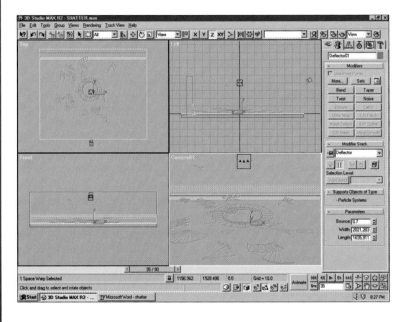

Figure 3
The placement and parameters of Deflector01.

3. Create a second Deflector that covers the entire wall and position it at x = 43.43, y = 603.65, z = 286.65: **Bounce** = 0.7

4. Bind the Deflector02 to object PArray01.

At this point, you should see the fragments of the plate bouncing off the wall and floor and continuing upward indefinitely.

Adding a Space Warp

In this section, you are going to create a Gravity space warp to keep the fragments from bouncing to infinity.

1. Create a Gravity space warp and position it at x = 196.31, y = 387.24, z = 384.13:
   Icon Size = 110
   Strength = 1.5, planar

2. Bind Gravity01 to PArray01.

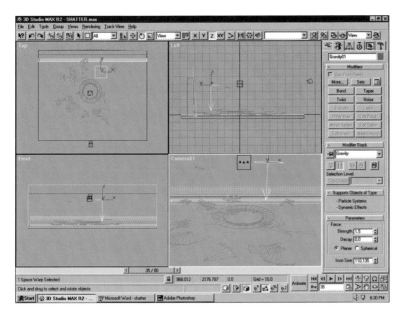

Figure 4
The parameters and placement of the Gravity space warp.

At this point, the falling plate breaks and the pieces go outward in a circular fashion, bouncing a few times and then stopping. The only problem is that you still see the original plate as one solid piece.

Setting Object Visibility

In this section, you create a Visibity Track in Track View to hide the original plate as the PArray is set to start.

1. Open up a Track View. Select object plate and create a Visibility Track by clicking the button that looks like an eye.

2. Click the Add Keys button and then create a key at Frame 15 (see Figure 5).

Note

The blue line that appears indicates that the object will be visible. In this case object plate will be renderable only in the first 15 frames. Then the PArray01 will be visible.

Mass Destruction

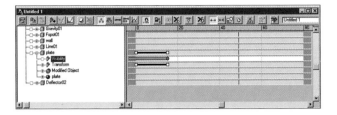

Figure 5
The Visibility track.

At this point you have finished the effect. Object plate falls and becomes hidden when the PArray01 begins to create the fragments. If you play around with the Image Motion blur setting and blur the image more, it will give the effect of the shattered pieces traveling faster. You can find the final MAX file, ShatterFinal.max in the Pre-load folder and the AVI file in the Images folder.

Missile Launch

by Greg Carbonaro

The dramatic elements of a large missile launch, including thick, dark, powerful smoke thrust and bright, pulsating engine glows are surprisingly easy to create. A simple particle system for the thrust and an omni light for the engine glow are the primary elements. Of course, there is a little more to it than that—any good effect requires several elements and a degree of subtle tweaking, but the beautiful simplicity of this effect will delight you.

Note

All position and rotational information is based on absolute world coordinates. When creating objects, use keyboard entry when possible. When positioning objects, use the Transform Type-In dialog box located in the Tools menu. These techniques ensure proper object placement and orientation.

Leave any settings that are not listed in the example at the MAX default values. Create objects in the Top viewport, unless otherwise indicated.

Preconfiguration

1. Before beginning this effect, please reset *or* restart MAX.

2. Copy the Missile Launch project map files from the accompanying CD-ROM to the MAX maps subdirectory.

3. Load the file Missile.max from this project's Pre-load folder on the accompanying CD.

4. Open the Material Editor. Right-click in any material slot and make sure Sample Windows are set to 3×2.

The scene consists of a missile and its launch vehicle placed on a landscape. The motion of the missile has already been animated. The animation length is preset to 300 frames.

Particle Systems and Materials

In this section, a particle system will be created to simulate the exhaust from the missile. A material is created and applied to the particle system to provide the desired smoky look to the exhaust.

Missile Thrust Creation

1. Create a Spray particle system located at the nozzle of the missile. Use the Transform Type-In dialog box to place it at x = –884, y = 1178, z = –245. Rotate to x = 0, y = 48, z = 48.5. Set the following parameters:
Render Count = 800
Drop Size = 12
Speed = 12
Variation = 0.5
Particles = Drops
Render = Facing
Start = 38
Life = 41
Emitter: Width = 5, Length = 5

2. Name the Spray **Missile Thrust**.

3. Open Track View and expand the hierarchy tree to display the Drop Size track for object Missile Thrust. Create the following animation keys:
Frame 0 (Keyframe 1) **Drop Size** = 12
Frame 240 (Keyframe 2) **Drop Size** = 12
Frame 300 (Keyframe 3) **Drop Size** = 36

4. Set the In and Out tangents to Linear for the above 3 keys.

5. Right-click on object Missile Thrust and choose Properties. Set the Object properties:
Cast Shadows = Off

6. Link the Missile Thrust particle system to the Missile object (see Figure 1).

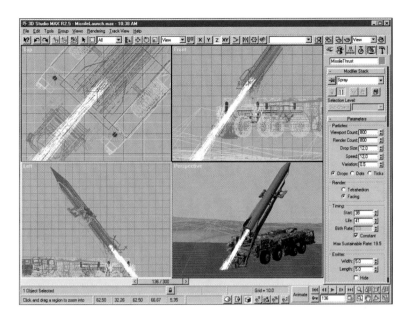

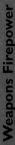

Figure 1
Placement of the thrust particle emitter in the body of the missile and setting of the linear tangents for thrust particle size animation in the track view.

Thrust Material

1. In the Material Editor, activate material slot 1 and set the Material Type to Standard.

2. Set the Basic Parameters as follows:
    Self-Illumination = 65
    Shininess = 0
    Shin. Strength = 0

3. Turn Animate on. In the Extended Parameters rollout, set Opacity Falloff: Amt = 0 at Frame 0. Advance to Frame 240 and shift-right click on the Amt spinner to create a key. Advance to Frame 300 and set Amt = 97. Turn Animate off.

4. Set the Amount for the Diffuse map slot to 100. Click the Diffuse map slot and set the Map Type to Noise. Set the Noise parameters:
    Noise Type = Fractal
    Size = 20

5. Set the Amount for the Opacity map slot to 100. Click the Opacity map slot and set the Map Type to Mask.

6. Click the Map map slot and set the Map Type to Noise. Set the Noise parameters:
Noise Type = Fractal
Size = 20

7. Return to the Mask map level. Click the Mask map slot and set the Map Type to Gradient. Set the Gradient Parameters:
Gradient Type = Radial

8. Swap Color #1 with Color #3.

9. Name the material **Thrust**.

10. Apply the Thrust material to the Missile Thrust particle system (see Figure 2).

At this point, the exhaust particle system and material have been defined.

Dynamic Forces and Space Warps

In this section, a Deflector space warp will be added to the scene, causing the exhaust to bounce off the ground. A Wind space warp will also be added to provide turbulence to the exhaust as it bounces off the ground.

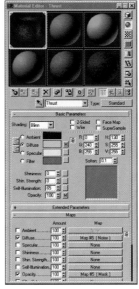

Figure 2
Creating a missile thrust material.

I. Create a Particles and Dynamics Deflector space warp located at ground level below and behind the missile exhaust. Use the Transform Type-In to position it at x = −1006, y = 1057, z = −279. Set the following parameters:
Bounce = 0.45
Width = 400
Length = 400

2. Bind the Missile Thrust particle system to the Deflector.

3. Create a Particles and Dynamics Wind space warp behind the missile exhaust. Use the Transform Type-In to position it at x = 0, y = 180, z = 0. Rotate to x = 0, y = 180, z = 0. Set the Wind parameters:
Turbulence = 10
Frequency = 2
Icon Size = 11

4. Bind the Missile Thrust particle system to the Wind (see Figure 3).

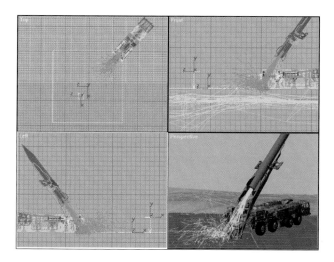

Figure 3
The Deflector and Wind space warp cause the exhaust to bounce in a chaotic manner off the ground.

At this point the exhaust particle system is now bouncing off the ground in a realistic manner.

Lighting Setup

Next, you will create the lighting effects for this scene.

1. Create an omni light located to the side of the missile nozzle at x = −881, y = 1163, z = −247.4.

2. In the Attenuation section, set the following parameters:
   Far Use = Checked
   Far Start = 21
   Far End = 70

3. Name the omni light **Engine Glow Light**.

4. Open Track View and expand the hierarchy tree to display the Multiplier track for object Engine Glow Light. Select Multiplier in the hierarchy tree, click on Assign Controller and choose Noise Float. Right-click on the Multiplier track to display the Noise Controller dialog box. (See Figure 4.) Set the following parameters:
   Frequency = 0.24
   Fractal Noise = Checked
   Strength = 5
   >0 = Checked

Note

The Noise Strength field is broken in MAX R2.5. In the following step, set the Strength value using the spinner.

Weapons Firepower

5. Create the following animation keys in Engine Glow Light's Color track:
Frame 0 (Keyframe 1) Color = (R = 0, G = 0, B = 0)
Frame 38 (Keyframe 2) Color = (R = 128, G = 128, B = 128)
Frame 42 (Keyframe 3) Color = (R = 255, G = 161, B = 0)

6. Set the In and Out tangents to Step for the above 3 keys.

7. Link the omni light to the Missile object.

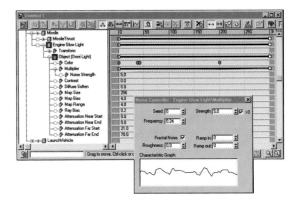

Figure 4
This omni light creates the engine glow. A very dynamic effect is achieved by animating both the color and multiplier.

8. Create an omni light to the side of and high above the launch vehicle. Use the Transform Type-In to position it at x = –613, y = 937, z = 266. Set the following parameters:
Color = (R = 180, G = 180, B = 180)
Multiplier = 0.75
Cast Shadows = On
Use Global Settings = On
Use Shadow Maps = On
Size = 1024

9. Name the omni light **FrontLight**.

10. In the Left viewport, create a target spot light to the left of and far above the landscape with the target at the launch vehicle. Position the body at x = –468, y = 3041, z = 1653. Position the target at x = –864, y = 1260, z = –204. Set the following parameters:
Color = (R = 180, G = 180, B = 180)
Multiplier = 1.12
Hot Spot = 10
Fall Off = 20
Overshoot = On

> **Cast Shadows** = On
> **Use Global Settings** = On
> **Use Shadow Maps** = On
> **Size** = 1024

11. Name the target spot light **SunLight**.

At this point the missile exhaust has been modeled and lighting applied to the scene.

Camera Setup

The final step is to set up the camera through which you will view the finished effect.

1. Create a target camera in front of and slightly above the landscape, with the target at the launch vehicle. Position the body at x = –915, y = 736, z = –179. Position the target at x = –874, y = 1205, z = –217. Set the following parameters:
   Lens = 74.89

2. Name the camera **MissileCam**.

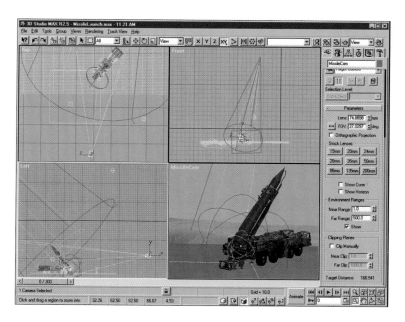

Figure 5
Completed Missile Launch effect.

You can find the final MAX file, MissileLaunch.max, in this project's Scene folder and the final AVI file in the Images folder.

Laser Cutting

by Greg Carbonaro

The effect of a laser cutting through an object is fairly easy to produce. The two easiest ways to achieve the effect are with an animated Opacity map or with an animated Boolean. Generally, the animated Boolean technique is the better way to go because it looks more convincing, as long as the object being animated is not too complicated. In contrast, when you use Opacity maps, the object doesn't appear to have true depth and can look incorrect when viewed from certain angles. The technique that you employ here is the animated Boolean.

Note

All position and rotational information is based on absolute world coordinates. When creating objects, use keyboard entry where possible. When positioning objects, use the Transform Type-In dialog box located in the Tools menu. These techniques ensure proper object placement and orientation.

Leave any settings that are not listed in the example at the MAX default values. Create objects in the Top viewport, unless otherwise noted.

Preconfiguration

1. Before beginning this effect, either reset *or* restart MAX.

2. Load the file Cutting.max from the accompanying CD-ROM.

Creating the Cut Doors

The first thing you have to do is create the pieces that make up the door.

1. Create a standard primitive box at x = 27.0, y = 571.9, z = 60.1.
    Set the following:
    Length = 250
    Width = 3
    Height = 30
    Length Segments = 20

2. Name the box **B Box02** because you are going to use this box
    to Boolean the door into two pieces.

3. In the Front viewport, rotate B Box02 25 degrees on the z-axis.

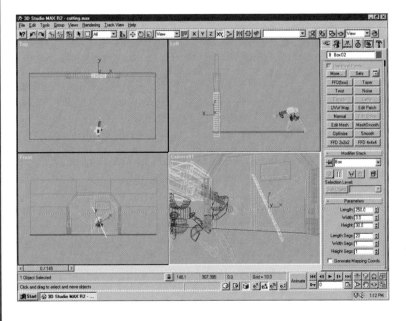

Figure 1
This image shows
object B Box02's
position relative to
object door whole.

4. Select door whole.

5. Select Compound Objects, Boolean from the Create pull-down
    menu. Click Pick Operand B and select B_Box02.

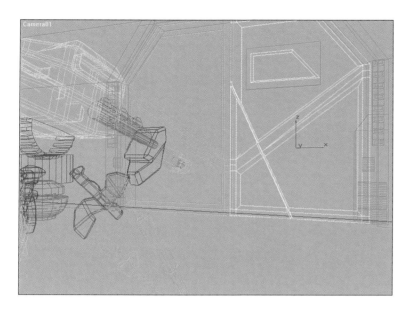

Figure 2
The completed
Boolean.

6. Clone the object door whole as a copy and call it **door small**.

7. In Modify, choose Edit Mesh. Select all the vertices on the piece that is going to be the large side of the door and delete them. All that remains is the little triangular piece of the door.

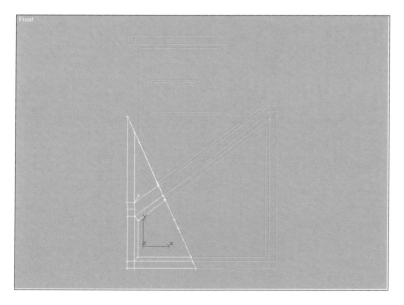

Figure 3
The remaining
smaller piece of
the door.

8. Clone the object door whole as a copy and call it **door large**. In Modify, choose Edit Mesh. Select all the vertices on the piece that is going to be the small side of the door and delete them. At this point, all that remains is the large piece of the door.

Animation

1. Advance to Frame 15 and choose object door whole.

2. Change the Reference Coordinate System to Local. Under the Modifier Stack, click Sub-Object. Select B: B_Box02 and move it along its y-axis to the bottom of the door so that it is not yet cutting into the door.

3. To animate the Boolean over time, click the Animate button.

4. Advance to Frame 100 and move Operand B along its y-axis to its final position, which would be after the laser has cut all the way through the door. After positioning Operand B, turn Animate off.

   Use door small and door large as guides. Use object laser as a reference to how far to move operand B: B Box02.

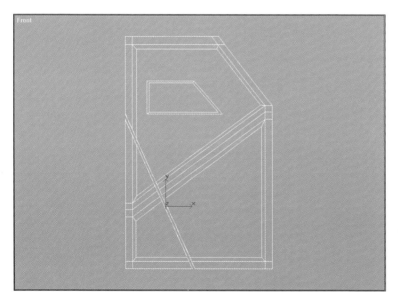

Figure 4
Frame 100, after the animation of the Boolean ends.

At this point, you should have three door pieces: door whole, door small, and door large. Door whole should have an animated Boolean going through it from Frame 15 to 100.

Lighting Setup

In this section, you create the lighting effects for the scene.

1. Create an omni light and position it in front of the door at X = 64.2, Y = 534.0, Z = –22.0. Set the following:
   Color = (R = 0, G = 0, B = 0)

2. Link the omni light to the object gun rotate.

3. In the Attenuation box set the following:
   Far Start = 0
   Far End = 30
   Use = checked

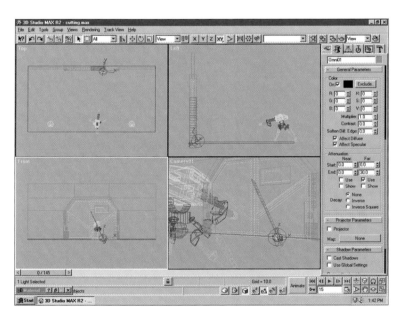

Figure 5
The position and settings for Omni01.

At this point, you created the light that will act like the hot glow from the laser. You will animate it later in the effect.

Creating a Super Spray Particle System

Now create the sparks for when the laser is cutting through the metal.

1. Create a Super Spray particle system. Position it by the Omni01 light at coordinates X = 64.2, Y = 547.6, Z = −26.2. In the Left viewport, rotate the Super Spray on the z-axis −40 degrees so that it is pointing slightly up.

2. In the Particle Formation box, set the following:
   Off Axis Spread = 45
   Off Plane Spread = 45

3. Set the Particle Quality parameters:
   Use Total = 550

4. Set the Particle Motion parameters:
   Speed = 6
   Variation = 0

5. In the Particle Generation rollout, set the Particle Timing parameters:
   Emit Start = 15
   Emit Stop = 100
   Display Unit = 200
   Life = 2
   Variation = 20

6. Set the Particle Size parameters:
   Size = 5
   Variation = 10

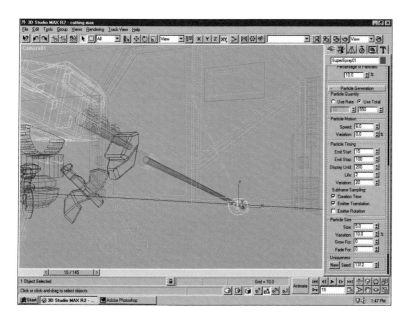

7. In the Particle Type rollout, click Tetra.

8. Link SuperSpray01 to object gun rotate.

You just finished animating for the sparks. Next, create the material for the sparks.

Creating the Laser Material

1. Select the particle system and object laser. In the Material Editor, create a material with the following parameters:
Ambient = (R = 255, G = 255, B = 0)
Diffuse = (R = 255, G = 255, B = 0)
Specular = (R = 255, G = 255, B = 0)
Filter = (R = 255, G = 255, B = 0)
Self–Illumination = 100
Material Effects Channel = 1

2. Name the material **Laser**.

3. Apply the material to both objects.

4. Under Space Warps, create a Deflector. Set the following:
Bounce = 0.7

5. Size and position the Deflector so that it covers the entire floor. Bind it to the particle system.

Weapons Firepower

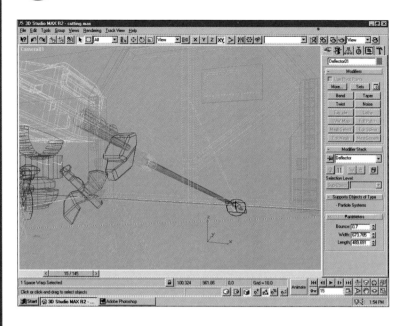

Figure 7
The setup and placement of Deflector01.

6. Create a Gravity space warp:
   Strength = 0.6, planar

7. Bind the Gravity space warp to the particle system.

Creating Hot Metal

When the laser cuts through the door, the metal is going to become really hot. By animating Omni01, you can fake the metal changing color.

1. Open up a Track View and click on Omni01.

2. Create a key at 8 and 15. If you right-click key 8, the color is already black: (R = 0, G = 0, B = 0)

3. At key 15, change the color to orange:
   Color = (R = 255, G = 174, B = 0)

4. Copy the key from 8 to 105.

5. Copy the key from 15 to 98.

6. Go to object door whole and create a Visibility track and a key at 100.

7. Go to object door small and create a Visibility track and a key at 0 and 100.

8. Select the Visibility track and copy it.

Figure 8
Set up the keys for Omni01.

9. Go to object door large and•create a Visibility track and paste the keys from door small.

You have just set keys so that from Frame 0 to 100, you will be rendering door whole while the Boolean is occurring. Then you will hide door whole and render door small and door large. This way, you can animate the two pieces independently from one another.

Creating Glows in Video Post

Now add the finishing glow effect on the sparks in Video Post.

1. Click Scene Event and pick Camera01.

2. To create glowing sparks, click Add Image Filter Event and choose Lens Effects Glow.

3. Click Setup and then click Properties.

4. In the Source box, choose Material ID.

5. Click Preferences, and set the following:
   Size = 1
   Color Box = User
   Color = (R = 255, G = 174, B = 0)
   Intensity = 4

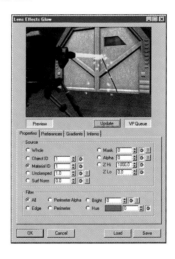

Figure 9
Set up the Properties window in Video Post.

As you can see, the door was quite simple to create, and the Boolean worked well. If the object you are cutting is too complicated, an Opacity map is the way to go, but remember that with an Opacity map you have to consider the angle at which the object will be viewed.

Laser Blast

by Jay Kapadia

Particle Array and Combustion are the keys to this Laser Blast effect. You could create this effect with the Bomb space warp in a third of the steps, but you won't be happy with the final results. The Particle Array takes the actual geometry and breaks it into chunks; you can give the chunks thickness, which you cannot do with the Bomb space warp. Thickness is the key. If you use the Bomb space warp to create this effect, the debris looks like paper-thin triangles, but with the PArray, the debris appears to have mass. In addition, you can use all of the space warps that affect particle dynamics, which is something you cannot do with the Bomb space warp.

Note

All position and rotational information is based on absolute world coordinates. When creating objects, use keyboard entry where possible. When positioning objects, use the Transform Type-In dialog box located in the Tools menu. These techniques ensure proper object placement and orientation.

Leave any settings that are not listed in the example at the MAX default values. Create objects in the Top viewport, unless otherwise indicated.

Preconfiguration

1. Before beginning this effect, please either reset *or* restart MAX.

2. Open the file blast.max from the project's Preload directory on the accompanying CD-ROM.

At this point, you should see a scene containing a room with a laser gun pointed at a sphere on a stand.

Objects and Materials

In this section, you are going to use some straightforward geometry, particle systems, and materials to create a laser.

Creating a Laser

1. Create a standard primitive cylinder and place it in the gun barrel. You can use the Transform Type-In dialog box to position it at x = 26.9, y = 223.1, z = 71.5. Set the following:
   Radius = 2.5
   Height = 30

2. Name the cylinder **laser blast**.

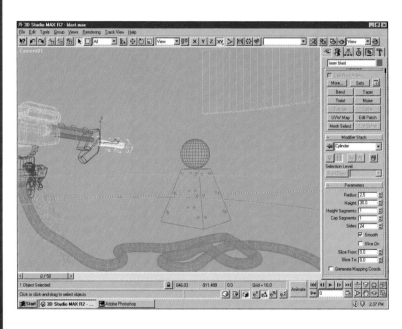

Figure 1
Place the object laser blast.

3. Open up the Material Editor and select slot 4.

4. In the Material Editor, create a material:
   Ambient = (R = 255, G = 216, B = 0)
   Diffuse = (R = 255, G = 78, B = 12)
   Filter = (R = 255, G = 78, B = 12)
   Self-Illumination = 100

5. Name the material **laser blast**.

6. In the Extended Parameters rollout, set the following:
Out = selected
Amt = 100

7. Apply the material laser blast to the object laser blast.

At this point, you have created the laser "blast" that will destroy the target.

Laser Blast Particle System Creation

Now you create the debris of the target being destroyed.

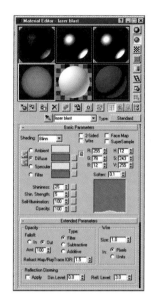

Figure 2
The parameters for the material laser blast.

1. Create a PArray (Particle Array), which is found with the rest of the particle systems. In the Basic Parameters rollout, click the Pick Object button and choose Target.

2. In the Viewport Display box, choose Mesh.

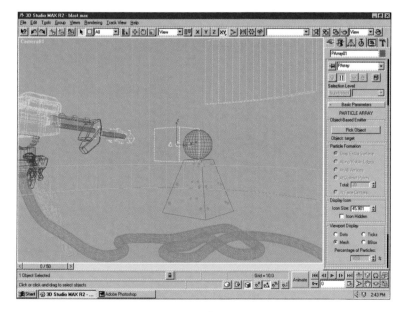

Figure 3
The basic creation of the PArray.

3. In the Particle Motion section of the Particle Generation rollout, set the following:
Speed = 15
Variation = 30
Divergence = 20

4. In the Particle Timing section, set the following:
Emit Start = 10
Display Unit = 100
Life = 70
Variation = 0

5. In the Object Fragments Controls section of the Particle Type rollout, set the following:
Thickness = 8
Number of Chunks = 50

6. In the Material Mapping and Source box of the Particle Type rollout, turn on Picked Emitter and click the Material From button. The material assigned to object target is applied to the PArray.

Figure 4
This image shows the Object Properties dialog box of the PArray01.

7. Right-click the PArray, select Properties, and turn on Image Motion Blur.

At this point, you have created the debris of the target scattering all around the room.

Creating the UDeflectors

Next you give the debris dynamic properties so that it acts like real debris.

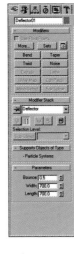

1. Create a Universal Deflector, UDeflector. Click the Pick Object button and select Stand. Set Bounce to 0.5 and bind it to PArray.

2. Create a second UDeflector. Click the Pick Object button and select Blaster tube. Change the Bounce to 0.1 and bind it to the PArray.

Figure 5
This image shows the Basic Parameters of Deflector01.

3. Create a third UDeflector. Click the Pick Object button and select Wall. Change the Bounce to 0.5 and bind it to the PArray.

4. Create a Deflector that covers the entire floor, change the Bounce to 0.5, and bind it to the PArray.

5. Create a Gravity space warp and bind it to the PArray. Set the following:
Strength = 1, Planar

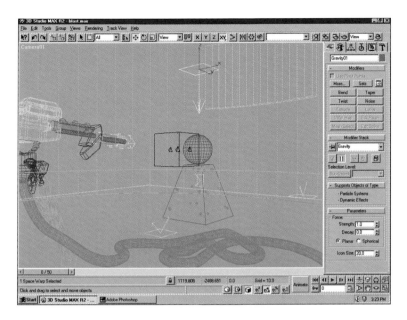

Figure 6
The parameters for Gravity01.

At this point, you have finished setting up the dynamics for the debris so that they bounce off the wall, the floor, and other solid objects in the room.

Animation

The next step is to animate the laser blowing up the target.

1. Turn Animate on and advance to Frame 10. Move object laser blast to the center of the target or use the Transform Type-In dialog box to position the blast at x = 26.9, y = 360.9, z = 61.8. Turn Animate off.

2. Open a Track View. Select object target and create a Visibility Track.

3. Create a key at Frame 11. (This makes the object renderable in only the first 11 frames. Then the particle array will be visible.)

4. Select object laser blast and create a Visibility track.

Figure 7
The final destination of object laser blast.

5. Create a key at Frame 10. (This makes the object renderable only in the first 10 frames.)

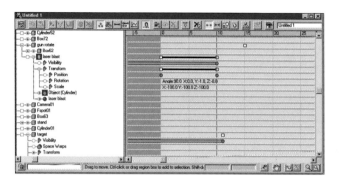

At this point, you have created the laser gun shooting the target and the debris should be bouncing all over the room. No laser blast would be complete, however, without a fiery explosion, which is what you create in the next section.

Creating a Fiery Explosion

You will use MAX's standard Combustion to create the fire effect.

1. Create a SphereGizmo; from the Create menu, choose Helpers, Atmospheric Apparatus. Position it at x = 34.8, y = 381.8, z = 64.8. Set the following:
   Radius = 80

2. In the Environment dialog box, click Add and choose Combustion.

3. Click Pick Gizmo and choose SphereGizmo01.

4. In the Explosion box, check Explosion, deselect Smoke, and then click Setup Explosion:
   Start Time = 10
   End Time = 40

Congratulations! You just created your own laser testing site. The Combustion along with the Image Blur really gives the blast a feeling of power. You might even want to try this effect by using the Bomb space warp to see what the difference would be. The final MAX file is in the project's Scene directory as Final_Blast.max.

Weld Sparks

by Jay Kapedia

Y ou can add Weld Sparks to any animation in which you need to
create sparks—sparks on train tracks, sparks from a lighter, sparks
from a laser, and so on. Basically, the effect makes use of a simple particle
system with a few dynamic space warps and a slight glow. By using
Deflectors, gravity, and wind, you can make the sparks bounce around or
fade away as they die off.

Leave any settings that are not listed in the example at the MAX default
values. Create objects in the Top viewport, unless otherwise indicated.

Preconfiguration

1. Before beginning this effect, please either reset *or* restart MAX.

2. Load the weld.max file from this project's Preload folder on the
   accompanying CD-ROM.

At this point, you should see a scene with two robotic arms and a conveyor belt carrying canisters between them. The animation is preset to
110 frames.

Modeling and Materials

First you are going to create the sparks by using a Super Spray particle system (see Figure 1).

Creating the Sparks

1. Create a Super Spray particle system with an Icon Size of 10. Position it at x = –538.27, y = 272.06, z = –689.02, which is directly in front of the canister 02.

2. Switch to the Left viewport and rotate the Super Spray 15 degrees on the z-axis and –20 degrees on the y-axis so that the Super Spray is pointing at the camera.

3. Name the particle system **Sparks01**.

4. In the Particle Formation box of the Basic Parameters rollout, set the following:
   Spread = 45
   Spread = 45

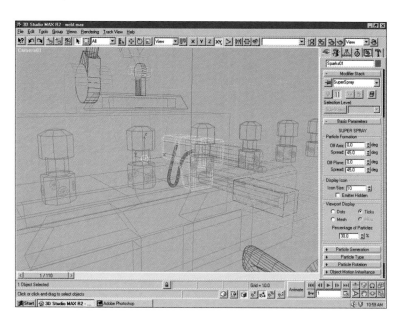

Figure 1
The location of object Sparks01.

5. In the Particle Timing box of the Particle Generation rollout, set the following:
   Emit Start = 10
   Emit Stop = 14
   Display Unit = 110
   Life = 20
   Variation = 20

6. In the Particle Size box, set the following:
Size = 10
Variation = 5
Grow For = 4
Fade For = 4

7. In the Particle Type rollout, click Tetra.

8. Clone the emitter as a Copy.

9. Name the copy **Sparks02**.

10. In the Particle Generation rollout, set the following:
Emit Start = 46
Emit Stop = 50

11. Click New Seed to make it unique.

Directing the Sparks

Now you create gravity to make the sparks fall downward (see Figure 2).

1. Create a Gravity space warp with an Icon Size of 10. Position it at x = −538.27, y = 173.31, z = −573.51. Set the following:
Strength = 1, planar

2. Bind the space warp to both particle systems.

Note

You can place the space warp wherever you like, but I personally like to keep the space warps close to the objects they are effecting, so I know what space warp is effecting what.

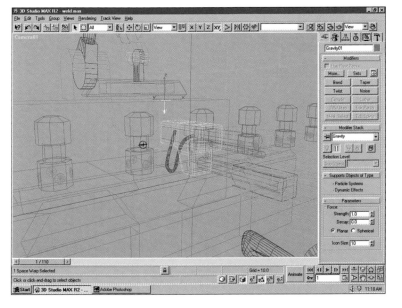

Figure 2
The placement for Gravity01 and its Basic Parameters.

At this point, when you move the slider bar across the bottom, you notice two particle bursts, from which the particles fall downward.

Creating UDeflectors

Now create the Deflectors so that the particles bounce off the objects in the scene (see Figure 3).

1. Create a UDeflector with an Icon Size = 70 . Position it at coordinates x = −533.35, y = 296.87, z = −859.88. Click the Pick Object button and pick Conveyor:
   Bounce = 1

2. Create a second UDeflector with an Icon Size = 70 . Position it at x = −533.35, y = −17.39, z = 31.24. Click the Pick Object button and pick table01:
   Bounce = 1

3. Create a third UDeflector with an Icon Size = 70 . Position it at x = −533.35, y = 541.65, z = −668.47. Click Pick Object button and pick Table02.
   Bounce = 1

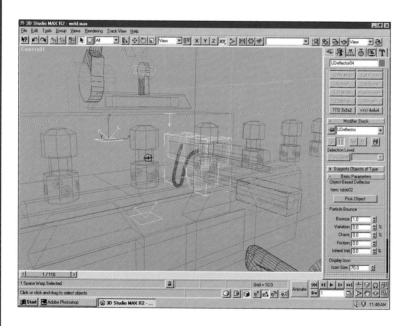

Figure 3
The placement of the third UDeflector and its Basic Parameters.

4. Bind the three UDeflectors to both particle systems by using the Bind to Space Warp icon.

Note

You can make as many UDeflectors as you want the particles to bounce off.

At this point, you should see both of the particle systems bouncing off the objects in the scene.

Creating the Sparks Materials

Now you create the material for the sparks.

1. Select both particle systems and open the Material Editor. Activate slot 11 and set the Basic parameters:
Ambient = (R = 235, G = 188, B = 0)
Diffuse = (R = 235, G = 188, B = 0)
Self-Illumination = 100
Material Effects Channel = 1

2. Name the material **Sparks**.

3. Apply the material to both particle systems.

Now if you render your scene, it is complete—except when the sparks appear, there is no burst of light.

Lighting Setup

In this section, you create the lighting effects for the scene.

1. Create an omni light and place it exactly where the sparks are emitted. Try x = −535.38, y = 257.15, z = −688.96:
Color = (R = 0, G = 0, B = 0)
Multiplier = 3.5
Attenuation Box: End = 700, Far = 700, and the others = 0
Use = on
Cast Shadows = on

2. Under Create Helpers, create a point and name it **pt for flare.** Place it where the sparks are emitted at coordinates x = −547.65, y = 267.60, z = −687.96 (see Figure 4).

Fires, Glows, and Sparks

Figure 4
The position of helper pt for flare.

Animation

In this section, you animate Omni01 to go on and off when the sparks appear (see Figure 5).

1. Open up a Track View and click Omni01, Color.

2. Create a key at Frame 9 and Frame 10:
   Key 9: Color = (R = 0, G = 0, B = 0)
   Key 10: Color = (R = 255, G = 255, B = 0).

3. Copy the key from 9 to 15, 46, 52.

4. Copy the key from 10 to 14, 47, 51.

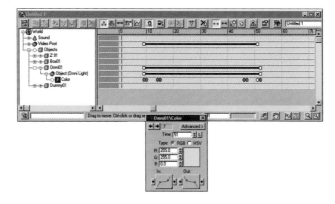

Figure 5
The keys for Omni01.

If you do a small test render, you see that you have completed the effect. Now go into Video Post to add a glow to the sparks and a lens flare, which will make this effect a good one.

Adding Glows in Video Post

You can use Lens Effects glow to enhance this effect. The glow gives the particles a nice soft edge.

1. Click Scene Event and pick Camera01.

2. To create glowing sparks, click Add Image Filter Event and choose Lens Effects Glows (see Figure 6).

3. Click Setup and then click Properties. Set the following:
   Source Box = Material ID

4. Click Preferences and set the following:
   Effect Box: Size = 1
   Color Box = User
   Color = (R = 255, G = 150, B = 0)
   Intensity = 5

5. To create the lens flare, click Add Image Filter Event and choose Lens Effects Flare. Click Setup.

6. Click Node Source and choose helper pt for flare:
   Glow = checked
   Rings = checked
   Man. Sec = checked
   Rays = checked

7. Click the Glows tab.

8. Double-click the second tab in Radial Color and change it to yellow (R = 255, G = 255, B = 0).

9. Now animate the lens flare on and off completely in Track View. Open up a Track View and click Video Post, Lens Effects Flare, Size.

10. Create a key at Frame 9 and 10:
    Key 9 = 0
    Key 10 = 30

11. Copy the key from 9 to 15, 46, 52.

12. Copy the key from 10 to 14, 47, 51.

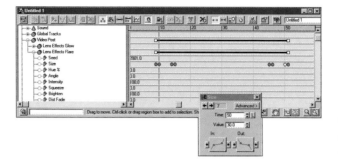

Figure 6
The location for the keys for the lens flare.

Now you can render your scene through Video Post—notice the difference the glow and the lens flare actually create. You can find the final MAX file in this project's Scene folder and the AVI file in the Images folder.

Jacob's Ladder

by Steve Alexander

I n this simple Jacob's Ladder effect, the main visual results from a
Noise modifier that you place on a spline for the jumpy plasma arc.
You then glow it with Lens Effects to create an electric feeling. Add a
light, projected on the background to enhance the arc's visual impact.
You can use the settings and overall idea for this effect in any situation in
which you need wild electricity, such as lightning or electrical sparks
emanating from some sort of device.

Note

All position and rotational information is based on absolute world coordinates. When creating objects, use keyboard entry where possible. When positioning objects, use the Transform Type-In dialog box located in the Tools menu. These techniques ensure proper object placement and orientation.

Leave any settings that are not listed in the example at the MAX default
values. Create objects in the Top viewport, unless otherwise indicated.

Preconfiguration

1. Before beginning this effect, please either reset *or* restart MAX.

2. Copy the Jacob's Ladder project map files from the accompanying CD-ROM to your MAX maps subdirectory.

3. Load the Jacobs.max file from this project's Preload folder on the accompanying CD-ROM. This file contains all of the basic setup

objects. There is a small wooden box with the Jacob's Ladder
antennae coming from the top. Watch the dial on the front of the
box; the dial is animated for a subtle effect.

Modeling and Materials

In this section, you create an arc with an animated noise to emulate an
electric spark (see Figure 1).

1. Create an Arc in the Front viewport at x = 0, y = 0, z = 54. Set
   the following parameters for Arc:
   General: Renderable, Thickness = 0.45
   Parameters: Radius = 15, From = 45, To = 135

2. Apply an Edit Spline modifier. Go to the segment level and on
   each segment, refine with 1 vertex. Turn off Sub-Object.

3. Apply a Noise modifier and in the Noise section of the
   Parameters rollout, set the following:
   Fractal = checked
   Roughness = 0.6

4. In the Strength section, set the following:
   x = 2, y = −40, z = 12

5. In the Animation section, set the following:
   Animate Noise = checked

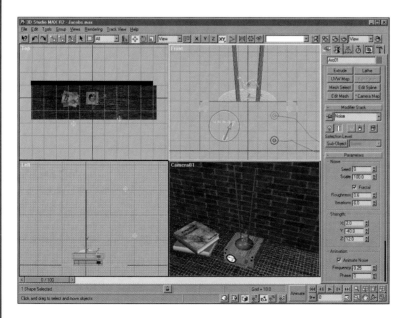

Figure 1
Jacob's Ladder arc
at the correct
position.

6. Apply an XForm modifier.

7. Create a new material and set the Basic Parameters as follows:
   Ambient = (R = 255, G = 255, B = 255)
   Diffuse = (R = 255, G = 255, B = 255)
   Self Illumination = 100
   Material Effects Channel = 1

8. Apply this material to the arc.

This material will be the cue for a glow in Video Post.

Lighting Setup

The following light casts an electric-like glow onto the wall, which makes the spark more believable (see Figure 2).

1. Create a free spotlight anywhere in the Front viewport and move it to x = 0, y = −14, z = 67. Set the following:
   Color = (R = 75, G = 165, B = 200)
   Multiplier = 1.25
   Hotspot = 27
   Falloff = 90
   Rectangle = on
   Aspect = 2.0

2. Link the light as a child object to the Arc.

3. In Track View, for the Multiplier track of the light, add a Noise Float controller. Go to the properties of the controller and set the following:
   Noise Type = Fractal
   Strength = 1.25
   >0 = checked

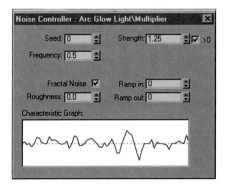

Figure 2
The Track View with the settings for the Arc Light's noise controller.

At this point, the light follows the arc when it is animated and casts a noise-controlled glow onto the wall.

Animation

In this section, you animate the position and scale of the arc so that it appears to move as a real Jacob's Ladder does (see Figure 3).

1. Animate the arc. At Frame 100, set the following:
   Position = (x = 0, y = 0, z = 278)

2. Animate the XForm, Sub Object: Gizmo, Frame 100
   Non-Uniform Scale: x = 260%
   Use the Selection Center for the transformation.

   This step scales the gizmo of the Xform modifier so the arc appears to grow on its ascent.

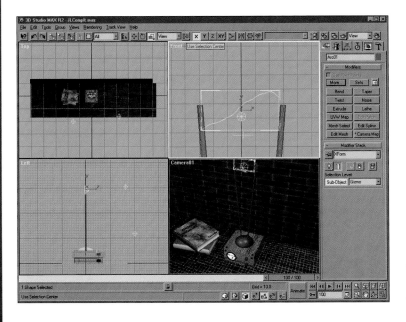

Figure 3
The arc at the correct scale and position.

Creating Glows in Video Post

Now create the effect of electricity using Video Post. The arc's material will be cued to glow with Lens Effects Glow (see Figure 4).

1. Click Scene Event and pick Camera01.

2. To create the glowing arc, click Add Image Filter Event and choose Lens Effects Glow.

3. Click Setup and then click Properties.

4. In the Source box, choose Material ID.

5. Click Preferences and set the following:
Size = 0.9
Color Box = User
Color = (R = 8, G = 17, B = 140)
Intensity = 100

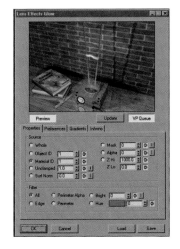

Figure 4
The Lens Effects window with the glowed arc.

Fireworks Burst

by Jay Kapadia

Fireworks bursts are simply particle systems with brilliant colors. By using particle dynamics, you can give them a very realistic motion, and with Video Post, you can add a great deal of color variation. The Super Spray, which was added to MAX R2, is the perfect particle system because particles can now emit other particles. You can cause particles to fade away with a simple click of a button, rather than playing with troublesome Opacity maps. This is a great way to add a glimmering trail behind your firework burst.

Note

All position and rotational information is based on absolute world coordinates. When creating objects, use keyboard entry when possible. When positioning objects, use the Transform Type-In dialog box located in the Tools menu. These techniques ensure proper object placement and orientation.

Leave any settings that are not listed in the example at the MAX default values. Create objects in the Top viewport, unless otherwise indicated.

Preconfiguration

1. Before beginning this effect, please reset *or* restart MAX.

2. Load the file burst.max from this project's Preload folder on the accompanying CD-ROM.

When you open this scene, you will find only a camera. The animation is set to 80 frames.

Creating the Super Sprays and Materials

In this section you are going to create a Super Spray that will serve as the source of all bursts.

Creating a Burst Particle System

1. Create a Super Spray particle system, positioned roughly in the center of the Camera view at x −262.05, y = 1112.14, z = 518.42.

2. Name the Super Spray **burst01**.

3. In the Particle Formation box of the Basic Parameters rollout, set the following:
Off Axis Spread = 90
Off Plane Spread = 90

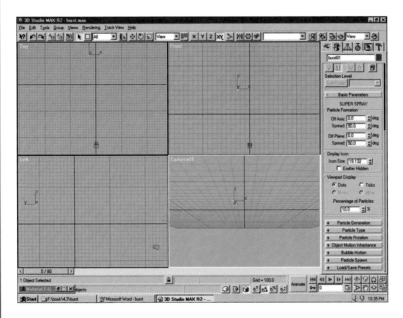

Figure 1
The location and Basic Parameters for burst01.

4. In the Particle Quantity box of the Particle Generation rollout set the following:
Use Total = 200.

5. In the Particle Motion box set the following:
Speed = 20

6. In the Particle Timing box set the following:
Emit Start = 0
Emit Stop = 3
Display Unit = 100
Life = 25
Variation = 20

7. In the Particle Size box set the following (see Figure 2):
Size = 5
Variation = 0
Grow for = 0
Fade for = 10

8. In the Particle Types box of the Particle Type rollout set the following:
Facing = Selected

9. In the Particle Spawning Effects box of the Particle Spawn rollout set the following:
Spawn Trails = Selected
Affects = 50
Variations = 20

10. In the Speed Chaos box, click Inherit Parent Velocity.

11. In the Lifespan Value Queue box, type **10** and click Add.

12. Switch to the Top viewport and create a Gravity space warp. Position it at x = −0.08, y = −54.42, z = 160. Set the following:
Icon Size = 25
Strength = 0.5

13. Bind the Gravity space warp to the particle system (see Figure 3).

14. Clone burst01 several times to create a sky full of fire works. Coordinates for the copies:
burst02 = x = −776.85, y = 870.13, z = 403.51
burst03 = x = −339.04, y = 404.35, z = −314.37
burst04 = x = −445.67, y = 1170.19, z = 1142.10
burst05 = x = 376.70, y = 230.38, z = 655.25
burst06 = x = 398.06, y = 726.25, z = −215.04
burst07 = x = 752.90, y = 1170.20, z = 623.70

Figure 2
The Particle Generation rollout of burst01.

Figure 3
The Parameters of Gravity01.

Fires, Glows, and Sparks

Creating Colors for the Bursts

You have just finished creating all the bursts. Now you're ready to create the different colors for the burst.

1. Open up the Material Editor, activate slot 01, and set the following:
   Ambient = (R = 255, G = 255, B = 0)
   Diffuse = (R = 255, G = 255, B = 0)
   Self Illumination = 100
   Material Effects Channel = 1

2. Name the material **burst01**.

3. Copy the material to slot 02 and call it **burst02**. Set the following Basic Parameters:
   Ambient = (R = 229, G = 229, B = 229)
   Diffuse = (R = 229, G = 229, B = 229)

4. Copy the material to slot 03 and call it **burst03**. Set the following Basic Parameters:
   Ambient = (R = 0, G = 255, B = 0)
   Diffuse = (R = 0, G = 255, B = 0)

5. Copy the material to slot 04 and call it **burst04**. Set the following Basic Parameters:
   Ambient = (R = 255, G = 0, B = 0)
   Diffuse = (R = 255, G = 0, B = 0)

6. Copy the material to slot 05 and call it **burst05**. Set the following Basic Parameters (see Figure 4):
   Ambient = (R = 0, G = 0, B = 255)
   Diffuse = (R = 0, G = 0, B = 255)

7. Assign the materials to the correct objects:
   Assign material burst01 to object burst01
   Assign material burst02 to objects burst02 and burst06
   Assign material burst03 to object burst03
   Assign material burst04 to objects burst04 and burst07
   Assign material burst05 to object burst05

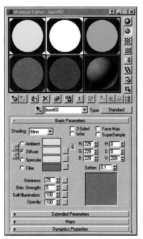

Note

You can change the values to whatever colors you want. Just remember to set the Material Effects Channel to 1.

Figure 4
The different colors for all the bursts.

8. Select all the particle systems, right-click, and select Properties.

9. In the dialog box under Motion Blur, click Image and change the Multiplier to 2.

At this point, you should see seven unique bursts occurring at different times. Create a test render to see the effect.

Adding Glows in Video Post

In this section you are going to use Video Post to add a glow to the fireworks bursts.

1. Click Scene Event and select Camera01.

2. Click Add Image Filter Event and select Lens Effects Glow.

3. Click Setup and then click Properties. In the Source box, select Material ID (see Figure 5).

4. Click Preferences and set the following:
   Size = 10
   Pixel = On
   Intensity = 75

You can also click User and change the color of the glow. For example, to create a white burst with a red glow, change the color to red and click User.

At this point you are finished with the effect. When you render it through Video Post, you will see what a difference the glows make.

You can find the final MAX file, BurstFinal.max, in this project's Scene folder and the final AVI file in the Images folder.

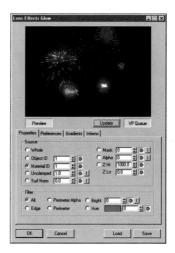

Figure 5
The Properties menu for Lens Effects Glow.

Note

You don't want all the fireworks to go off at the same time, so change the particle systems' Emit Start and Emit Stop times. For uniqueness, click the New seed button. You might also want to change the Lifespan Value Queue so that some bursts have longer trails and some shorter. Change the direction in which the particle systems are pointing to make it look more unique. You can also change the spread to produce a different look and animate the color over time to achieve a nice effect.

Fires, Glows, and Sparks

Fireworks Pinwheel

by Kim Lee

W ith this effect, you can recreate the firework displays that you see at carnivals and state fairs. In this scene, the display takes place at dusk to emphasize the lighting and glow of the effect. You will use particle systems to create the trails of sparks thrusting from each rocket of the pinwheel. Finally, you will carefully apply Lens Effects Glow and Hilight within Video Post to complete the illusion.

Note

All position and rotational information is based on absolute world coordinates. When positioning objects in your scene, always use the Transform Type-In dialog box located in the Tools menu. This ensures proper object orientation.

Leave any settings that are not listed in the example at the MAX default values.

Create the Pinwheel and Environment Objects

You will begin by creating the structure of the pinwheel and the stand that it is mounted on, as well as setting up the background and environment.

First, change the length of the animation to 200 in the Time Configuration dialog box.

Create the Wheel

1. Create a standard primitive cylinder in the Front viewport at (x = 0, y = 0, z = 0) using the following parameters:
   Radius = 88
   Height = –30
   Height Segments = 1
   Cap Segments = 2
   Sides = 12

2. Add an Edit Mesh modifier to the stack and in the Top viewport, then select the top row of vertices.

3. Press delete to delete these vertices.

4. Deselect the Sub-Object button and add a Lattice modifier to the stack. Set the following Struts parameters:
   Sides = 6
   Smooth = On

5. Rename the object **Wheel**.

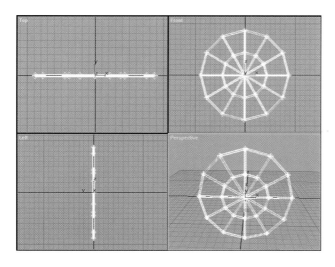

Figure 1
Creating the Wheel object.

Create the Base

1. Create a standard primitive box in the Front viewport at x = –0.483, y = 8.731, z = –109.113. Set the following parameters:
   Length = 225
   Width = 125

Height = 25
Length Segments = 4
Width Segments = 2
Height Segments = 1

2. Rename the object **Base**.

3. Add a Taper modifier to the stack with the following parameters:
Amount = −1.8
Curve = 0
Primary Taper Axis = Y
Effect = XZ

4. Add a Lattice modifier to the stack with the following Struts parameters:
Smooth = On

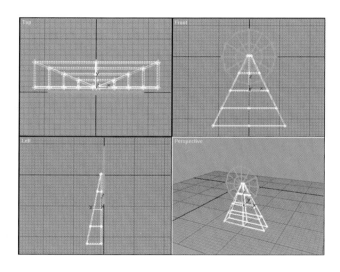

Figure 2
Adding a Lattice modifier.

Create a Firecracker

1. Create a standard primitive cylinder in the Top viewport with the following parameters:
Radius = 3
Height = 18
Height Segments = 1
Cap Segments = 1
Sides = 10

2. Rename this object **Firecracker01** and position it at
   x = −88.735, y = −7.161, z = 1.841.

3. Link the firecracker to the wheel, using the Link tool.

Create the Particle Systems

1. Create a Super Spray particle system in the Top viewport, centered on the firecracker at x = −88.735, y = −7.161, z = −9.521.

2. In the Front viewport, rotate the Super Spray emitter 180
   degrees so that it is directed downward. Link the Super Spray to
   the Wheel.

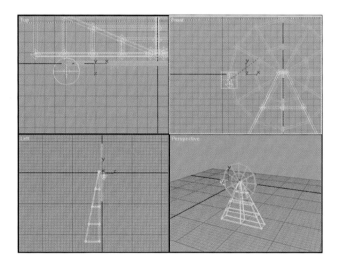

Figure 3
Linking the Super
Spray.

3. Click the Modifier tab and set the following Super Spray Basic
   Parameters:
   Off Axis Spread = 8.0
   Off Plane Spread = 180
   Viewport Display = Optionally Ticks or Mesh

4. In the Particle Generation rollout, set the following:
   Use Rate = 20
   Emit Start = 10
   Emit Stop = 200
   Display Until = 200
   Life = 20
   Variation = 3
   Size = 5.0
   Variation = 0
   Grow For = 5
   Fade For = 0

5. Set the Particle Type parameters:
Particle Type = Standard Particles
Standard Particles = Tetra

6. Set the Particle Rotation parameters:
Spin Axis Controls = Direction Of Travel/Mblur
Stretch = 0

7. Set the Object Motion Inheritance parameters:
Influence = 0

8. Select the wheel, firecracker, and Super Spray objects. Right-click any of the selected objects and select Properties from the pop-up menu. Turn on Image Motion Blur.

9. Select only the Super Spray object and right-click. Again Select Properties and turn off both Cast Shadows and Receive Shadows (see Figure 4).

10. Select the firecracker object. Change the Reference Coordinate System to Pick and click the wheel object.

Figure 4
Select the
Properties tab.

11. Change the Transform center setting to Use Transform Coordinate Center.

12. Select the Array tool. Click the arrow button on the Totals side of the Rotate label. Set the Z axis total rotation to 360 degrees. Set the following:
Array Dimensions = 1D
Count = 12
Type of Object = Instance

13. In the Top viewport, create a QuadPatch:
Length = 950
Width = 1700

14. Name the QuadPatch **Ground** and position it under the base object.

15. Create a free camera in the Front viewport and position it at x = −271.895, y = −745.413, z = 33.623. Move and rotate the Ground object so that its far edge is level with the horizon of the camera view. The absolute world coordinates for the ground are x = 219.226, y = 270.09, z = −227.963 (see Figure 5).

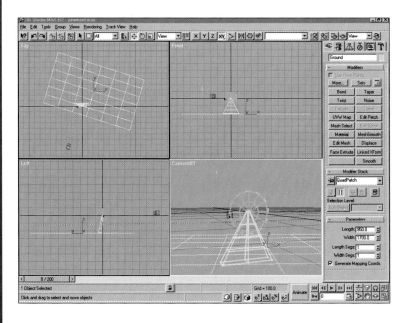

Figure 5
Creating a camera.

16. In the Front viewport, create an omni light with the following values:
Color = (R = 255, G = 253, B = 186)
Multiplier = 1.5

17. Set the Attenuation parameters:
Start/Far = 26
End/Far = 115
Use = on
Cast Shadows = checked

18. Position the light near Superspray01, at x = −87.465, y = −13.819, z = −20.671).

19. Turn Animate on and at Frame 20, set a key for the omni light's color value (V) of 255. Advance to Frame 10 and animate the light's color value to 0.

20. Turn Animate off and link the light to the wheel object.

21. Select the omni light object. Change the Reference Coordinate System to wheel. Change the Transform center setting to Use Transform Coordinate Center.

22. Select the Array tool. Click on the arrow button on the Totals side of the Rotate label. Set the Z axis total rotation to 360 degrees. Set the following:
Array Dimensions = 1D
Count = 12
Type of Object = Instance

23. Create a target spotlight in the Left viewport, directed down toward the pinwheel. The spotlight should be at absolute world coordinates (0, −338.549, 183.134) and the target should be at (0, 143.987, −242.152). Set the following:
Color = (R = 180, G = 180, B = 180, V = 180)
Hotspot = 60
Falloff = 90
Cast Shadows = on
Use Shadow Maps = on
Size = 1024

24. Open the Track view and right click on the filters button. Select Selected Objects Only from the list. Open the Object tracks for Spot01 and select the Multiplier track.

25. Click on the assign controller button and select Float List.

26. Open the Multiplier track and select the track labeled Available. Click on the assign controller button and select Noise Float.

27. Select the new track labeled Available which appears below the Noise Float track. Click on the assign controller button and select bezier Float.

28. Press the Function curves button and select the Noise Float track. Right click on the label Noise Float and select properties. Use the following parameters:
Seed = 1
Frequency = 1.0
Strength = 0.289
>0 = checked
Ramp In = 10

29. Select the bezier Float track and create keys at the following frames with the corresponding values:
Frame 10: Value = 0
Frame 25: Value = 0.914
Frame 200: Value = 0.914

30. Close the Track View.

Fires, Glows, and Sparks

At this point all of the geometry is in place as well as the environmental elements.

Animate the Scene

Now you will animate the actual wheel as well as the particle systems. You will also clone the particles after animating them in order to avoid the repetitious task of animating each one individually.

1. Select the wheel object. Advance to frame 20 and right-click the time slider. Select only rotation from the Create Key dialog box and click OK.

2. Turn Animate on and advance to frame 100. Turn on angle snap and rotate the wheel 180 degrees clockwise around the z local axis.

3. Advance to frame 200 and rotate the wheel 360 degrees clockwise around the z local axis.

4. Select SuperSpray01 and go to the Particle Generation rollout in the Modify command panel. Go to frame 20 and change Speed to 5.

5. Turn off Animate and go to frame 0.

6. Select the Super Spray object. Change the Reference Coordinate System to wheel. Change the Transform center setting to Use Transform Coordinate Center.

7. Select the Array tool. Click the arrow button on the Totals side of the Rotate label. Set the Z axis total rotation to 360 degrees. Set the following:
   Array Dimensions = 1D
   Count = 12
   Type of Object = Copy

You are now finished building the scene and adding animation.

Creating Materials

Now you will create materials and apply them to the objects.

Wheel and Base Materials

1. In the Material Editor select an empty slot and click Get Material.

2. In the Material/Map Browser, choose Mtl Library to browse from and select Brushed Metal.

3. Apply Brushed Metal to both Wheel and Base objects.

Firecracker Material

1. In the Material Editor, select an empty slot and rename it **Firecracker**.

2. Click the Diffuse slot button and set the Map Type to Bitmap. Click Bitmap and select Fcracker.tga.

3. Apply this material to all 12 of the Firecracker objects (see Figure 6).

Ground Material

1. In the Material Editor, select an empty slot and rename it **Ground**.

2. Click the Diffuse slot button and choose Map Type Bitmap.

3. Click the Bitmap button and select gravel.jpg. Set the following:
   U Tiling = 1.7
   V Tiling = 2.0

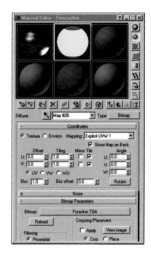

Figure 6
Applying the material.

4. Go to the parent level of the Ground material and copy the diffuse map to the bump map slot. Set the bump amount to 73.

5. Apply the Ground material to the Ground object.

Fireworks Material

1. In the Material Editor, select an empty slot and rename it **Fireworks**.

2. Click the Diffuse slot button and set the Map Type to Particle Age.

3. Set the Particle Age colors as follows:
   Color #1: Age = 10, Color = (R = 255, G = 255, B = 255)
   Color #2: Age = 30, Color = (R = 255, G = 246, B = 0)
   Color #3: Age = 70, Color = (R = 255, G = 120, B = 0)

4. Go to the parent level of the material and set the following:
   Material Effects Channel = 1
   Self-Illumination = 100

5. Apply the Fireworks material to all 12 Super Spray objects.

Background Environment

1. Select Environment from the Rendering drop-down menu.

2. Click Environment Map and choose Map Type Bitmap.

3. Drag and instance copy the Environment Map button to an empty slot in the Material Editor.

4. Rename the material **Background**.

5. Set Mapping to Screen and select Sunset.tga as the bitmap. Set the V offset to 0.3, which will align the distant mountains just over the edge of our ground plane.

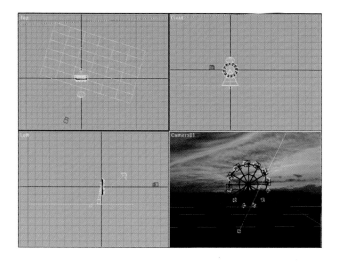

Figure 7
Aligning the mountains.

The effect is almost complete. You have all of your geometry, materials, and animation set.

Apply Video Post Effects

In this section, you will apply the glow and highlight effects to put the finishing touch on your animation.

1. Select Video Post from the Rendering drop-down menu.

2. Click Add Scene Event, select the Camera01 view, and click OK.

Add the Glow Effect

1. Deselect all entries, click Add Image Filter Event, and choose Lens Effects Glow from the drop-down menu. Click OK.

2. Double click the Lens Effects Glow entry in Video Post and click Setup.

3. In the Properties tab, set the following:
Source = Material ID 1
Filter: Hue = checked, All = unchecked

4. Click the color swatch next to Hue set the following:
Color = (R = 250 G = 241 B = 0)
Variance = 20

5. In the Preferences tab, set the following:
Size = 1
Color = Gradient

6. In the Gradients tab, double-click the right-most slider on the Radial Color gradient. Set the following:
Color = (R = 255 G = 246 B = 0)

7. In the Radial Transparency gradient, drag a new slider to position 69 and set all of the color values to 4.

8. Go to Frame 36 and click VP Queue and Preview to view the effect. Click OK (see Figure 8).

Figure 8
Preview the effect.

Add the Highlight Effect

1. Deselect all entries, click the Add Image Filter Event button, and choose Lens Effects Hilight from the drop-down menu. Click OK.

2. Double-click the Lens Effects Hilight entry in Video Post and click Setup.

3. In the Properties tab, set the following:
Source = Material ID 1
Filter: Edge = unchecked, Bright = checked, Bright Value = 224

4. In the Preferences tab, set the following:
Size = 7
Color = Pixel

5. Click VP Queue and Preview to view the effect. Click OK (see Figure 9).

6. Click Add Image Output Event. Click Files and name the output file **pinwheel.avi**.

7. Click Execute Sequence and set the output size to 320×240.

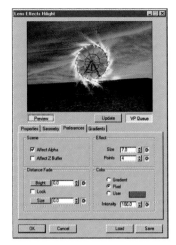

Figure 9
Preview the effect.

Note that the Lens Effects Glow and Hilight results are strongly dependent on the rendering resolution that you use. The settings used to create the 320×240 Avi are significantly different than those used for a 1024×768 resolution rendering. Due to the limited preview size available within the interface of each effect, I found it necessary to do full-size renders as part of the tweaking phase of developing this effect for anything over 320×240 because many of the parameters for these effects are based on pixels (such as glow size). Therefore, a Glow with Size of 10 affects a larger portion of a 320×240 frame than a 1024×768 frame. It is a good idea to use the preview window as a rough sketch of the final effect and depend only on full-frame test renders when working with any Lens Effects.

You can find the final MAX file, pinwheel.max, in this project's Scene folder and the final AVI file in the Images folder.

Rocket Engine Glow

by Jay Kapadia

By combining Video Post and Combustion, you can create a believable animation of an engine firing up. In the Lens Effects Glow, you use Inferno to add noise to the glow, creating a heat distortion effect. You create the flame coming from the back of the engine by using Combustion. By playing around with the Inferno and Combustion parameters, you can make an ordinary engine look very powerful.

Note

All position and rotational information is based on absolute world coordinates. When creating objects, use keyboard entry where possible. When positioning objects, use the Transform Type-In dialog box located in the Tools menu. These techniques ensure proper object placement and orientation.

Leave any settings that are not listed in the example at the MAX default values.

Preconfiguration

1. Before beginning this effect, either reset *or* restart MAX.

2. Copy this project's map files from the accompanying CD-ROM to the MAX maps subdirectory.

3. Load the Glow.max file from this project's Preload folder on the accompanying CD-ROM.

At this point, you should see a scene containing a spaceship and a ramp. The animation is preset to 60 frames.

Objects and Materials

In this section, you create the engine glow for the scene (see Figure 1).

1. In the Front viewport, create a Hemisphere:
   Radius = 30
   Segments = 20

2. Name it **engine glow01**.

3. In the Left viewport, select Non–Uniform Scale and scale the object to 16% on the x-axis. Rotate it on the z-axis –20 degrees and place it at x = 0.53, y= 5.42, z = –75.85.

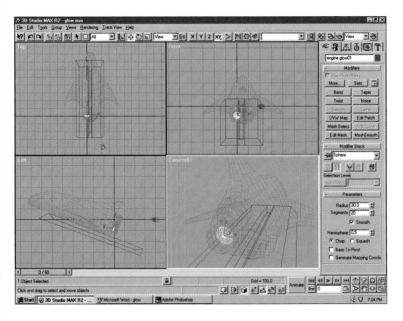

Figure 1
The final position of object engine glow01.

4. Copy the object two more times and position them inside the other two engines. Place object engine glow02 at x = 97.03, y = 5.42, z = –75.85. Place object engine glow03 at x = 49.27, y = –22.80, z = 1.68.

5. Select all three engine glows and then open the Material Editor. Activate slot 1 and set the Basic Parameters:
   Ambient = (R = 255, G = 0, B = 0)
   Diffuse = (R = 255, G = 166, B = 0)
   Specular = (R = 255, G = 255, B = 0)

Self–Illumination = 50
Material Effects Channel = 1

6. Name the material **engine glow**.

7. Apply the material engine glow to all three objects.

At this point, when you render your scene, you see hot spots in the center of all three engines.

Lighting Setup

In this section, you use an omni light to light up the back of the ship when the engines fire (see Figure 2).

1. Create an omni light and position it between all three engines at x = 44.75, y = –59.88, z = –70.21. Set the following:
Color = (R = 0, G = 0, B = 0)
Multiplier = 2.5

2. In the Attenuation section of the General Parameters rollout, set the following:
End Far = 200
Start Far = 80
Far Use = checked

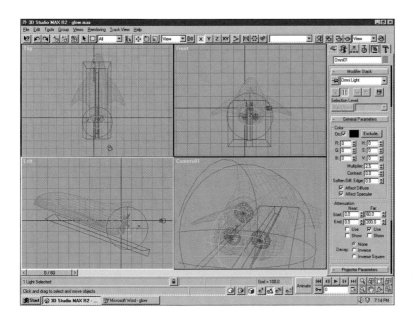

Figure 2
The position of Omni01.

Animating the Flames and Light

In this section, you use Combustion to create the flames and animate Omni01 (see Figure 3).

1. In the Front viewport, create an atmospheric apparatus helper SphereGizmo:
   Radius = 40
   Hemisphere = selected

2. In the Left viewport, select Non-Uniform Scale and scale it to 46% on the x-axis. Rotate it on the z-axis −20 degrees and place it at x = −0.32, y = −17.62, z = −83.81. Click the New Seed button.

3. Switch to the local coordinate system. Turn Animate on and advance to Frame 35. Scale SphereGizmo01 on the z-axis 1766% and turn Animate off.

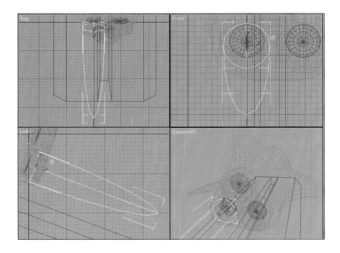

Figure 3
The scaling of
SphereGizmo01.

4. Return to Frame 0. Clone the SphereGizmo01 twice and position them behind each engine. Place SphereGizmo02 at x = 97.11, y = −17.62, z = −83.81. Place SphereGizmo03 at x = 49.35, y = −45.85, z = −6.27.

5. Open up a Track View and select SphereGizmo01, SphereGizmo02, and SphereGizmo03.

6. Move the keys from Frame 0 to Frame 30.

7. While still in the Track View, select Omni01, Object (Omni Light), Color (see Figure 4).

8. Create keys at Frame 20 and Frame 35:
   Frame 20 = (R = 0, G = 0, B = 0)
   Frame 35 = (R = 255, G = 255, B = 0)

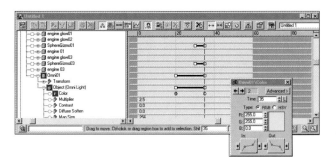

Figure 4
The Track View for
Omni01.

9. Open the Environment dialog box. Click Add and choose
   Combustion.

10. Click the Pick Gizmo button and choose SphereGizmo01. Click
    the Pick Gizmo button again and choose SphereGizmo02. Click
    the Pick Gizmo button a third time and choose SphereGizmo03.
    Set the following Combustion Parameters:
    Flame Type = Tendril
    Density = 0

11. Open Track View and choose Environment, Combustion.

12. Choose Density and create keys at Frame 30 and Frame 35. Set
    the following:
    Frame 30 = 0
    Frame 35 = 10

13. Choose Phase and create keys at Frame 0 and Frame 60. Set the
    following:
    Frame 0 = 0
    Frame 60 = 30

14. Copy the keys from Phase track and paste them into Drift track.

At this point, the effect is basically done. Fire obviously gives off light, so
as the combustion appears, Omni01 lights up the back of the ship.

Creating Glows in Video Post

In this section, you use Lens Effects Glow to make the engines look
extremely hot and cause heat distortion.

**Fires, Glows, and
Sparks**

1. Click Scene Event and select Camera01.

2. Create glowing engines by clicking Add Image Filter Event and choosing Lens Effects Glows.

3. Click Setup and when the dialog box appears, click the Preview button and then the VP Queue button. Next, click the Properties tab. In the Source box, select Material ID. The Material ID default is 1 and that is the Material Effects Channel for Material engine glow (see Figure 5).

4. Click the Preferences tab. In the Effect box, set Size to 10.

5. In the Color section, set the following:
   User = selected
   Color = (R = 255, G = 162, B = 0)
   Intensity = 10

6. Click the Inferno tab, and set the following:
   Red = checked
   Green = checked
   Blue = checked
   Fiery = selected

Figure 5
The Properties menu in Video Post.

7. Click Reseed. This adds a slight glow to the core of the engine and noise, which will look like heat distortion.

Animating the Glow

Now you animate the glow of the engine firing up in Track View.

1. In Track View, select Video Post, Lens Effects Glow, Size (see Figure 6).

2. Create keys at Frame 0 and Frame 30:
   Frame 0 = 0
   Frame 30 = 10

3. Copy the keys from Size and paste them in Intensity.

Figure 6
The keys for the
Video Post.

Now you're all set to render through Video Post to see what a glow can
do to intensify a scene. If you play with the Inferno settings, you can create incredible effects. The final MAX file, FinalGlow.max, is in this project's Scene folder on the CD-ROM.

Candle Flame with Wax Translucency

by Greg Carbonaro

Yºou can easily achieve believable raytraced object translucency with the proper materials. A wax candle complete with flame creates the necessary backdrop to illustrate this technique. First, you create a dancing flame animation with the use of a fractal noise and then synchronize the motion of the various lights to create moving shadows and translucency gradations through the candle object.

Note

All position and rotational information is based on absolute world coordinates. When creating objects, use keyboard entry when possible. When positioning objects, use the Transform Type-In dialog box located in the Tools menu. These techniques ensure proper object placement and orientation.

Leave any settings that are not listed in the example at the MAX default values. Create objects in the Top viewport, unless otherwise indicated.

Preconfiguration

1. Before beginning this effect, please reset *or* restart MAX.

2. Copy the Candle Flame project map files from the accompanying CD-ROM to your MAX maps subdirectory.

3. Set the animation length to 100 frames.

4. Open the Material Editor. Right-click in any material slot and make sure Sample Windows are set to 3×2.

Modeling and Materials

Candle Object Creation

1. Activate the Top viewport.

2. Create a standard primitive cylinder roughly in the center and use the Transform Type-In dialog box to position it at x = 0, y = 0, z = 0. Set the following:
Height = 7
Radius = 2

3. Set the Object properties:
Receive Shadows = Off

4. Click the Edit Stack button and choose Convert to NURBS Surface from the menu that appears (see Figure 1).

5. In the Modifier Stack, set Sub-Object to Surface CV. Emulate a melted/dripped wax candle by selecting and pulling control vertices around the top circumference of the candle. Indent and form the flame "pocket" by selecting the top center vertices and pulling downward (see Figure 2).

Figure 1
Converting standard cylinder geometry into a NURBS object.

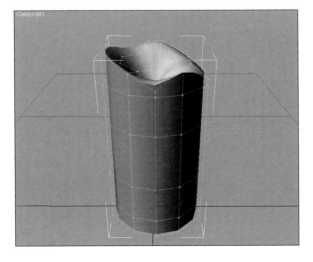

Figure 2
Sculpting the top of the candle object by pulling control points.

6. Add a UVW map = cylindrical.

7. Name the object **Candle**.

Candle Material

1. In the Material Editor, make material slot 1 active.

2. Set the Material Type to **Raytrace** material.

3. Set the Basic Parameters as follows:

   Diffuse = (R = 253, G = 177, B = 96)
   Specular Color = (R = 254, G = 213, B = 131)
   Shininess = 51
   Shin. Strength = 131

4. In the Basic Parameters area, turn on the Bump check box and set the amount to 999. Click on its Map slot next to the amount and set it to Bitmap. Use the Candlebump.bmp as the Map (see Figure 3).

5. In the Maps area click the Translucency map slot and set the Map Type to Gradient. On the Gradient level set the following:
   Color1 = (R = 252, G = 184, B = 0)
   Color2 = (R = 128, G =128, B = 128)

6. Name the material **Wax**.

7. Apply the Wax material to the Candle object.

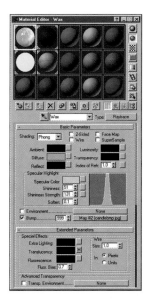

Figure 3
The location of the Bump channel is different in a Raytrace material.

Wick Object Creation

1. Activate the Top viewport.

2. Create a standard primitive cylinder roughly in the center of the flame pocket and then use the Transform Type-In to position it exactly at x = 0, y = 0, z = 5.897. Set the following:
   Height = 1
   Radius = 0.05
   Height Segments = 4

3. Add a Bend modifier:
Angle = 20.5 degrees

4. Name the object **Wick**.

Wick Material

1. In the Material Editor, make material slot 2 active and set the Material Type to Standard.

2. Set the Basic Parameters as follows:
Ambient = (R = 45, G = 45, B = 45)
Diffuse = (R = 45, G = 45, B = 45)

3. Name the material **Burnt**.

4. Apply the Burnt material to the Wick object (see Figure 4).

Flame Object Creation

Now you are going to create the basis of the Flame object with a closed spline.

1. Activate the Front viewport.

Figure 4
Creating the wick and the burnt material to apply to it.

2. Create a closed Spline with 7 vertices near the end of the Wick object. Make it in the roughly in the shape of a flame.

3. Add an Edit Spline modifier and fine tune the points so it looks flame-like.

4. Now we are going to smooth out the straight lines and sharp vertices of the flame spline. Go to the splines Modifier Stack, click the Sub-Ojects drop-down list, and select the Spline Sub-Object level.

5. Right-Click the Flame object and select Curve.

6. To fine-tune the flame shape, you can go back to the Sub-Object Vertex level and move vertices around.

7. Now use the Transform Type-In to position the flame precisely at x = 0.202, y = 0, z = 7.522 (see Figure 5).

8. Name the spline object **Flame**.

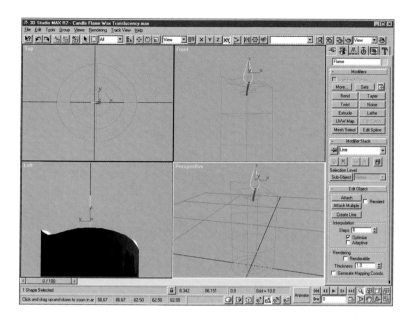

Figure 5
Flame shape after a
Sub-object spline
level curve is
applied.

Now you will complete the flame animation.

Flame Animation Technique

You will impart a realistic animation to the flame simply by adding a
Noise modifier to its vertices.

Flame Animation

1. Activate the Front viewport.

2. Select the Flame, go to the Modifier Stack, and Select Sub-
   Object Vertex level.

3. Select all the vertices except the one vertex at the base of the
   flame and Add a Noise modifier:
   Strength = (x = 0.5, y = 0.5, z = 0.5)
   Fractal = on
   Animate Noise = on

4. Turn off the Sub-Object button.

5. Add an Extrude modifier to the Flame spline to make it a 3D
   object:
   Amount = 0.5

Flame Material

1. In the Material Editor, make material slot 4 active and set the Material Type to Standard.

2. Set the Basic Parameters as follows:
   Ambient = (R = 16, G = 40, B = 46)
   Diffuse = (R = 255, G = 223, B = 49)
   Shininess = 0
   Shin. Strength = 0
   Self-Illumination = 100

3. Set the following:
   Material Effects Channel = 1

4. Name the material **Hot** (see Figure 6).

5. Apply the Hot material to the Flame object.

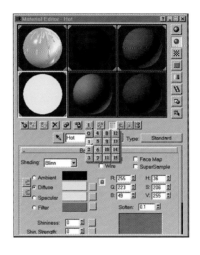

Figure 6
Assign the material to Material Effects Channel 1 so you can make it glow in Video Post.

Now the candle, wick, and flame animation are complete. At the end, you will add the flame glow.

Lighting Setup

In this section, you will add the lighting effects for the scene.

1. Create an omni light roughly centered over the flame and then use the Transform Type-In dialog box to position it precisely at x = 0.19, y = 0, z = 11.286. Set the following:
   Color = (R = 250, G = 233, B = 180)
   Multiplier = 1.15
   Attenuation = Use
   Far Start = 3
   Far End = 17
   Cast Shadows = On

2. Add a Noise modifier to the omni:
   Fractal = On
   Strength = (x = 1, y = 1, z = 1.5)
   Animate Noise = On

Note

Adding a Noise modifier to an omni light causes it to move around. This movement simulates the natural movement a real flame might have.

3. Name the omni light **ShadowLight**.

4. Create an omni light roughly centered on the flame. Then use the Transform Type-In to position it precisely at x = 0.19, y = 0, z = 7.35. Set the following:
   Color = (R = 250, G = 233, B = 180)
   Multiplier = 0.5
   Attenuation = Use
   Far Start = 2
   Far End = 5
   Cast Shadows = On

5. Add a Noise modifier to the omni light:
   Fractal = On
   Roughness = 0.2
   Strength = (x = 1, y = 1, z = 1)
   Animate Noise = On

6. Name the omni light **FlameLight**.

7. Create an omni light roughly centered above and in front of the flame then use the Transform Type-In dialog box to position it precisely at x = 0.155, y = −12.6, z= 14.521. Set the following:
   Color = (R = 250, G = 233, B = 180)
   Multiplier = 0.3
   Cast Shadows = Off

8. Click the Exclude button and select Both (Shadow Casting and Illumination). Select all objects for exclusion except Plate.

9. Name the omni light **RoomLight**.

You have just added 3 omni lights which should all appear in your scene in a vertical line stacked on and above the candle flame.

Camera Setup

Next you set up the camera through which you will view the final effect.

1. Create a target camera at x = 4.17, y = −17.56, z = 10.59. Position the target at x = 0.37, y = −2.55, z = 5.18.

2. Change the perspective to your Camera viewport and turn on Smooth and Highlight Shading.

Fires, Glows, and Sparks

Environment

1. Merge the Wall background into the scene by using the Merge command located in the File drop-down menu. The file Wall.max can be found in the project pre-load directory on the accompanying CD-ROM.

Adding Glows in Video Post

Now you will use Video Post LensFX to generate a nice flame glow.

1. In the Rendering drop-down menu, select Video Post.

2. Add a scene event and select the Camera viewport.

3. Add an Image Filter event and select LensFX Glow from the drop-down list.

4. Set the glow properties:
   Source = Material ID#1
   Filter = All

5. Set the Glow preferences:
   Effect Size = 20
   Color = Pixel
   Intensity = 60

6. Add an image output event and set it to AVI by using the Autodesk RLE compressor codec (see Figure 7).

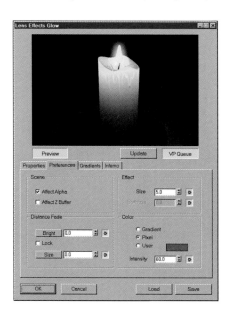

Figure 7
A convincing glow is added to the candle flame in Video Post as a finishing touch.

To generate the desired results, you must render from within Video Post. I have found that because of the subtle raytraced translucency of the wax candle, the only AVI codec that does this animation justice is the AutoDesk RLE compressor. All of the other AVI codecs produce very bad color banding.

You can find the final MAX file, CandleFlame.max, in this project's Scene folder and the AVI file in the Images folder.

Black Billowing Smoke

by Greg Carbonaro

Black billowing smoke is one of the most dramatic elements of convincing fatal damage. Whereas white or gray smoke usually indicates minor damage, black smoke is an undeniable sign that the damage is complete and final. You achieve the drama of this effect with a particle system and a specially designed black smoke material.

Note

All position and rotational information is based on absolute world coordinates. When creating objects, use keyboard entry where possible. When positioning objects, use the Transform Type-In dialog box located in the Tools menu. These techniques ensure proper object placement and orientation.

Leave any settings that are not listed in the example at the MAX default values. Create objects in the Top viewport, unless otherwise indicated.

Preconfiguration

1. Before beginning this effect, either reset *or* restart MAX.

2. Copy the Billowing Smoke project map files from the accompanying CD-ROM to the MAX maps subdirectory.

3. Load the Clouds.max file from this project's Preload folder on the CD-ROM. This file consists of a box mapped with a cloud texture map that you can use as the scene background. The animation length is already set to 300.

4. Open the Materials Editor, right-click in any material slot, and make sure Sample Windows is set to 3×2.

Environment Setup

In this section, you add a volumetric fog to the scene to help provide the illusion of depth in the scene (see Figure 1).

1. Create an atmospheric apparatus helper BoxGizmo at x = 543, y = 1801, z = −103. Set the following:
   Length = 1000
   Width = 3500
   Height = 200

2. Name the BoxGizmo **Falloff**.

3. In Rendering/Environment, add a Volume Fog effect. Set the following parameters:
   Gizmos: Pick Gizmo = Falloff, Soften Gizmo Edges = 1
   Volume: Color = (R = 115, G = 149, B = 223), Density = 2
   Noise: Uniformity = 1, Size = 1

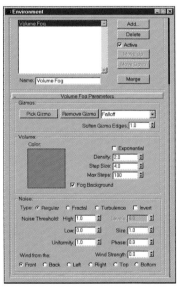

At this point, the scene consists of the volumetric fog located beneath the background box.

Modeling and Materials

Note

An atmospheric apparatus with volume fog was used to create camera distance cue because standard camera distance cue techniques interfere with smoky materials.

Figure 1
The volume fog settings for the distance cue.

In this section, you create the ground object and material. Noise is used both in the object and material definitions to provide the randomness found in nature.

Ground Object Creation

1. Create a QuadPatch at x = 394, y= 1015, z = 0. Set the following:
   Length = 2500
   Width = 2500
   Length Segments = 10
   Width Segments = 10
   Generate Mapping Coords. = on

2. Name the object **Ground**.

3. In the Modify panel, add a Noise modifier to object Ground. Set the following parameters (see Figure 2):
   Seed = 45324
   Scale = 10
   Fractal = on
   Roughness = 0.15
   Strength = (x = 0, y = 0, z = 35)

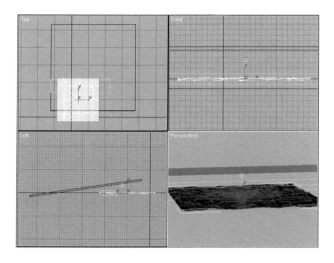

Figure 2
The noise-modified Ground object positioned in the scene.

Ground Material

1. In the Material Editor, make material slot 1 active and set the Material Type to Standard.

2. Set the Basic Parameters as follows:
   Ambient = (R = 158, G = 148, B = 129)
   Diffuse = (R = 235, G = 226, B = 205)
   Specular = (R = 246, G = 242, B = 232)
   Self-Illumination = 25

3. Set the Amount for the Diffuse slot to 100. Click the Diffuse slot and set the Map Type to Noise.

4. Set the following Noise parameters:
   Noise Type = Fractal
   Size = 1
   Color #1 =(R = 149, G = 143, B = 133)
   Color #2 =(R = 235, G = 226, B = 205)

5. Set the Amount for the Bump slot to 20. Click the Bump slot and set the Map Type to Noise.

6. Set the Noise parameters:
Noise Type = Turbulence
Size = 75
Color #1 =(R = 149, G = 143, B = 133)
Color #2 =(R = 235, G = 226, B = 205)

7. Name the material **Sand**.

8. Apply the Sand material to the Ground object (see Figure 3).

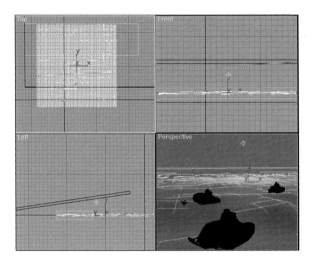

Figure 3
The scene with the Sand material applied to the Ground object.

At this point, the scene consists of the texture mapped Ground object located partially within the volumetric fog and both located beneath the background box.

Animation

In this section, you create a particle system and a material to model the smoke. You also add the geometry for three tanks to the scene.

Smoke Particle System Creation

1. Create a Spray particle system near the lower-left corner of the Ground object. Use the Transform Type-In dialog box to position the particle system at x = –2.8, y = –17.6, z = 37.7. Set the rotation to x = 0, y = 180, z = 0. Set the following parameters (see Figure 4):
Render Count = 1500
Drop Size = 12
Speed = 5
Variation =1.75
Particles = Drops
Render = Facing

Life = 301
Emitter: Width = 8, Length = 8

2. Name the Spray **Smoke Particles**.

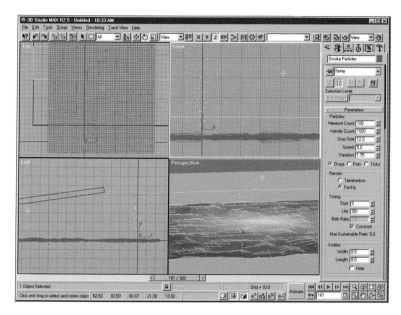

Figure 4
The Smoke Particles object positioned in the scene and its parameters.

Smoke Particle System Material

1. In the Material Editor, make material slot 2 active and set the Material Type to Standard.

2. Set the following Basic Parameters:
   Filter = (R = 60, G = 60, B = 60)
   Self-Illumination = 25

3. Set the Amount for the Diffuse slot to 100. Click the Diffuse slot and set the Map Type to Noise.

4. Set the following Noise parameters:
   Noise Type = Fractal
   Size = 20

5. Set the Amount for the Opacity slot to 100. Click the Opacity slot and set the Map Type to Mask.

6. In the Mask map, click the Map slot and set the Map Type to Noise. Set the following Noise parameters:
   Noise Type = Fractal
   Size = 25

7. Return to the Mask map, click the Mask slot, and set the Map Type to Gradient. Set the following Gradient parameters: **Gradient Type** = Radial

8. Swap Color #1 with Color #3.

9. Name the material **Smoke**.

10. Apply the Smoke material to the Smoke Particles object.

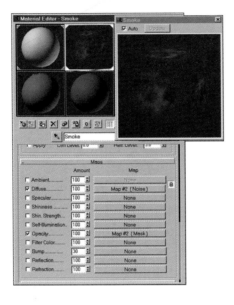

Figure 5
Creating a smoky material.

Tank Object

1. Using File/Merge, load file FT17-BER.max into the scene from the project's Preload directory on the accompanying CD-ROM.

2. In the Merge dialog box, select all three objects to merge. This loads three tank objects into the scene.

At this point, the scene consists of three tanks positioned on the Ground object. The Smoke particle system originates within one of the tanks.

Lighting Setup

In this section, you create the lighting effects for the scene.

1. Create an omni light below the Ground object. Use the Transform Type-In dialog box to position the light at x = 168, y = –604, z = 127. Set the following parameters:
Color = (R = 180, G = 180, B = 180)
Multiplier = 1.5

2. Click the Exclude button and select Illumination. Select Smoke Particles for exclusion.

3. Name the omni light **Front Light**.

4. Create an omni light to the left of the center tank. Use the Transform Type-In dialog box to position the light at x = –365, y = 260, z = 427. Set the following parameters:
   Color = (R = 180, G = 180, B = 180)
   Multiplier = 1.25
   Cast Shadows = on

5. Click the Exclude button and select Illumination. Select Smoke Particles for exclusion.

6. Name the omni light **Sun Light**.

7. Create an omni light to the left of Front Light at x = –191, y = –640, z = 127. Set the following parameters:
   Color = (R = 180, G = 180, B = 180)
   Multiplier = 0.4

8. Click the Exclude button and select Both (Illumination and Shadow Casting). Select FT17-BER for exclusion.

9. Name the omni light **Smoke Light**.

At this point, the scene consists of three tanks positioned on the Ground object, smoke coming from one of the tanks, and lighting for the scene (see Figure 6).

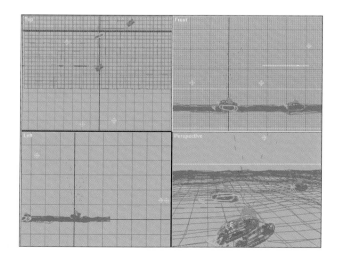

Figure 6
The placement of lights in the scene.

Camera Setup

The final step is to set up the camera through which you can view the finished effect.

1. Create a target camera with the camera body at the bottom center of the Ground object and the target at the lowest tank. Position the camera at x = −55.62, y = −264.26, z = 120.11. Position the target at x = −17.4, y = −87.21, z = 93.49.

You can find the final MAX file, BlackBillowingSmoke.max, in this project's Scene folder on the CD-ROM (see Figure 7).

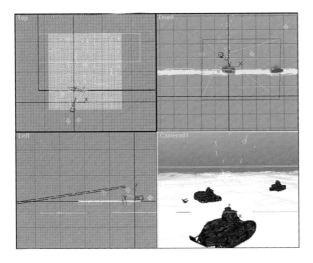

Figure 7
Completed Black Billowing Smoke sequence.

Rocket Smoke Trail

by Greg Carbonaro

Particle systems combined with the right materials can easily reproduce jet engine thrust as well as the unique smoke trail generated
by solid fuel burning rockets. Creating a realistic look by using particle
systems with moving projectiles includes some unique challenges.

Note

*All position and rota-
tional information is
based on absolute
world coordinates.
When creating
objects, use keyboard
entry when possible.
When positioning
objects, use the
Transform Type-In
dialog box located in
the Tools menu. These
techniques ensure
proper object place-
ment and orientation.*

Leave any settings that are not listed in the example at the MAX default
values. Create objects in the Top viewport, unless otherwise indicated.

Preconfiguration

1. Before beginning this effect, please either reset *or* restart MAX.

2. Copy the Rocket Smoke project map files from the accompanying CD-ROM to the MAX maps subdirectory.

3. Load the Jet.max file from this project's Preload subdirectory on
   the CD-ROM. The animation length has been preset to 300
   frames.

4. Open the Material Editor. Right-click in any material slot and
   make sure Sample Windows are set to 5×3.

Once the file is loaded, you will see a jet in your camera viewport. If you move your Time Slider, the jet flies past the camera.

Environment Setup

You are now going to set up some simple environmental elements.

1. In the Rendering drop-down menu, click Environment to open the Environment dialog and set the Global Lighting:
   Ambient = (R = 77, G = 77, B = 77)

2. Add an atmosphere fog effect:
   Color = (R = 217, G = 244, B = 255)
   Fog Background = On
   Type: Standard = On

Particle System Animation and Materials

In the next few steps, you will create the particle system that will produce the jet's thrust.

Jet Engine Thrust

1. Set the Time Slider to Frame 230. Activate the Left viewport and zoom into the jet so you can see the back of the engine exhaust (see Figure 1).

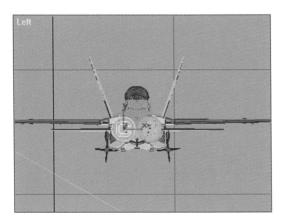

Figure 1
Zoom in to the back of the jet so you can position the particle emitters.

2. Still working in the Left viewport, create a PCloud roughly centered over the left engine exhaust, then use the Transform Type-In to position it precisely at x = −213, y = −5.5, z = 15.5. Set the following:

Particle Formation = Cylinder Emitter
Display Icon: Rad/Len = 1.4, Height = 0.5
Percentage of Particles = 10%
Particle Generation Quantity: Use Rate =15
Particle Motion: Speed = 10, Variation = 25%
Enter Vector: (x = 0, y = 0, z = 1), Variation = 2%
Particle Timing: Emit Stop = 300, Display Until = 300, Life = 8, Variation = 5
Particle Size: Size = 2, Variation = 40%, Grow For = 1
Particle Type: Standard Particles = Facing

3. Name the PCloud **JetThrust01**.

4. Copy JetThrust01 to a position roughly centered over the right engine exhaust, then use the Transform Type-In dialog box to position it precisely at x = −213, y = −7.5, z = 15.

5. Name the PCloud copy **JetThrust02** and set the following in the Particle Timing section of the Particle Generation rollout:
Emit Start = 8

6. Link both JetThrust01 and JetThrust02 to the Jet object (see Figure 2).

Thrust Material

1. In the Material Editor, make material slot 1 active and set the Material Type to Standard.

Figure 2
Creation of the two PCloud jet engines.

2. Set the Basic Parameters:
Ambient = (R = 0, G = 0, B = 0)
Diffuse = (R = 255, G = 255, B = 255)
Face Map = on
Self-Illumination = 25

3. Set the Extended parameters:
Opacity Falloff = 85

Smoke and Steam

4. Set the amount for the Diffuse map slot to 50. Click the Diffuse map slot and set the Map Type to Noise. Set the Noise Parameters:
Noise Type = Regular
Size = 2.5
Swap Color#1 with Color#2

5. Go back up to the Parent level of the material. Click the Opacity slot and set the Map Type to Mask. On the Mask level of the material, click the Map slot and set the Map Type to Noise.

6. On the Noise level Set the Noise parameters as follows:
Noise Type = Regular
Size = 2.5
Swap Color #1 with Color #2

7. Go back up to the Mask level of the material. Click the Mask slot and set the Map Type to Gradient. On the Gradient level, set the Gradient parameters as follows:
Gradient Type = Radial
Swap Color #1 with Color #3

8. Go back up to the parent level of the material and Name the material **SmokeJet**.

9. Apply the SmokeJet material to the JetThrust01 and JetThrust02.

Rocket Smoke Trail

Now create the particle emitter that will produce the rocket's smoke trail.

1. Set the Time Slider to Frame 125. Activate the Left viewport and zoom into the jet so you can see the back of the left wing's rocket exhaust (see Figure 3).

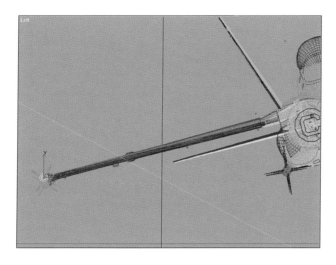

Figure 3
Zoom in to the
back of the left
rocket so you can
position the parti-
cle emitter.

2. Create a PCloud at x = –211, y = 5.5, z = 19.3. Set the
   following:
   Particle Formation = Cylinder Emitter
   Display Icon: Rad/Len = 0.35, Height = 0.5
   Percentage of Particles = 10%
   Particle Generation Quantity: Use Rate = 25
   Particle Motion: Speed = 5, Variation = 25%
   Enter Vector: (x = 0, y = 0, z = 1), Variation = 1%
   Particle Timing: Emit Start = 152, Emit Stop = 300, Display
   Until = 300
   Life = 148
   Variation = 10
   Particle Size: Size = 10, Variation = 25%, Grow For = 40
   Particle Type: Standard Particles = Facing
   Object Motion Inheritance: Influence = 50%,
   Multiplier = 0.913

3. Name the PCloud **RocketThrust**.

4. Link the RocketThrust PCloud to the Jet object.

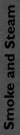

Smoke and Steam

Rocket Thrust Material

1. In the Material Editor, make material slot 3 active and set the Material Type to Standard.

2. Set the Basic Parameters as follows:
Ambient = (R = 0, G = 0, B = 0)
Diffuse = (R = 255, G = 255, B = 255)
Filter = (R = 75, G = 75, B = 75)
Face Map = On
Self-Illumination = 0

3. Under Extended Parameters, animate Opacity Falloff:
Frame 0 (Keyframe 1) Opacity = 0
     IN tangent and OUT tangent = linear
Frame 152 (KeyFrame 2) Opacity = 0
     IN tangent and OUT tangent = linear
Frame 225 (Keyframe 3) Opacity = 97
     IN tangent = slow, OUT tangent = linear
Frame 300 (Keyframe 4) Opacity = 97
     IN tangent and OUT tangent = linear

> **Note**
>
> *The best way to set these animation values is to use the Track View.*

4. Set the Amount for the Diffuse map slot to 85. Click the Diffuse map slot and set the Map Type to Noise. Set the Noise parameters:
Noise Type = Fractal
Size = 2
Swap Color #1 with Color #2

5. Go back up to the parent level of the material. Click the Opacity map slot and set the Map Type to Mask. On the materials Mask level Click the Map slot and set the Map Type to Noise.

6. On the noise level of the Mask Set the Noise parameters as follows:
Noise Type = Fractal
Size = 2
Swap Color #1 with Color #2

7. Go back up to the Mask level and Click the Mask's map slot and set the Map Type to Gradient. On the Gradient level, set the Gradient parameters:
Gradient Type = Radial
Swap Color #1 with Color #3

8. Go back up to the Parent level of the material and name the material **SmokeRockets** (see Figure 4).

9. Apply the SmokeRockets material to RocketThrust.

Rocket Engine Glow

Next you'll create the rockets engine ignition and flame propulsion with the addition of a simple omni light.

1. Create an omni light roughly centered behind the left wing rocket engine exhaust, and then use the Transform Type-In dialog box to position it precisely at x = –210, y = 6.4, z = 19.6. Set the following:
   Color = (R = 0, G = 0, G = 0)
   Multiplier = 3
   Attenuation = Use
   Far Start = 0
   Far End = 7

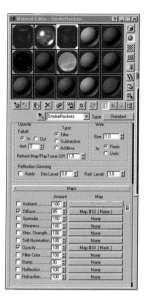

Figure 4
Creating the smoke material for the rocket thrust.

2. Animate the omni light's color:
   Frame 0 (Keyframe 1) Color = (R = 0, G = 0, B = 0)
      IN tangent and OUT tangent = digital
   Frame 152 (KeyFrame 2) Color = (R = 255, G = 255, B = 255)
      IN tangent and OUT tangent = digital
   Frame 156 (Keyframe 3) Color = (R = 255, G = 161, B =0)
      IN tangent = digital, OUT tangent = linear
   Frame 300 (Keyframe 4) Color = (R = 255, G = 161, B =0)
      IN tangent and OUT tangent = linear

3. Name the omni light **Rocket Engine GlowLight**.

4. Link the Rocket Engine GlowLight to the Jet object (see Figure 5).

Note

The best way to set these animation values is to use the Track View.

Smoke and Steam

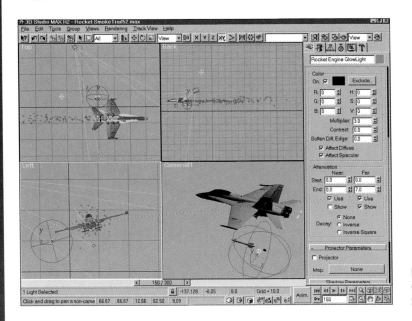

Figure 5
Completed Rocket Smoke Trail effect.

One of the most difficult aspects of this animation is finding the correct balance between particle motion and object speed. If you experiment with the jet's speed or the particle speeds, you will see a variety of problems develop that create undesirable visual effects—everything from particle stuttering and staggering to particle/emitter motion anticipation. Fortunately, you can solve most of these problems by tweaking the settings.

You can find the final MAX file, RocketSmokeTrail.max, in this project's Scene folder and the final AVI in the Images folder.

Drain Vortex

by Greg Carbonaro

There are many ways to create illusions in MAX. Before doing the Drain Vortex effect, take a look at the animation and try to figure out the technique used here. How was this done? Is it a particle system with a special material? Maybe it is MetaParticles with a Motor Space Warp. What about the sink—is that a Universal Deflector? No—those techniques require too much processing power to be practical and the render times would be outrageous. The actual technique that you are about to use might surprise you. Sometimes an animator is forced to come up with shortcut solutions, which is the case here. This effect is a quick, clean solution to a tough animation problem.

Note

All position and rotational information is based on absolute world coordinates. When creating objects, use keyboard entry when possible. When positioning objects, use the Transform Type-In dialog box located in the Tools menu. These techniques ensure proper object placement and orientation.

Leave any settings that are not listed in the example at the MAX default values. Create objects in the Top viewport, unless otherwise indicated.

Preconfiguration

1. Before beginning this effect, please reset *or* restart MAX.

2. Copy the project map files from the accompanying CD-ROM to the MAX maps subdirectory.

3. Load the file Sink.max from the project preload subdirectory on the CD-ROM. The animation has been preset to 300 frames.

4. Open the Material Editor. Right-click in any material slot and make sure Sample Windows are set to 5×3.

Once the file is loaded, you should see a bathroom sink and faucet in your viewports.

Modeling and Materials

In the following section, you will create all the Water used in this scene.

Water Surface Creation

1. Activate the Top viewport.

2. Create a standard primitive cylinder roughly centered in the sink, then use the Transform Type-In to position it precisely at x = 3.141, y = −37.889, z = 2.915. Set the following:
Radius = 93
Height = 3.5
Height Segments = 2
Cap Segments = 64
Sides = 64
Smoothing = on
Generate Mapping = on

3. Name the object **WaterSurface**.

Water Surface Material

1. In the Material Editor, make material slot 1 active and set the Material Type to Standard.

2. Set the Basic parameters as follows:
Shading = Blinn
Ambient = (R = 45, G = 55, B = 65)
Diffuse = (R = 104, G = 121, B = 136)
Specular = (R = 255, G = 255, B = 255)
Filter = (R = 41, G = 24, B = 14)
Shininess = 41
Shin. Strength = 100
Opacity = 30

3. In Extended Parameters set the following:
Refract Map/RayTrace IOR = 1.3

4. Set the Amount for the Bump slot to 25. Click the Bump map slot and set the map Type to Noise. Set the Noise parameters as follows:

Coordinates = UVW1
V Tiling = 4
Noise Type = Turbulence
Size = 0.2

5. Animate the Noise Coordinates W Offset:
Frame 0 (Keyframe 1) W offset = 0
   IN tangent = normal, OUT tangent = slow
Frame 300 (Keyframe 2) W offset = 4.5
   IN tangent = fast, OUT tangent = normal

Note

The best way to set these animation values is to use the Track View.

6. Set the Amount for the Refraction slot to 40. Click the Refraction slot and set the map type to Thin Wall Refraction. Set the following:
Refraction: bump map effect = 2

7. Go back up to the parent level of the material and name the material **WaterSurface**.

8. Apply the WaterSurface material to the WaterSurface object (see Figure 1).

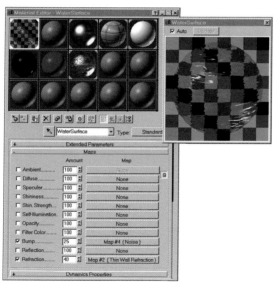

Figure 1
When rendered, the bumpy noise animation of the material will make the water appear to move inward toward the center.

You should now see a sink filled with water in your scene.

Smoke and Steam

Water Surface Animation

1. Select the WaterSurface object and add a Noise modifier to it. Set the following Noise Parameters:
   Seed = 342342
   Scale = 3.2
   Fractal = on
   Roughness = 0.5
   Iterations = 10
   Strength: Z = 3.2 5
   Animate Noise = on
   Frequency = 0.1

2. Activate the Top Viewport.

3. Create a Geometric/Deformable Displace space warp roughly centered on the WaterSurface and use the Transform Type-In to position it precisely at x = 3.141, y = −37.889, z = 39.031. Set the Displacement parameters as follows:
   Strength = 96
   Decay = 6.175
   Map = spherical
   Length = 5
   Width = 5
   Height = 50

4. Animate the Displacement Decay:
   Frame 0 (Keyframe 1) Decay = 6.175
       IN tangent = linear, OUT tangent = fast
   Frame 78 (Keyframe 2) Decay = 1.886
       IN tangent = bezier, OUT tangent = bezier
   Frame 250 (Keyframe 3) Decay = 0.35
       IN tangent = slow, OUT tangent = linear
   Frame 300 (Keyframe 4) Decay = 0.6
       IN tangent = linear, OUT tangent = linear

5. Accept the default name for the space warp **Displace01**.

6. Select the Displace01 space warp first, and then Bind it to the WaterSurface object.

7. Select the WaterSurface first, and then Link it to the Displace01 space warp (see Figure 2).

Once the Displace is bound to the water surface, the water deforms and the VORTEX is born.

Note

The best way to set these animation values is to use the Track View. Open Track View and expand the hierarchy tree for Displace01. Click Add Keys and add the following keys to the Decay track. Right click on the keys to set the values and the IN and OUT tangents.

Note

The purpose of this link is to cause the displace space warp to follow the WaterSurface object when it is animated. It is important to follow the selection and binding instructions in the exact order as above or MAX will not allow the link and give you a dependency loop error message.

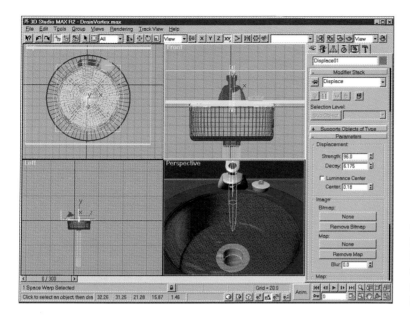

Figure 2
Bind and link the
Displace space
warp to the Water
Surface object.
Follow the selec-
tion and bind/link
order as outlined
in the steps.

Animating the Water

Next you'll rotate and move the WaterSurface downward to simulate
draining.

1. Animate the WaterSurface Z position:
   Frame 0 (Keyframe 1) Z position = 2.915
   Frame 150 (Keyframe 2) Z position = –6.963
   Frame 250 (Keyframe 3) Z position = –18.689
   Frame 300 (Keyframe 4) Z position = –76.474

2. With Track View still open select the WaterSurface Rotation
   track, click Assign Controller, and select the Euler XYZ rotation
   controller.

3. Expand the hierarchy tree for the Rotation track. Using Add
   Keys, set the following Z rotation keys (see Figure 3):
   Frame –30 (Keyframe 1) Z rotation = –20
       IN tangent = linear, OUT tangent = Slow
   Frame 300 (Keyframe 2) Z rotation = –560
       IN tangent = fast, OUT tangent = Linear

Note

*The best way to set
the following anima-
tion values is to use
the Track View. Open
Track View and
expand the hierarchy
tree for
WaterSurface. Click
Add Keys and add
the following Z posi-
tion Key Frame val-
ues to the position
track. Right-click on
the keys to set the
values. Leave the X
and Y position values
set as they are.*

Smoke and Steam

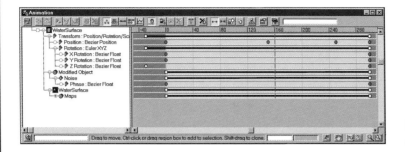

Figure 3
Animate the water.

Lighting Setup

Next, you will create the lighting for the scene.

1. Activate the Top viewport.

2. Create a target spot light roughly in front of and pointing toward the sink, then use the Transform Type-In to position the body precisely at x = –192, y = –413, z = 422. Position the target at x = 20, y = –24, z = 0. Set the spotlight parameters as follows:
   Multiplier = 2
   Hot Spot = 29
   Fall Off = 60

Camera Setup

The final step is to set up the camera through which you will view the finished effect.

1. Create a target camera roughly in front of and pointing towards the sink, and then use the Transform Type-In to position the body precisely at x = 5, y = –188, z = 129. Position the target at x = 5, y = –6, z = –9 (see Figure 4). Set the camera parameters as follows:
   Lens = 35mm

When you render the final effect, you will appreciate the speed at which it renders. A traditional approach that includes an elaborate particle system and material might take hours per frame to render and the final results might not look as good. Unconventional approaches and solutions are what being an animator is all about.

You can find the final MAX file, DrainVortex.max, in the Scene folder and the final AVI file in the Images folder.

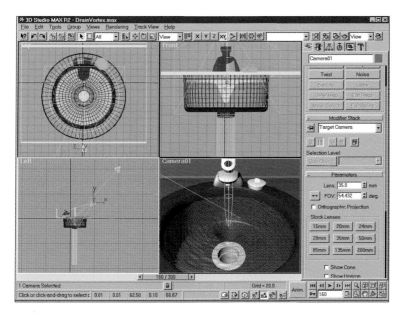

Figure 4
Completed Drain
Vortex effect.

Steam

by Steve Alexander

In the Steam effect, you use particle systems to provide the flowing motion of steam by setting up particles as facing particles and mapping the faces with a noisy Opacity map to emulate the wispy characteristics of steam. The basic file includes a kitchen scene with a teapot from which the steam boils. The teapot is actually two teapots. The first was created without the body, handle, and spout. This is the "lid." The second was created with everything but the lid and is the "pot." This was done so that the lid can animate as the steam boils up.

Note

All position and rotational information is based on absolute world coordinates. When creating objects, use keyboard entry where possible. When positioning objects, use the Transform Type-In dialog box located in the Tools menu. These techniques ensure proper object placement and orientation.

Leave any settings that are not listed in the example at the MAX default values. Create objects in the Top viewport, unless otherwise indicated.

Preconfiguration

1. Before beginning this effect, please either reset *or* restart MAX.

2. Copy the maps from the CD to your maps folder.

3. Load the Steam.max file from this project's Pre-load folder on the accompanying CD. The scene consists of a stove in a kitchen. A teapot on the stove will be the source of the steam for the effect. The animation is preset to 300 frames.

Modeling and Materials

In this section you will create three spray particle systems, which will be the mapable objects for the steam material.

1. Activate the Bottom viewport.

2. Create a spray particle system anywhere and move it to x = 45, y = 0, z = 37. Set the following:
   Emitter Width = 6
   Emitter Length = 3.5
   Render Count = 250
   Drop Size = 3.2
   Speed = 7.0
   Variation = 1.0
   Render = Facing
   Timing: **Start** = 30, **Life** = 20
   Constant = Checked

3. Create a second particle system anywhere and move it to x = 0, y = 20, z = 37. Set the following:
   Emitter Width = 25
   Emitter Length = 1.0
   Rotate: x = 173
   Render Count = 250
   Drop Size = 5.0
   Speed = 5.0
   Variation = 1.5
   Render = Facing
   Timing: **Start** = 32, **Life** = 30
   Constant = Unchecked
   Birth Rate = 15

4. Create a third particle system anywhere and move it to x = 0, y = −20, z = 37. Set the following:
   Emitter Width = 25
   Emitter Length = 1.0
   Rotate: x = −162
   Render Count = 250
   Drop Size = 4.0
   Speed = 6.0
   Variation = 0.5
   Render = Facing
   Timing: **Start** = 30, **Life** = 30
   Constant = Checked

Creating the Particle Material

1. In the Material Editor, select a slot and name the material
   Steam.

2. Set the Basic Parameters:
   Filter Color = (R = 170, G = 170, B = 170)
   Shininess = 0
   Shin. Strength = 0
   Self-Illumination = 60

3. Set the Amount for the Diffuse map slot to 50. Click the Diffuse
   slot and set the Map Type to Noise.

4. Click the Opacity map slot and set the Map Type to Mask.

5. Click the Map map slot and set the Map Type to Noise.

6. Click the Mask map slot and set the Map Type to Gradient. Set
   the Gradient parameters:
   Swap Color#1 and Color#3
   Gradient Type = Radial
   Noise = Fractal
   Amount = 0.5
   Size = 15.0

7. Apply this material to all three spray systems (see Figure 1).

8. Create the Hot Burner Material. Set the
   following: **Diffuse** = (R = 110, G = 55,
   B = 25)

Figure 1
The Steam material
hierarchy.

9. Name the material **Burner**.

10. Turn Animate on and set the following for Frame 30:
    Self-Illumination = 100
    Color = (R = 255, G = 130, B = 60)

At this point the particles will render as facing squares with the noisy
steam material applied. Since the material makes use of a Gradient mask,
which makes use of the Opacity channel, the outer square edges of the
facing particles will disappear.

Animation

In this section you'll complete the illusion and make the teapot's lid bounce and rotate as if the force of the steam were coming out and doing it.

1. Animate the teapot lid:
   Track View: Object Lid Transform Position = Noise Position controller
   Noise Strength = (x = 2, y = 2, z = 5)
   >0 = Checked
   Fractal = Checked

2. **Lid Transform Rotation** = Noise Rotation controller
   Noise Strength – (x = 3, y = 3, z = 3)
   Fractal = Checked

3. Move the white squares for the noise position and the noise rotation controllers to Frame 30 so that the lid starts moving and rotating (see Figure 2).

Figure 2
Track View of the noise controller starting points.

You can find the final MAX file, SteamPot.max, in this project's Scene folder and the final AVI file in the Images folder.

Photoshop Magic Premier Collection

Save over $50 on five of the most popular Magic books and get *The Complete Guide to Photoshop Native Filters*—complete coverage of all 97 of Photoshop's filters—and a poster showing the effects of all of them.

The boxed set includes *Photoshop Web Magic, Photoshop Type Magic 1, Photoshop Type Magic* 2, *Photoshop Effects Magic,* and *Photoshop Textures Magic.* It's the perfect way to achieve special effects for the Web, create amazing type treatments, design stunning graphics and illustrations, and appkly eye-catching textures.

ISBN: 1-56830-442-0   **$149.99 USA/$214.95 CAN**

Illustrator Type Magic

by Greg Simsic

Every page of *Illustrator Type Magic* makes a visual promise: you will be able to create this! The book's highly effective, recipe-style approach walks you through the procedures of creating special effects with type, and the stunning four-color illustrations are sure to inspire any designer.

ISBN: 1-56830-334-3   **$39.99 USA/$56.95 CAN**

Photoshop Web Magic, Volume 1

by Ted Schulman, Renée LeWinter, and Tom Emmanuelides

This 4-color book provides numerous examples of dazzling Web graphics, textures, backgrounds, buttons, and animations in a recipe format with simple step-by-step instructions. Specific graphic techniques for customizing Web design to fit client needs and expert advice for print designers moving to the Web is included.

ISBN: 1-56830-314-9   **$45.00 USA/$63.95 CAN**

Photoshop Web Magic, Volume 2

by Jeff Foster

This companion volume to Photoshop Web Magic, Volume 1, includes 45 all-new techniques and provides step-by-step directions to create dazzling effects for the Web. A new section covers Java rollovers, animation tools, and WYSIWYG HTML editors.

ISBN: 1-56830-392-0   **$45.00 USA/$63.95 CAN**

Photoshop 5 Web Magic

by Michael Ninness

An all-new collection of animations, textures, edge treatments for images, buttons, and backgrounds! The companion CD-ROM will be filled with demos and live software for creating buttons quickly and easily!

ISBN: 1-56205-913-0   **$39.99 USA/$56.95 CAN**

What's on the CD-ROM...

The value-packed CD-ROM contains the following:

- Four fantastic **bonus effects**:
  Brook
  Stream
  Wrinkles
  Flamethrower

- Original MAX files that you will use to re-create the effects in this book (Pre-load folder)

- Map files (Maps folder)

- The MAX files that the authors used to render the finished effects (Scene folder)

- AVI files showing the finished effects (Images folder)

Disclaimer

By opening this package, you are agreeing to be bound by the following agreement:

Some of the software included with this product may be copyrighted, in which case all rights are reserved by the respective copyright holder. You are licensed to use software copyrighted by the Publisher and its licensors on a single computer. You may copy and/or modify the software as needed to facilitate your use of it on a single computer. Making copies of the software for any other purpose is a violation of the United States copyright laws.

This software is sold as is without warranty of any kind, either expressed or implied, including but not limited to the implied warranties of merchantability and fitness for a particular purpose. Neither the publisher nor its dealers or distributors assumes any liability for any alleged or actual damages arising from the use of this program. (Some states do not allow for the exclusion of implied warranties, so the exclusion may not apply to you.)

Windows 95 and Windows NT: If you have AutoPlay enabled, insert the CD-ROM and choose installation options from the displayed splash screen.

NOTE: If you have AutoPlay disabled on your computer, the CD-ROM will *not* automatically display the installation splash screen. To browse the CD-ROM manually, double-click on My Computer on the desktop, then right-click on your CD player icon, and choose Explore from the shortcut menu. By doing this, you can immediately access the files for this CD-ROM.